CAMBRIDGE LATIN AMERICAN STUDIES

GENERAL EDITOR
SIMON COLLIER

ADVISORY COMMITTEE
MALCOLM DEAS, STUART SCHWARTZ,
ARTURO VALENZUELA

70

THE POLITICS OF MEMORY

For a list of other books in the
Cambridge Latin American Studies series,
please see page 225

THE POLITICS OF MEMORY

Native historical interpretation in the Colombian Andes

JOANNE RAPPAPORT

University of Maryland, Baltimore County

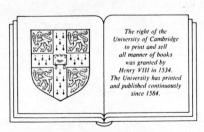

The right of the
University of Cambridge
to print and sell
all manner of books
was granted by
Henry VIII in 1534.
The University has printed
and published continuously
since 1584.

CAMBRIDGE UNIVERSITY PRESS

Cambridge

New York   Port Chester

Melbourne   Sydney

Published by the Press Syndicate of the University of Cambridge
The Pitt Building, Trumpington Street, Cambridge CB2 1RP
40 West 20th Street, New York, NY 10011, USA
10 Stamford Road, Oakleigh, Melbourne 3166, Australia

First published 1990

Printed in Great Britain by the University Press, Cambridge

British Library cataloguing in publication data

Rappaport, Joanne
The politics of memory: native historical interpretation in the Colombian Andes
– (Cambridge Latin American studies)
1. South American studies
1. Title
305.8′98

Library of Congress cataloguing in publication data

Rappaport, Joanne.
The politics of memory: native historical interpretation in the Colombian
Andes/Joanne Rappaport.
p.   cm.
Bibliography.
ISBN 0-521-37345-X
1. Paez Indians – History. 2. Indians of South America – Colombia – Cauca
(Dept.) – History. 1. Title.
F2270.2.P3R36   1990
986.1′53004982 – dc20   89-9756   CIP

ISBN 0 521 37345 X

C.U.P.

IN MEMORY

HELEN RAPPAPORT
AND
JOSEPH B. CASAGRANDE

When Rabbi Baer was five years old, a fire broke out in his father's house. Hearing his mother grieve and cry about this, he asked her: "Mother, do we have to be so unhappy because we have lost a house?"

"I am not grieving for the house," she said, "but for our family tree which burned up. It began with Rabbi Yohanon, the sandal-maker, the master in the Talmud."

"And what does that matter!" exclaimed the boy. "I shall get you a new family tree which begins with me!"

(Martin Buber, *Tales of the Hasidim*)

Contents

Illustrations

Preface

This book will trace the historical vision of the Páez of the highlands of Cauca, Colombia over three centuries. In it, I examine the political, social and economic forces, both internal to the Páez and those originating in the dominant society, that have impinged upon native thought, causing age-old symbols to be deployed in new ways and innovations to be cast as historical. This process of historical renovation has served as an ideological means of resisting ethnocide. My analysis is a product of the times in which I came to know the Páez, an era in which they were under attack from landowners and army, accused of political subversion because they had organized themselves as Indians. Living with the Páez from 1978 to 1980, sharing with them their fear of the soldiers who were occupying their territory, I listened to their thoughts on the past, and on how their history might help them to survive the present. Originally, I meant to study their notion of sacred space, but quickly came to realize that Páez cosmology was inextricably bound up in resistance tactics, and thus could not be studied in isolation.

My first attempt at analyzing the information I collected from 1978 to 1980 in Tierradentro, Cauca, was a dissertation (Rappaport 1982) that focused heavily on the contemporary Páez and the colonial roots of their historical vision. Since then, as I worked with nineteenth-century historical materials, I began to realize that traditional Andean scholarship was flawed in its insistence upon cultural continuity from precolumbian times to the present as an example of the persistence of unconscious structures in the minds of Andean peoples. I discovered that the nineteenth century, frequently neglected by anthropologists, was key to an understanding of contemporary oral tradition. On the one hand, it is in this period that the conscious reappropriation of the past is most clearly manifest in the activities of indigenous politicians. On the other hand, the nineteenth-century reinvention of tradition is not so much the persistence of mental structures, as a reapplication of older models to quite distinct social circumstances. In short, it became evident that a detailed analysis of contemporary oral tradition would have to be historical in focus. As I came to this realization, my ethnographic data became less a central focus of analysis, than a means of culturally anchoring myself in the Páez historical experience that permitted me, as it were, to view my historical materials "from the inside." This book, then, is not so much an ethnography, as an ethnographically-informed intellectual history of the Páez.

First, I would like to thank the Instituto Colombiano de Antropología (ICAN) and its director in 1978, Alvaro Soto Holguín, for granting me permission to conduct ethnographic research in Colombia, by waiving then-existing restrictions on foreign anthropological research. Dr. Soto and later directors of ICAN, Drs. Alberto Rivera, Iván Posada and Roberto Pineda Giraldo, graciously opened the resources of the Instituto to me. I would also like to thank the Fundación de Investigaciones Arqueológicas Nacionales (Banco de la República) and the Universidad del Cauca for agreeing to fund my research, at a time when North American foundations hesitated to support ethnographic investigation in Colombia. In the summer of 1984, after restrictions on the activities of foreign anthropologists had been lifted, my archival and bibliographic research was supported by a grant-in-aid from the Wenner-Gren Foundation for Anthropological Research and a faculty summer research fellowship from the University of Maryland Baltimore County for which I am grateful.

I also wish to acknowledge the collaboration of the directors of the various archives and libraries in which I conducted historical research in Colombia and in Ecuador, including the Archivo de la Academia Colombiana de Historia, the Archivo Central del Cauca, the Archivo Fundación Colombia Nuestra, the Archivo Histórico de Tierradentro, the Archivo del Instituto Colombiano de la Reforma Agraria, the Archivo Jijón y Caamaño, the Archivo Nacional de Colombia, the Archivo Nacional de Historia, the Archivo Provincia Franciscana de Santafé, the Archivo Provincial de los Padres Vicentinos de Colombia, the Biblioteca Luis Angel Arango, and the Biblioteca Nacional de Colombia. In all of these repositories, directors and staff went out of their way to alert me to important materials, making the historical portion of my research both productive and enjoyable. Documents from the Archivo General de Indias were consulted from a microfilm collection compiled by

Joseph B. Casagrande, with the support of the National Science Foundation.

I also received extensive support from local people while in the field. I would especially like to thank the Prefectura Apostólica de Tierradentro and Monsignors Enrique Vallejo and Germán García, the Hermanas Misioneras de la Madre Laura of Calderas and Vitoncó, Miguel Palomino and Fr. Jorge Escobar for their support. Two Colombian anthropology students, Sofía Botero and Gustavo Antonio Legarda, ably served as my assistants during various phases of the research.

In Colombia, I met a circle of anthropologists, historians and political activists with whom I shared interests, both with regard to the Páez and ethnohistory in general. Although I run the risk of forgetting some of them, I thank Segundo Bernal, Víctor Daniel Bonilla, Ana María Falcetti, María Teresa Findji, Ximena Pachón, Roberto Pineda Camacho, Clemencia Plazas, Gerardo Reichel-Dolmatoff, Kathleen Romoli, Carlos Alberto Uribe, María Victoria Uribe and Luis Guillermo Vasco for sharing hours of conversation and analysis with me.

In North America, a number of individuals served as teachers, colleagues and sounding-boards at different stages of the development of the ideas in this book. They include Catherine Allen, Ruth Behar, Gonzalo Castillo, David William Cohen, David Earle, Donald Lathrap, Richard Price, Frank Salomon, Jack Sinnigen, Michael Taussig 'and R. Tom Zuidema. My special thanks also go to those who have read and commented upon my manuscript at various stages in its preparation: Stephen Hugh-Jones, Grant Jones, Catherine LeGrand, Sutti Ortiz, Deborah Poole and Linda Seligmann. I would especially like to thank Wendy Guise of Cambridge University Press for her collaboration in turning my manuscript into a book.

Gonzalo Castillo Cárdenas, editor of Quintín Lame's treatise, and author of the introduction to the 1971 edition of *Los pensamientos*, graciously granted me permission to quote extensively from the work.

Julie Perlmutter contributed the maps and illustrations in this volume.

My father, Irving Rappaport, provided constant support and motivation from the very beginning of the project.

This book is dedicated to the memory of two people who would have taken pleasure in seeing the completed book, but died too soon for me to share it with them. Without the support of my mother, Helen Rappaport, and my dissertation director, Joseph B. Casagrande, it would never have been possible.

Of all those who contributed in some way to the final product, I must single out the Páez of Calderas, Jambaló, San José, Togoima and Vitoncó, who shared with me their homes, their time, their ideas, their hopes for the future and their knowledge of the past. I hope that, once translated into an appropriate medium and language, my analysis might become an arm in their struggle for autonomy and dignity. My immense gratitude goes to these men and women, sons and daughters of the Star.

1

Introduction: interpreting the past

In *Los funerales de la Mamá Grande*, Gabriel García Márquez declares that he must tell his story "before the historians have time to arrive." But in reality, the historians arrived long ago, and the novelist is righting the wrongs of Colombian historiography by giving life and breath to long-forgotten incidents which should have been at the center of the Colombian historical consciousness, but were omitted by historians. Throughout the Americas indigenous peoples are working toward these same ends, revalidating their own historical knowledge as an arm against their subordinate position in society. For them, history is a source of knowledge of how they were first subjugated and of information about their legal rights, the beginnings of a new definition of themselves as a people, a model upon which to base new national structures (Barre 1983).[1] For them as for García Márquez, Western historiography has severed the Indians from their past by neglecting to mention them except as exotic beings or as savages. Western historiography thus justifies the European invasion. Nevertheless, from the perspective of aboriginal peoples, the writings of historians are more legendary than accurate (Wankar 1981: 297–81). European myths of the Americas have served as tools for dominating Native Americans by denying them access to a knowledge of their own past so necessary for organizing in the present. In the words of one native writer: "The whites block our road toward the future by blocking our road to the past" (Wankar 1981: 279).

This book will trace the process by which the Páez of southern highland Colombia have revalidated their historical vision since the eighteenth century by defining, stating, reformulating and acting upon their own notion of their place in the historical process. I will examine their process of historical definition, highlighting selected periods in which native historians elaborated on their past in a form accessible to us, and tracing the continuities in narrative themes that link late twentieth-century storytellers to their colonial counterparts.

Although Páez narrative exhibits a clear continuity from past to present, it is also the product of the historical conditions under which it was elaborated. The historical consciousness of the people of Tierradentro is most clearly understood when interpreted in conjunction with an analysis of the changing relationship of the aboriginal population to the State, both the Spanish colonial state and the modern Colombian nation. Since the advent of European rule Páez political action has always aimed at defining and empowering the group in relation to the dominant society. Páez history incorporates the memory of the various junctures at which the community confronted the Crown and the State. Nevertheless, neither whites nor the State are the center of these historical narrations. Instead, the Páez historical vision dwells upon indigenous activities in the past, documenting the successes and failures they have encountered in their struggle to maintain themselves as a people. History is a double-edged sword for the Páez. The eighteenth- and early twentieth-century accounts available to us are written: thus, they were originally aimed at literate non-Indian audiences or at future generations of literate Indians, employing literary conventions to convey indigenous principles as well as to empower the community. Nevertheless, much of their argumentation uses Páez images, making allusions to topographic sites and mythological occurrences which would only be understood by other Indians. Moreover, they are not organized chronologically. Thus, in a sense, the examples we have of Páez interpretations of the past are, like their Peruvian counterparts, "chronicles of the impossible," indigenous attempts at integrating their own brand of historical and cosmological thought within Western-style discourse, both of which are effaced in the process because they contradict each other (Salomon 1982).

THE PÁEZ

The Páez live on the slopes of Colombia's Central Cordillera in the northeastern corner of the department of Cauca (Maps 1,2,3). Linked to the Colombian nation by commerce, transportation, technology, wage labor, religion and political process, as well as by a common historical experience, their everyday lives are also charged with a history of their own.[2] The villages that dot the landscape (Plate 1), connected until recently by bridlepaths and today by roads in

Map 1   The Páez within their broader geographic context

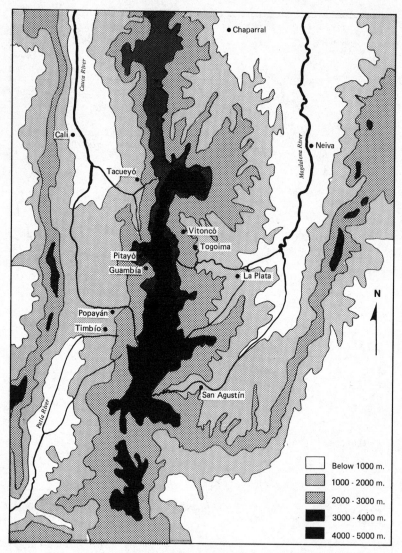

Map 2   Topographic map of the Colombian Central Cordillera

varying states of disrepair, were established in the seventeenth
century by Spanish authorities who hoped thereby to control the
Indians as a source of labor and of tribute; the communities
themselves only came into existence when the Páez were forced to

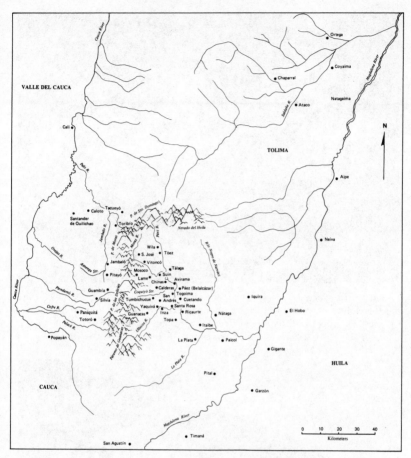

Map 3   General map of the Páez area

ascend the Cordillera, after having been uprooted from the warmer valleys to the east around La Plata, and after the Spaniards founded new villages following the depopulation of conquest. The 60,000 people who today identify themselves as Páez do not live in these villages, but in dispersed homesteads in the high mountains, and visit town centers only infrequently to attend festivals or on their way to the regional market centers of Silvia or Belalcázar (Plate 2).

Most Páez are members of *resguardos*, political and territorial units that communally own lands granted them by the Crown in the eighteenth century; individuals enjoy usufruct rights to parcels, and

Plate 1   *The village of Tálaga.* The site of Father Castillo y Orozco's mission in the eighteenth century, Tálaga's town center is today mainly inhabited by mestizos. Most Indians do not live in town, but dispersed throughout the *resguardo.*

Plate 2   *A festival in Togoima.* A celebration to dedicate a new religious image. Most Páez towns serve largely as ceremonial centers, having few inhabitants between festivals.

Plate 3   *Cabildo members from the* resguardo *of Quichaya. Cabildo* members carry
staffs of office, which are refreshed annually in a ceremony that recreates history.

cannot sell their lands to outsiders. Although the Indians trace a
connection between modern-day *resguardos* and their colonial
forebears, in reality the institution has changed considerably in the
past 300 years. The *resguardo*'s land base was diminished with the
expansion of great estates in the nineteenth century, it now includes
colonization zones settled by mestizos and is smaller and weaker
than its eighteenth-century progenitor as a result of post-Independence legislation that changed councils, or *cabildos*, from being
independent political authorities into intermediaries between communities and the State (Plate 3).

Plate 4   *A family from San José.* San José was decimated during the civil war of
the 1950s, its *cabildo* murdered, its population dispersed, and its church
destroyed.

   The Páez cultivate coca and manioc, maize or potatoes, depending
upon the elevation at which they live, ranging from 1,000 to 3,500
meters above sea level. But cash crops have also been introduced,
including coffee at the turn of the century and hemp since the 1970s,
and coca cultivation has diminished as a result of Colombia's anti-
cocaine policy. During the seventeenth and eighteenth centuries, a
substantial layer of *resguardo* residents spent time working on Spanish
plantations surrounding Popayán, while in the nineteenth century,
many were absent from their communities extracting quinine from
the forests for the Colombian and international markets. Today, they
periodically abandon their homes to engage in wage labor on nearby
coffee and sugar plantations, and some have no land at all, but live
as tenant farmers on mestizo-owned haciendas.
   Although they no longer engage in the internecine warfare that
characterized sixteenth-century Páez chiefdoms, the Páez heartland
of Tierradentro has been a stage for violent confrontation since then.
The dominant Colombian society promotes a warlike image of the
Páez, and outsiders seeking to achieve change through violent means
have harnessed a presumed Páez ferocity over the years, first during

the nineteenth-century civil wars, later in the wave of violence that swept the nation in the 1950s and most recently in the political persecution that has cut down over 100 Indian leaders since the early 1970s (Plate 4).

The Páez tradition of resistance finds its roots deep in the past. The people of Tierradentro have encoded their history of struggle in their sacred geography, so that past meets present in the very terrain on which they live, farm and walk. Memory has built upon memory, connecting events of the distant past, the more recent past and the present in the topography of Tierradentro. Many contemporary Indians belong to one of a number of ethnic rights organizations established during the past two decades to confront the dominant society through land claims, the proclamation of sharecroppers' rights, the strengthening of *cabildo* authority and the revitalization of culture and language. Indian rights activists are fully conscious of the lessons they must draw from the memories of precolumbian battles with aboriginal enemies, the military resistance their ancestors offered in response to the Spanish invasion of 1572, the judicial battles that established the *resguardos* and that assured their existence until today. Of all the fighters of yesteryear, those who occupy the center of the historical memory are the eighteenth-century chiefs, or *caciques*, who created *resguardos* and left behind land titles. Their example has been revived countless times since their deaths, most prominently by nineteenth-century Páez politico-military leaders who commanded Indian battalions in the civil wars and by Manuel Quintín Lame, whose early twentieth-century pan-Indian organization lay the basis for today's ethnic demands.

The historical consciousness of the people of Tierradentro is founded on a moral link with the past that is operationalized in the interests of achieving political goals in the present. As we shall see, Páez history has its own internal logic embodied in time-worn patterns that are regenerated, century after century, to confront new political conditions. In other words, the Páez historical vision can be legitimately studied as a symbolic system internal to the community. But this is only half the equation: the moral history articulated by contemporary Páez activists is operationalized at the interface of the native community and the broader Colombian society, and must address both internal and external ideological needs. Consequently, Páez historical consciousness must be examined within the context of historical developments in the broader society, including the transformation of political systems, the changing nature of historical evidence in the legal system and the history of Colombian historiography. In order to comprehend the internal logic of Páez history, then, we must also understand the history of Colombia.

NON-WESTERN HISTORICAL CONSCIOUSNESS

To what extent have anthropologists developed the analytic tools needed to examine Páez historical consciousness? Let us look at how ethnohistorians have studied native histories, a task most notably undertaken in recent years by historians of Africa (Vansina 1973; Miller 1980; Cohen 1989) and Afro-America (Price 1983), and which is also catching on among students of Asian (Errington 1979; Rosaldo 1980) and Pacific societies (Harwood 1976; Morphy and Morphy 1985; Borofsky 1987; Parmentier 1987). Students of indigenous societies of the Americas have made their own mark upon this literature, examining the writings of colonial and nineteenth-century indigenous historians (Bricker 1981; Salomon 1982; Zuidema 1982; Adorno 1986) or contemporary Native American historical interpretation (Rivera 1986; Fowler 1987).

Most of these scholars agree that while non-Western histories are about the past, they do not generally isolate earlier events from contemporary concerns. In Morphy and Morphy's words (1985: 462), these accounts are images *of* the past and not *from* the past, reflections by inhabitants of our own time on what might have occurred earlier. Instead of documenting "what really occurred," they bring up images of "what should have happened." Many times non-Western historians employ mythic images or metaphors to represent and explain historical events; mythic vehicles frequently overshadow the events themselves, making it difficult for us to locate them in time and in space.[3] Studies of classical memory techniques demonstrate that striking images were frequently used in the Greco-Roman world as mnemonic devices for remembering more commonplace referents (Yates 1966). Building upon classical scholarship, Harwood (1976) and Miller (1980) suggest that symbols play a similar role in non-western myth: fantastic images are mnemonic devices for generating more scantily-clad historical facts which would otherwise remain inaccessible to the oral memory.

Native histories differ most markedly from our own in their narrative structure. A number of current writers have suggested that they cannot properly be called "narratives," since they are frequently not stylized and are brief or episodic, taking forms ranging from proverbs, to references to former house-sites, to songs (Rosaldo 1980; Price 1983; Cohen 1989). Allen (1984) and Cohen (1989) maintain that historicity is not lodged in a static text, but in an ongoing process of interpretation whereby accounts are constantly assembled and reassembled; Allen speculates that this process is to a great degree determined by aesthetic norms. Poole (n.d.) finds Andean narratives to be diffuse and confusing to the non-Andean, precisely because they cannot be understood as isolated texts, but only in conjunction with a whole range of activities, including ritual, pilgrimage and dance which clarify, elaborate upon and provide keys to the reinterpretation of narratives.

Many of these accounts are not chronological. Their creators juxtapose time-frames, omitting causal explanation, refraining from narrating events in linear form, or locating them outside of chronological time. This does not mean that native historians have no notion of causation. Linear notions of historical process are understood by the narrator and listener, perhaps discussed by them in another context and in a different mode, but not necessarily conveyed within the narration itself. Finally, much of this history is encoded in physical space, and geography does more than carry important historical referents: it also organizes the manner in which these facts are conceptualized, remembered and organized into a temporal framework (Harwood 1976; Rosaldo 1980).

If historical knowledge is bound to the present through its non-linear expression in space and in ritual, this is because it has practical uses. Knowledge of the past is a fundamental component of land disputes, political agreements and arguments over inheritance.[4] It is also central to efforts at strengthening a communal identity, indispensable in the maintenance of autonomy in the face of European domination (Rosaldo 1980; Price 1983; Cohen 1989; Lederman 1986; Fowler 1987). The non-narrative, non-stylized and episodic nature of the historical vision is fundamental to its usefulness: flexibility and ambiguity permit knowledge to be used in a variety of forms across a broad array of situations.

THE PROBLEM OF CLASSIFICATION

Although it is useful to outline the general attributes of non-Western historical traditions, it is less productive to classify them in distinction to our own historical canons. We commonly define historicity as embodied in chronological or linear narratives, without accepting that these are characteristics of the European theory of time, inextricably bound up in the process of the European conquest of the globe (Cohn 1981: 227–29). As an outgrowth of these circumstances we have come to accept our own temporal framework as natural and given, according second place to the historical schema of the conquered.[5]

Anthropologists have drawn upon classical studies in their development of classificatory schemes, consequently de-emphasizing the cultural, social and historical specificity of the Euroamerican historical vision. This is played out *par excellence* in typologies that label our own construction of the past as "history," while alien modes are called "myth." Seminal to this discussion is M. I. Finley's "Myth, Memory, and History" (1965), which traces the development of historical thought from Greek myth. For Finley, the distinction is very clear: history is chronological, organized on the basis of a coherent dating scheme and using evidence derived from documents that are then formulated into a systematic presentation; myth is the antithesis of history: non-linear, atemporal, fictional, non-systematic. Goody (1977) has expanded upon Finley's argument by suggesting that the potential for historical thought exists exclusively in literate society where objective, analytic and chronological thinking is fostered through the distancing that is only possible when a range of conflicting reports about a single event can be read and ruminated over.[6] When transported to native South America, the myth–history distinction was transformed into the supposition that our own society is "hot" and has history, while primitive society is "cold" and timeless (Lévi-Strauss 1966; Kaplan 1981). Using this sort of formulation, detailed analyses were undertaken of native texts in order to demonstrate that Andean peoples do not think in historical terms, but integrate the memory of events into a mythical framework reflecting mental structures more than temporal process (Ossio 1977; Zuidema 1982).

What is most useful to the anthropologist caught in the myth–history snare is a return to the historical literature, where we can see how theorists of history define their own discipline. They suggest that definitions of history are moving closer and closer to our own notions of myth or literature. In *The Idea of History*, one of the classics of historical theory, Collingwood (1946) defines the historical enterprise as the analysis of evidence within the framework of a universal plot-structure that is mythic in nature. To the more contemporary Hayden White (1973, 1978), the mythic framework is imposed by the very language used by historians. Prisoners of the times in which they live, they will choose one of a variety of styles of exposition that, in turn, will determine their analysis. History is not a matter of "truth," but of the choice of a particular expository style that is itself determined historically. White's definition of history, then, erases the dividing line between history and literature:

Viewed simply as verbal artifacts histories and novels are indistinguishable from one another. We cannot easily distinguish between them on formal grounds unless we approach them with specific preconceptions about the kinds of truths that each is supposed to deal in. But the aim of the writer of a novel must be the same as that of the writer of a history. Both wish to provide a verbal image of "reality." The novelist may present his notion of this reality indirectly, that is to say, by figurative techniques, rather than directly, which is to say, by registering a series of propositions which are supposed to correspond point by point to some extratextual domain of occurrence or happening, as the historian claims to do. But the image of reality which the novelist thus constructs is meant to correspond in its general outline to some domain of human experience which is no less "real" than that referred to by the historian. It is not, then, a matter of a conflict between two kinds of truth (which the Western prejudice for empiricism as the sole access to reality has foisted upon us), a conflict between the truth of correspondence, on the one side, and the truth of coherence, on the other. (White 1978: 110)

White's work is an attempt to distinguish the various mythic modes which structure historical interpretation.

Discussions among historians break down our own anthropological notion of the distinction between "structure" and "event," in which we ascribe structure to the mythic mode, while history deals with "true events" (Sahlins 1981). Contemporary historians force us to recognize that historical thought is equally determined by structural considerations. In sum, the anthropologist cannot make a distinction between "myth" and "history" until both terms are adequately defined, and historians are now clouding our once-clear typology.

A second, more radical approach used by popular historians is also useful in breaking down the anthropologist's preconceived notion of the limits of historical thought. Much of the history we learn from the communities we study is not professional history written by full-time historians, but popular history produced by individuals who do not submit to disciplinary standards. Indeed, much popular history is not encoded in formal narrations, but in public activities and ritual, in an entirely non-chronological fashion (Popular Memory Group 1982; see also Löwy 1985: 56–57). This alternative means of representing temporal process is no less

historical than our own written narrations although it does not
submit to the same canons. By disassociating them from "history"
because they do not conform to our own preconceived standards of
the historical enterprise, we do not explain these histories, we only
classify them (Sperber 1975).

CONTEXTS FOR STUDYING HISTORIES

Our own difficulties in accepting the historicity of non-Western
accounts of the past stem in part from the fact that we have not
adequately contextualized them, beyond drawing comparisons
between their structure and a more general social structure. We have
not situated them in their historical or sociopolitical contexts, but
have analyzed them as timeless texts. In an attempt to address this
problem, Bloch (1977) suggests that our difficulties in explaining
why some societies have notions of linear durational time while
others do not, can be traced to our own anthropological biases in
favor of studying the ritual sphere, while disregarding the
importance of temporal reckoning in practical activity. While Bloch
draws an unnecessarily rigid distinction between the two spheres, he
is correct in urging us to consider the practical implications of
ritualized texts and to examine their utilization in the more practical
domains of community and intercommunity life. Even more, we
must consider the importance of temporal structures informed by
ritual in the everyday activities of working, walking, eating,
sleeping, etc. We are not dealing with static "texts," but with everchanging interpretations that are applied in practice, whose form and
contents are determined both by the memory of earlier interpretations and by the exigencies of the situation.

If historical thought is itself a product of historical process, as
much related to the present as to the past, how then should we as
ethnographers approach history in the communities in which we
conduct our fieldwork? How can we ground the attributes of non-
western historical thought described above in historical process,
without neglecting the very real differences that exist among
historical visions? In an often-quoted passage, Walter Benjamin
(1968: 255) gives us a clue as to the meaning of history outside of
the walls of Academe:

To articulate the past historically does not mean to recognize it "the way it really
was" (Ranke). It means to seize hold of a memory as it flashes up at a moment of
danger... The danger affects both the content of the tradition and its receivers...

In every era the attempt must be made anew to wrest tradition away from a conformism that is about to overpower it...

Applying the thoughts of Benjamin, and of Silvia Bovenschen (1978) on the witch as an image of empowerment in the feminist movement, Michael Taussig (1984: 88) suggests that South American shamans' use of historical imagery is not meant to be understood as a link in a causal sequence, but as a metaphorical application of what is known from the past:

They are mythic images reflecting and condensing the experiential appropriation of the history of conquest, as that history is seen to form analogies and structural correspondences with the hopes and tribulations of the present...

The magical power of history lies in the contrasts and contradictions between the past as it was experienced and the structure of the present world.

This issue has been raised in the broader arena of the uses of literature and history in the Third World. History has a power in newly-formed nations because it fuels the creation of non-European definitions of society:

The capacity to control the past, by defining it as history, and to establish classifications, which differentiate Europeans from others are central to the revolutions and transformations which are part of what we call the history of the modern world.   (Cohn 1981: 244)

History is a question of power in the present, and not of detached reflection upon the past. It can serve to maintain power, or can become a vehicle for empowerment.

The power derived from controlling the past in order to redefine the future is of fundamental concern to Third World novelists who, like Taussig's shamans, produce a vision or an image of the past, as opposed to a chronology. In their novels, past, present and future interpenetrate one another:

Later generations selectively create or re-create a sense of the past, largely – though not totally – through art, and this created, simplified past in turn helps to create a sense of what the future could be. To paraphrase Stephen Dedalus, artists do forge the uncreated conscience and consciousness of their race. If that collective consciousness is sometimes a forgery, it is no less potent for that.
                                                    (Dasenbrock 1985–86: 312–13)

For these writers, the locus of the historical memory is not the past, but the present and the future:

We live today. Tomorrow we shall have an image of today. We cannot ignore this, as we cannot ignore that the past was lived, that the origin of the past is the present:

we remember here, today. But we also imagine here, today. And we should not separate what we are able to imagine from what we are able to remember. Remember the future; imagine the past: I believe that this is the truthful articulation of time as it is lived, inevitable, in the present...   (Fuentes 1985–86: 338)[7]

If the vision of history as a thing of the present which confers power is anywhere felt deepest, it is in the writings of Gabriel García Márquez. In his novels he re-writes Colombian history, interweaving legendary and mythic images with historical fact, thus sharpening the truth he wishes to convey:

The well-read reader, properly plumped with information, can distinguish the real from the invented and mark the changes worked on the real. His sense of the difference between an imagined and an actual reality is not blurred, but sharpened. The fictions that are most misleading become those that seem most real and most natural, not those that seem most artificial. Perhaps most important, such a rewriting of the past unmoors our sense of the reasonableness, naturalness, and inevitability of such a history. It has occurred, but must it continue to do so?

(Janes 1985–86: 300)

Perhaps for this very reason, many Colombian intellectuals see García Márquez as one of the few who is able to convey the true meaning of Colombianness, and to do it in a form more gripping than those "real and natural" histories. This is why he rushes to tell his stories "before the historians have time to arrive."

And this also explains the power of the mythic images so frequently encountered in non-Western narrations of the past. It is not that indigenous peoples have no sense of the flow of time, nor that they are unable to distinguish fact from fiction, nor that they prefer to confront universal and logical problems as opposed to problems on the ground, but that fictive and fantastic images may help them to reflect more fully upon the real. By using mythic or cyclical images to highlight the "holes" in the historical memory, they emphasize more powerfully the importance of the past because it is more readily recognizable. Moreover, by stressing the repetitive structure of historical process, they link the past to the future, providing a template for understanding where we came from, but also where we are going. For this reason, native North and South American histories have mirror images in futuristic visions, especially apparent in those models which gauge time as moving across a fixed number of generations from past to future, with the present as a pivot.[8]

But what is it that native histories actually focus upon? And how does historical process determine the analytic tools that native historians use to interpret their circumstances? The nature of any particular example of this blending of past, present and future, fact and fantasy, must be examined within its own historical and social context. A useful conceptual framework can be drawn from Marxist literary criticism. Eagleton (1978) has outlined the various elements which must be taken into account in the analysis of a literary text, underlining the importance of an understanding of the complex series of interactions among the broader social formation, the particular mode by which literary texts are produced and consumed, the ideology which determines standards of canonicity and controls the production and distribution of literary artifacts, the biographical attributes of the author and the aesthetic norms under which he or she works.

Eagleton's approach to literature can guide us in formulating a series of questions guiding the study of Páez historical narrative, taking us beyond a formal analysis of an isolated mythic text and into the intermediate ground where native histories and the history of the dominant society interact: What is the relationship between the insertion of indigenous peoples into the State and the form of historical interpretation they develop in their struggle to survive as an autonomous people? Under what circumstances will indigenous peoples produce histories in written forms amenable to the conceptual framework of the dominant society? How do these written histories influence the intepretive and narrative approaches of local histories made by and for community members? Under what circumstances do authors/historians arise in these communities and what is their influence on historical production within the local community? To what extent and under what conditions does the historical vision of the dominant society influence the indigenous historical vision? What is the relationship between ideology as it is expressed in these histories and as it is enacted in political practice? How do the aesthetic norms or the range of genres in which these histories are expressed affect the very nature of historical interpretation? These questions will be addressed in the chapters that follow as we trace the development of a distinctly Páez historical consciousness from the eighteenth century to the present.

PÁEZ HISTORY

This book is a history of Páez historical consciousness, tracing over the years the images and patterns that were created and revived by indigenous politicians and intellectuals as they struggled to uphold their identity and land base. It is also a history of Páez relations with the dominant society, examining the space of historical interpretation that lies at the interface of the two worlds. This will be accomplished through a juxtaposition of political and textual analysis, in an effort to illustrate the historical constraints that have determined the aboriginal vision of the past at several junctures in the history of Tierradentro.

The Páez present an interesting case for the study of historical consciousness because of the time-depth of available documentation of their historical thought, beginning in the early eighteenth century in the form of *resguardo* titles, continuing through the nineteenth and early twentieth centuries with published treatises, and ending in the present day with widespread storytelling by individuals of great insight and talent. Many of the assertions of Páez historians since the eighteenth century can be checked against other documentary evidence, helping us to determine the historicity of their accounts. Moreover, this documentation contains a vast quantity of information on the political tactics of native historymakers, giving us further indications of how their historical vision was translated into practice.

What is perhaps most intriguing about the Páez example is the fact that it is relatively easy to reconstruct a clear chain of transmission of historical data from one historian to the next: each of the succeeding generations we will be examining had at its disposal documents from the previous generation and used them as a basis for historical interpretation. Thus, we have a continuous range of historical evidence with which to analyze the structure of Páez historical thought and its translation into an ideology that informs activity aimed at the physical and cultural maintenance of the group.

The chains of transmission of the Páez historical vision permit the drawing of a moral continuity between the precolumbian inhabitants of Tierradentro and the twentieth-century population that lives there. Moral continuity is expressed in Páez definitions of their own identity, as much in myth as in toponymy, genealogies and chiefly titles. Whether or not they are the same group as fought the Spaniards in 1572 is immaterial: what matters is that they perceive this link as existing, and have fashioned their ideology so as to legitimize it.

Three key sources will be used to document the development of historical consciousness among the Páez:

1 Colonial *resguardo* titles

Eighteenth-century *resguardo* titles were written with the participation of *caciques*, the most well-known of whom was Don Juan Tama of Vitoncó. While establishing a territorial and political base for communities, they also provide a Páez interpretation of intertribal relations and the rise of a new political authority.[9] Although the titles appear on the surface to be chronological narratives of events that transpired during the coming to power of these rulers, a careful reading suggests that the narrators condensed time-frames, giving us accounts that combine information from the pre-Conquest era with colonial data. These sources, which are official colonial documents, were written in Spanish.

2 Political treatises

At the beginning of the twentieth century *indigenista* leader Manuel Quintín Lame wrote a treatise entitled *The Thoughts of the Indian Educated in the Colombian Forests* (Lame 1971),[10] which remained as a handwritten manuscript until it was published in the early 1970s by the Comité de Defensa del Indio. Written in Spanish, this document utilizes Páez history to justify the political activities of its author. Its style represents a blending of the chronological and factual historical tradition of non-Indian Colombian society with a more mythical Páez vision of the past. Lame's activities are well documented in Colombian archives and newspapers (Castrillón 1973; Sevilla Casas 1976b; Tello 1982), allowing us to trace the political implementation of his historical knowledge.

3 Contemporary historical interpretation

The contemporary Páez express their historical tradition through political rhetoric, myth, ritual and visual images, conveyed in both Spanish and Páez, and act upon this knowledge through their political institutions, drawing upon the earlier historical visions described above. But talented and observant individuals, such as Julio Niquinás,[11] a follower of Lame and a long-time political activist who participated in the founding of contemporary ethnic rights organizations, more carefully articulate oral and written evidence to create interpretations that fuel grassroots historical consciousness.

Páez historiography is best examined through the contributions of individual intellectuals. Given the marginal status of the Páez within the colonial and national systems, only intellectuals were able to bridge the gap between oral and written communication, permitting the utilization of a vast range of sources of evidence and the transmission of historical interpretations from one generation to the next. These individuals were frequently also political leaders, disseminating their theories as they organized their followers, thus fostering a lively oral tradition which we can observe today, but whose past contents we can only guess at. These men made history in a double sense: they altered the course of historical events through political action and reinterpreted historical process through narrative. We will study both in the coming chapters.

None of these individuals was a professional historian in the Western sense of the term. In fact, none enjoyed a lengthy formal education and it is not even clear as to whether all were literate. The colonial *caciques* dictated their thoughts to scribes.[12] Quintín Lame could read, but he could not write well and he routinely used Indian secretaries to take dictation for his treatise, for the many newspaper articles he composed and for the myriad legal documents he drew up in defense of the Páez and surrounding communities. Of all the historians to be examined here, only Julio Niquinás was literate in the full sense of the word, having spent a few years at school and later honing his skills in the Indian movement.

The power of the historical interpretations made by these men was not due to any professional qualifications. Nevertheless, I would suspect that they were all good listeners and that their histories are syntheses of traditions known by their contemporaries, developed into coherent narratives through their own interpretive skills. Most importantly, all of these historians were political activists: Tama forged the *resguardo* system in Tierradentro, Lame revived its importance across three Colombian departments, Niquinás participated in pan-Indian politics from 1915 through the 1970s, joining an internationally recognized movement. It was political participation on a regional or national scale that afforded these men the opportunity to acquire a more global perspective on the thoughts, actions and problems of their people, a knowledge that lent a power and a sophistication to their historical narratives. Their political stature also permitted their voices to be heard within and beyond the confines of Tierradentro. Moreover, their political activities provided a clear context in which history was a source of inspiration in the formulation of tactics and strategy.

What is intriguing about these historians is that each was intimately linked to whoever came before or after him. Colonial *resguardo* titles were a source of inspiration for Quintín Lame, who was an avid archival researcher, and the example of the colonial *caciques* gave him a framework for the formulation of political demands and a clear picture of the territorial boundaries of the communities he aimed to reconstruct. Contemporary oral tradition is an elaboration upon these documents, originating I suspect, in Quintín Lame's revalidation of their contents some 50 years ago. There are also direct links between the material produced by Lame and the histories of Julio Niquinás, for Niquinás was Lame's secretary for several years while the two served prison sentences together.

Chains of transmission of historical knowledge are only important insofar as they help their recipients to elicit powerful images of the past, images which move people to action. Among the Páez, the power of historical sources not only stems from the sophistication of their historians, but even more from the magical power they commanded. Don Juan Tama of Vitoncó claimed to be the son of the stars of the Tama Stream, born of the supernatural. Quintín Lame repeatedly asserted that he was a direct descendant of the *cacique* of Vitoncó, and although it is probable that he was not related to Don Juan Tama, the exclusive information to which he was privy as a result of his archival investigations lent him an aura of power that undoubtedly led many to believe that he was indeed linked to the culture hero. The people of northern Tierradentro believe that Tama was born in a stream near the hamlet of Cabuyo and that his only living descendants are the members of the Cabuyo-based Niquinás family to which Julio Niquinás belonged. While on one level the power of these historians derived from their descent from Juan Tama and thus indirectly, from the supernatural, on a deeper level it is clear that all have an attribute in common: they were all cultural brokers, with one foot in Páez society and the other planted in Colombian national life. A careful comparison in the following chapters of the two titles drawn up by Don Juan Tama indicates that the *cacique* was probably not Páez, and possessed a much more broad cross-cultural experience than did his subjects. Manuel Quintín Lame was not reared on a *resguardo*, but was brought up as a sharecropper near the departmental capital of Popayán and served as a soldier in Panama in the War of the Thousand Days at the turn of the century. Julio Niquinás was brought up in Cabuyo, but spent periods working with Lame outside of Tierradentro and had extensive experience with attorneys. Novel and powerful images were created by these men, who were undoubtedly perceived as extraordinary because of their ease in moving through the bureaucratic apparatus of the State.

Although descent from the culture heroes is one of the components in the making of a Páez historian, it is not a sufficient condition for an individual to reach the heights of a Quintín Lame or a Julio Niquinás. In Togoima, members of the Guyumús family, the descendants of the Gueyomuse *caciques*, speak with a certain authority about historical matters. But they are unable to produce the sophisticated interpretations of the historians we will be examining. They repeat stories they have heard, but cannot weave new ones, nor integrate narrations about local matters into a more universal account. This is undoubtedly due to their lack of active participation in political activity beyond the local level. Herein lies one of the key areas in which the nature of the State determines the level of historical awareness among the Páez. History is an arm for the communal definition and resistance which arise as an adaptation to State expansion. As broader political units are forged in an attempt to contend with State power, historical interpretation must assume a more global vision if it is to be of any use in these projects. A universal perspective means, in this case, an understanding of the interrelationships between historical process in an array of communities, as well as a clear image of the major developments in the dominant society that have bearing on local history and political process. I do not mean to say that a more universal history is present in all indigenous communities, for it is most emphatically not. But it must be assumed that in cases in which a broad-based organization is needed, a universal history will begin to surface. This is as true for the precolumbian states of the Americas as in indigenous communities living under the Spanish colonial State or the nation-states of contemporary Latin America.

The nature of the State is central to the analysis of native historical interpretation for other reasons. The mode of narration and even the language chosen by the historian are intimately linked to the character of the State which he confronts. Thus, colonial Páez historians transmitted their interpretations through royal titles whose purposes were other than that of disseminating history, documents composed for the most part by non-Indians; the scribes only permitted *caciques* to make brief allusions to the history that empowered them. The written product of their thought was inaccessible to all but the chiefs themselves and the colonial authorities: the documents were written in Spanish and were stored in repositories in an era in which documentary investigation was by official appointment and not open to the population in general. Moreover, while the colonial system afforded indigenous communities a certain degree of political and territorial autonomy, it also isolated them from the dominant society in order to maintain an easily accessible labor pool. So the resources and contacts available to those Páez who were not *caciques* were quite limited and if any of them produced histories, their voices have not survived the flow of time.

In contrast, Quintín Lame and Julio Niquinás lived in a different era. Both were fluent in Spanish, as many Páez are nowadays. State policies that conferred citizenship upon Indians in order to integrate them into the nation and control their lands and allegiances, also gave them access to a broad range of media in which their histories could be transmitted. The Páez were active in the Colombian military and in political parties, and several of them were accorded the rank of General or Colonel. By the turn of the century an Indian could write newspaper articles, as did Lame, or even aspire to writing longer treatises (although his power to publish them was still limited). There was a broad audience for the Indian activist who communicated with the news media. Anxious to define an identity for the new Colombian nation, as well as to acquire empirical support for Colombia's place in the nineteenth-century march of "progress," history became an important vocation and academies of history complete with archives were established at the local, regional and national levels. Given these conditions, it is not surprising that Quintín Lame should have engaged in archival research, both to write history and to change it. In response to State policy, the notion of what it meant to be an Indian had also expanded in Lame's time. Lame forged a broad organization of Páez, Guambiano and the descendants of the Pijao in Tolima. In this new context, effective pan-Indian communication could only be achieved in the Spanish language. A sharecropper whose family had been uprooted from Tierradentro before he was born, Lame himself could not speak Páez and was thus a product of his times.

The context of Julio Niquinás' historical thinking was yet broader. At the time he was interviewed, indigenous organizations began to spring up throughout the continent. The Consejo Regional Indígena del Cauca (Regional Indian Council of Cauca) was in formation, ultimately producing its own newspaper that is circulated throughout Colombia as well as internationally. Here was a yet broader stage for pan-Indian communication, in which Indians did not only use the media, but in some cases actually controlled it. Their audience expanded to include international support groups and foundations. Although Niquinás' history is in oral form, it draws upon this increased media support and broader audience. The very orality of the Niquinás narratives is of a different nature than are other examples of contemporary storytelling, because it has been tape-recorded. Electronic recording of speech allows for a more faithful reproduction of the speech event, including in addition to the complete text, information regarding voice quality and tone. With the advent of inexpensive recording devices, the spoken word acquires a fixity which surpasses that of written communication (Ong 1982). Recordings are being actively used by the Indian movement in Páez language radio programs. This is by no means the same orality as that of the pre-electronic era.

But as the State intruded further and further into Páez life and the Páez widened their vistas, identifying themselves with other Indians and seeking an international audience, the very nature of their relationship with the outside also fostered the maintenance of an oral tradition on the local level, a mode of transmission which undoubtedly thrived throughout Páez history, although we have no record of it. The oral tradition is encoded in the geography of Tierradentro, surfacing in the form of myth and references to sacred sites. New interpretations of the past also appear in court cases, where historical knowledge is used as evidence. The oral accounts also serve as mnemonic devices for remembering *resguardo* boundaries, since most of the mythicized events occur along frontiers. The oral nature of this history lends it a flexibility of interpretation necessary if it is to be applied to everyday life. Orality also permits the community to maintain some history as its own, not shared with the dominant society and told in the Páez language. Finally, given that the writing of history is now firmly in the hands of a broad pan-Indian movement with its own media apparatus, Páez historians wishing to interpret the distinctly Páez experience for their own people choose an oral mode of transmission which is currently bolstered by the production of picture maps (Bonilla 1982) and symbols of the Páez nationality, which are powerful images evoking memories of the Páez past in novel genres.

The array of examples of Páez historical interpretation available to us represents a broad range of genres, extending from the mythical to the factual, some influenced by Colombian historiography and some more autochthonous in nature. The choice of which genre and which mode of interpretation to apply is not made in a vacuum: it is a conscious and strategic choice, determined in light of the nature of the political juncture and the character of the audience. The experience of the individual historian in both the local and national arenas will also influence the mode in which he expresses his thoughts. Thus, the study of Páez historical consciousness is not so much the creation of a myth–history typology, as the careful examination of how culturally-specific modes of historical interpretation articulate with political activity at the interface of two cultures.

In the following pages, the complex interplay of chains of transmission, genre, and political and historical juncture will be explored in the work of Don Juan Tama, Manuel Quintín Lame and Julio Niquinás. Their historical vision – which I will call "Páez history" – will be contrasted with my own reconstruction of their past – "the history of the Páez." In this way we will be better able to gauge the historicity of indigenous accounts on the one hand, and on the other, to reconstruct the constraints that determined the nature of aboriginal history in each period.

I

The creation of a chiefly ideology: Páez historical thought under Spanish rule

2

The rise of the colonial *cacique*

The patterns of Páez historical expression that we will trace from the eighteenth century to the present find their origins in the precolumbian period. Colonial *caciques*, who reforged the nature of political rule in Tierradentro, used the living memory of their precolumbian predecessors to fashion a model of the chiefdom relevant to their day and age. Their revitalization of the precolumbian *cacicazgo* was based more on the spirit than the letter of the political systems of the past, obeying the limitations of the colonial conditions under which they operated. Before examining the reinvention of the chiefdom under Don Juan Tama, though, let us consider the nature of political process in Tierradentro at the time of the Spanish invasion to acquire a picture of the historical substratum upon which Tama built his rule.

THE PRECOLUMBIAN *cacicazgo*

When the Spaniards arrived in Tierradentro in the mid-sixteenth century, they entered a recently-colonized territory, a frontier. According to the Spanish chronicler Juan de Velasco (1977–79 [1789]: 2: 65),[1] at the time of the Spanish invasion the two loci of Páez settlement were near La Plata and in Tierradentro. The Indians of La Plata were, in Velasco's words, less "rustic" than their cousins in Tierradentro, implying that the La Plata settlement was older and more well-established than the colony in Tierradentro. Archaeological evidence indicates that Velasco's contention was accurate, and dates Páez settlement in Tierradentro to the fourteenth century, AD (Pérez de Barradas 1943; Nachtigall 1955; Long and Yánguez 1970–71; Cháves and Puerta 1976, 1980). In 1564 a rebellion hit the environs of La Plata, organized by the Páez residing in the area. While the organizers sought support from other indigenous nations, they eschewed a military alliance with the Páez of Tierradentro, who were not seen as capable of serving as useful allies (Velasco 1979: 2: 66). The Páez settlements in Tierradentro were frontier posts, with their political center in La Plata; La Plata's influence extended from the eastern slopes to the edges of the tropical forest, where the Páez shared a border with the Timaná (ibid.: 70; Friede 1953: 140).

Sixteenth-century Tierradentro was multiethnic, its territory shared by the linguistically unrelated Páez, Guanacas and Pijao (Aguado 1956 [1575?]).[2] Although settlement was dispersed, there were some nodes of population concentration. For example, Aguado (ibid.: 524) described the Mesa de Páez (in the general vicinity of the modern village of Wila) in the following words:

It was an attractive plain, at that time well-cultivated and planted, half a league in length and half of that in breadth, and in it there were many hamlets...

The *cacique* (hereditary chief) Suyn, who lived along the lower Moras River, ruled over 500 houses (ibid.: 556). Nevertheless, the territory was characterized – and continued to be so throughout the colonial and post-Independence era – by a dispersed pattern of settlement (Hazañero 1645: 211; Rodríguez 1684: 25; ANC/B [Archivo Nacional de Colombia, Bogotá] 1751). In most cases, the people abandoned their homes upon the birth or death of an inhabitant (FDNR [*Fuentes documentales para la historia del Nuevo Reino de Granada*] 1975–76 [1564]; Rodríguez 1684: 73; Magnin 1964 [1725]: 54; Castillo 1877 [1755]: 86).

These scattered households of maize and manioc farmers did not yield easily to Spanish rule. The European invaders labored for a century to pacify the people of Tierradentro. Their dispersed mode of settlement impeded successful Spanish control of localities. Moreover, well-schooled in the arts of war, the Páez always noted the arrival of invading troops, spying them from the high mountains in which they made their homes (Hazañero 1645: 218). During the first century of resistance the Páez maintained their autonomy by engaging in guerrilla warfare, as well as by forging alliances with neighboring groups, such as the Pijao and Yalcón.[3]

Organization of sixteenth-century Páez *cacicazgos*

According to Aguado, there were three principal *parcialidades*, or regional political units in sixteenth-century Tierradentro (Map 4), led by the *caciques* Páez (to the north along the upper Páez River), Suyn (in the Moras drainage) and Abirama (to the south, along the

Map 4   Precolumbian *cacicazgos* of Tierradentro

lower Páez River). Probably, sixteenth-century chiefly territories
corresponded to the modern-day locations of the Mesa de Páez, Suin
and Avirama. The toponyms, which conserve the name of the
ancient *caciques*, were applied by the Spaniards; modern Páez place-
names describe characteristics of the sites.[4]

There were other political leaders under the three supreme rulers,
the minor *caciques* or *principales*:

Tarabira was ruled by a female *principal*, sister of the lords Páez, Tálaga and
Simurga, who were *principales* and *caciques* in those lands: they all belonged to a
different community from that of Abirama, because Abirama warred with them.
And Esmisa, with Suyn, his father, were the heads of another community. Thus,
three *parcialidades* existed in the province, and their *principales* were followed by the
rest of the *caciques* in the territory, each according to his preference.

(Aguado 1956: 518–19)

At first reading, this resembles the political organization of pre-Incaic Quito (Moreno 1978; Salomon 1986) and the Chibcha of the Bogotá area (Villamarín and Villamarín 1979), where kin groups claiming mythical ancestors were lorded over by *caciques*, and *cacicazgos* were subdivided into units headed by *principales*. Political leadership among the Pubenense of Popayán was similarly subdivided, so that under the supreme chief or *yasgüen*, were *caciques* ruling sections of villages, *caschu* heading smaller portions of communities, and *carabic* commoners given temporary responsibility for village administration (Mosquera 1866: 48; Earle n.d.b: 13–15).[5]

The first Jesuits to enter Tierradentro discovered 24 *caciques* in the area, probably including both minor *caciques* and *principales* (Hazañero 1645). Most of these were Páez. A tributary list dating from the end of the seventeenth century includes more than 28 *caciques* and *principales* in Tierradentro, indicating that each of these leaders enjoyed the allegiance of, on average, 60 to 80 followers (ANH/Q [Archivo Nacional de Historia, Quito] 1703 [1663]). These figures coincide with calculations made on the size of similar units in Quito (Salomon 1986: 117–22).

The colonial data present us with a labyrinth of poorly-defined terms, corresponding more to a European than a Páez terminology. *Caciques* were both contrasted with *principales* and described as interchangeable with them; levels of socio-political integration were thus continually confused. The chroniclers linked political leaders to territorial or population units called *parcialidades*, which were never well defined. Nevertheless, a careful analysis of the colonial sources, especially of Aguado's chronicle, provides a partial picture of the nature of the *cacicazgo* in this period.

At the outset we must define the extent of chiefly authority shared by the three major *caciques* at the time of the Spanish invasion.[6] An eighteenth-century Páez–Spanish dictionary (Castillo 1877: 64) provides us with some indication of the attributes of these leaders, calling them *netoth*, or "superiors in governing or power." Inferior political leaders were linked to the supreme rulers through kin-ties, the chiefly hierarchy defined by age or generational criteria. Thus, Aguado (1956: 518) noted a series of five siblings, all *caciques*, living along the upper Páez River: Páez, Tarabira, Tálaga, Simurga and Nuesga. Páez was the most powerful of the five, heading the *parcialidad*. In the Páez language a distinction was made among siblings according to birth order. In the eighteenth century, the youngest sibling was called *pevi* (Castillo 1877: 72) and the oldest, *netée* (ibid.: 64); the same root appears in the word *netoth*, used to describe the supreme *caciques*. The *cacique* Páez was *netoth*, the supreme ruler. He was probably also the eldest – *netée* – of his sibling group, and for this reason reigned over his brothers and sisters.

Chiefly rank was also determined by generational criteria. There were a number of father–son chiefly teams, where the father occupied the superior position. For example, Suyn was the *cacique* of an entire *parcialidad*, while his son Esmisa ruled with him (Aguado 1956: 519). Esmisa most probably occupied a hierarchical position similar to that of minor *caciques* and *principales* unrelated to one of the three supreme rulers. Aguado (ibid.: 540) suggests as much in his description of a banquet in which *principales* were seated together with the sons of the supreme *caciques*, in an order that appears to have been defined according to political rank. That is to say, the occupants of lower positions stood in relation to the higher ranks in the same way that the son of a supreme ruler stood in relation to his father. Nevertheless, if we try to compare the number of followers subject to *caciques*, *principales* and the children of supreme rulers, we discover that there was little difference in this respect, the same range of variation applying in all cases (ANH/Q 1703).

In sixteenth-century Quito the brothers of rulers occupied a special status, frequently intervening in the political activities of their siblings (Salomon 1986: 133). This does not appear to have been the case among the groups of chiefly siblings in Tierradentro, but was quite possibly true for father–son teams. Esmisa, the son of Suyn, and Itanquiba, son of Abirama, both assumed chiefly responsibilities at critical junctures (Aguado 1956: 538). But not all chiefly children achieved political hegemony on their native soils. A seventeenth-century list of Páez tributaries on the western slopes of the cordillera includes the *cacique* Tobalo of Toribío, who had 120 subjects; he was the son of the *cacique* Tálaga of Tierradentro (ANH/Q 1703: f.47v). Perhaps Tobalo colonized the western slopes as an emissary sent by his father. But he might also have left Tierradentro because he was unable to consolidate power in the area. It might be that the supreme *caciques* of Tierradentro were in fact the younger sons of the Páez chiefs of La Plata, sent to the higher altitudes of Tierradentro to found border settlements.

The nature of cacical power

How powerful were the sixteenth-century Páez supreme *caciques*? This is a difficult question to answer. If we compare them to the *caciques* of Quito (Salomon 1986: 125), they were not severe rulers: their subjects did not fear them. As in Quito, their homes were centers of the cosmic order: according to Castillo (1877: 85; ANC/B 1751: 228r), they presided over ceremonies, providing all the *chicha* or corn beer consumed by the guests. But it was only during wartime that they made decisions, commanded armies or assumed diplomatic duties. As commanders of armies they undertook long and difficult fasts before going on military incursions (Hazañero 1645: 213). Nevertheless, Hazañero complained that the Páez lived "without submitting to their Caciques, obstinately rebelling against the Spaniard" (ibid.: 214). According to Aguado (1956: 214), *principales* allied themselves with the regional rulers according to their own appraisal of the *cacique*'s capacity as a leader. Political loyalty was not determined by geographical proximity or membership in a kin group, and no leader commanded a fixed group of followers. Nor are there any indications that *caciques* controlled lands or that they collected tribute from their followers. In fact, the missionary descriptions of the period, written during fleeting eras of peace, only mentioned *cacicazgos* infrequently; in contrast, Aguado, who recounted the events of wartime, spoke more often of the *caciques* of Tierradentro. Moreover, the missionaries never mentioned the regional *cacicazgos*, citing only those leaders we would call lesser *caciques* or *principales*.

In the Andean regions adjacent to Tierradentro, that is, in Bogotá, Quito and Popayán, a fixed political hierarchy defined the political jurisdictions of social units. Individual rank was determined by genealogical distance from rulers. Some of these rulers were isolated from everyday life and some intervened in the lives of their subjects, even choosing their marriage partners (Trimborn 1949; Salomon 1986; Villamarín and Villamarín 1979). Among Tierradentro's neighbors who lived in the foothills of the Andes, the situation was quite different. There were 72 Pijao *caciques*, their supreme rulers chosen apparently by consensus (Ordóñez 1942: 184). Historians have similarly found little evidence for a rigid political hierarchy among the Andakí, whose *caciques* enjoyed only very restricted political authority (Friede 1953: 86–88).

Instead of explaining the character of political authority in terms of chiefly control over subjects, Clastres (1977) suggests that in lowland South America the opposite was in fact the case. Here, in civil matters, it would be best to speak of control by the group over its *cacique* or *cacica*, who was more an arbitrator than a ruler, the extent of their power determined by group consensus; should they overstep the bounds of their authority or shirk their duties, they would be abandoned by their subjects. In this system, chiefly authority became institutionalized only during wartime.

Similarly, the Páez exerted political control over their *caciques*. Authority was divided among a number of rulers who only appeared in the chronicle record during wartime. Group composition was fluid and leaders were subject to the whims of their followers, even during wars.

The same sorts of distinctions can be made within the economic sphere. As in the political realm, the lowland chiefs exercised little economic power over their followers, and in contrast, the latter controlled them (Clastres 1977). The *cacique* was a generous person, giving more than he received. Under these circumstances, there was no redistribution of goods collected in the form of tribute, given that there was nothing to redistribute.

Reichel-Dolmatoff (1978: 69) argues that the Andean chiefdom arose in conjunction with an evolution in social complexity made possible by the introduction of maize cultivation on the recently-colonized mountain slopes, thus permitting the consolidation of an easily-stored agricultural surplus. This economic complex gave rise to a political system based on the redistribution of foodstuffs by *caciques*, replacing an earlier form of reciprocal exchange that characterized these groups before their migration to the sierra. Similar redistributive norms appeared in Bogotá, Quito and in the nearby Cauca Valley, where moreover, *caciques* controlled a greater proportion of the means of production than did their subjects (Trimborn 1949: 212). According to Aguado (1956: 534) the Guambiano *cacique* Calambar, who allied himself with the Spaniards in their invasion of Tierradentro, easily raised 400 *cargas* of maize to use in his task of diplomacy. The Páez *caciques* were never mentioned as having had access to such a quantity of goods.

But among the tribes of the Andean foothills near Tierradentro such economic hegemony was unknown. Friede (1953: 86) found no documents mentioning tributary relations among the tribes of the Magdalena Valley. Although the Pijao were involved in the conquest of neighboring lands, there is no indication that they exacted tribute

from those they conquered. Similarly, there is no mention of tribute
collection among the Páez, whose *caciques* do not seem to have led a
more luxurious life than their subjects.

Nevertheless, Páez *caciques* enjoyed other sources of power. Like
neighboring Pijao chiefs (Lucena 1962: 148), they engaged in
ceremonial preparations before making war, playing an important
supernatural role in their communities. The first Jesuits to reach
Tierradentro met one of the *caciques* of Taravira, Paimoco, who was
renowned as a shaman (Hazañero 1645: 216). Chiefly power was
undoubtedly defined in part through shamanistic activity. This was
probably equally true in the Popayán area, for which Earle (n.d.b:
13–15) has done an interesting derivation of *yasgüen*, the word for
supreme ruler, translated as the "wand of power" or "magical
seminal plant."

In summary, the most reasonable characterization of chiefly
authority in sixteenth-century Tierradentro is a system of diffuse and
non-centralized political and economic power, depending upon a
base of popular support maintained through the supernatural
authority wielded by the chief (Rappaport, 1987a). Similar to the
non-Andean communities of the foothills of the cordillera with
whom the Páez cemented alliances against the Spaniards, the Páez
polity can be contrasted with the more institutionalized political
hierarchies of its Andean neighbors which, while more rigid, were
also more easily dismantled by the Spanish invaders.

Interethnic relations

At the time of the Spanish invasion of what is today southwestern
Colombia, a high degree of interaction and exchange existed among
the multiple ethnic groups that shared a common territory. To the
west lived various groups belonging to the Guambiano-Coconuco
linguistic family, some maintaining close relations with the *caciques* of
Tierradentro, while others warred with them. To the east, in the
foothills of the cordillera, were the tropical forest tribes of the
intermontane valleys who cemented military alliances within the
Páez. Of these myriad communities surrounding Tierradentro, those
who are of greatest importance to the Páez historical vision are the
highland Guambiano of the western slopes of the Central Cordillera
and the intermontane Pijao of the Magdalena Valley.

There is no conclusive agreement among scholars as to the nature
of the Guambiano polity. Some chroniclers (Escobar 1938 [1582])

note that in the Popayán plateau reigned a man called Popayán as supreme chief or *yasgüen*. His rule was linked to that of his brother (or possibly his classificatory brother) Calambás, who lorded over the cordillera itself. Some modern scholars contend that Popayán was a kingdom in which younger male siblings occupied positions of authority in subordinate communities (Trimborn 1949) or that it was a pre-state formation (Llanos 1981). Others suggest that there existed a confederation of linguistically-related tribes with their center in Popayán (Lehmann 1963). Still others maintain that political rule was decentralized, with local rulers exercising control over economic surplus and maintaining diplomatic and trade relations with surrounding communities; although not linked in a confederation *per se*, chiefs were related to each other through bonds of kinship (Hernández de Alba 1963; Earle n.d.b; Botero 1982). Analytic differences aside, the Guambiano polity was evidently more highly consolidated than that of the Páez: the chronicler Castellanos (1944: 458) and the colonial official Anuncíbay (1963 [1592]: 198) describe a population density unknown to Tierradentro and an architectural style which, while perhaps exaggerated, was certainly more grandiose than that of the Páez .

The Páez were not associated politically with the Guambianos: instead, they warred with each other. Aguado's description of the 1562 war between the Páez and Captain Domingo Lozano includes a detailed sketch of the Guambiano *cacique* Diego Calambar, perhaps a close relation of the Calambás mentioned by Escobar for the 1530s. Calambar lived in Tierradentro at some point subsequent to the Spanish invasion and must have incurred the wrath of the Páez at that time, because he joined ranks with Captain Lozano against the people of Tierradentro. Perhaps the Guambiano–Páez enmity arose over control of territory, given that at the time of the Spanish invasion both groups were establishing frontier settlements in the upper reaches of the cordillera (Botero 1982). The Páez feared Calambar, a powerful man who commanded vast armies and was able to raise huge quantities of supplies from his subjects. At various points during the war he demonstrated his political hegemony, dominating the local *caciques*. He served in one instance as the representative of all the indigenous forces (Aguado 1956: 537). At another point he offered an elaborate feast, thus assuming the role of supreme *cacique* while on alien soil (ibid.).

The Páez responded to Guambiano hegemony with military action. The Spanish colonial administration complained repeatedly of Páez attacks on Guambiano communities, resulting in death and destruction (FDNR 1559, 1576; AGI/S [Archivo General de Indias, Sevilla] 1582; ACC/P 1583–89). The Guambiano–Páez enmity outlived the Spanish invasion.

In contrast, Páez relations with the tribes to the east were more friendly. They forged alliances with the Pijao and Yalcón armies, as is repeatedly stated in the chronicle and documentary record. In fact, in many instances colonial observers confused Páez with Pijao. Nevertheless, Páez–Pijao relations were never cemented on a regional basis, but were the prerogative of local groups. Thus, while Aguado documented intertribal military alliances in response to the invasion of the Lozano forces, some of the lesser *caciques* sought cooperative arrangements to defend themselves from their inter-montane neighbors:

> Out of the Spanish quarters came the Indian, with only one eye, which did not augur well for cementing the peace, and he brought as a gift to the Captain, an arroba [*c.* 25 lbs.] of salt, and he told how he and another widow-woman were the lords of certain salt springs which were located in that valley, from which they artificially made salt by boiling and evaporation, and thus supplied themselves with the amount they needed. But all of the *caciques* and Indians of that province who wanted to make salt were not impeded from the task, and those that did not want to do the work were given it in return for aiding them in fighting the Pexaos, their principal enemies who came to assault them and destroy them and kidnap their women and children and sisters, and they had killed many people.
>
> (Aguado 1956: 527)

Thus, the Pijao, who were as decentralized as the Páez, were better able to relate to particular Páez *cacicazgos* than were the more powerful Guambiano chiefs.

THE SPANISH INVASION

By the end of the fourth decade of the sixteenth century the Spanish armies began to encroach on Páez territory, initiating a century of war. The Spanish invasion, euphemistically labelled a series of "entries" or *entradas*, began in 1538, with Pedro de Añasco's attack on the eastern Páez borders near Timaná, a confrontation that precipitated the military alliance of Páez and Yalcón and ended in Añasco's death. Military confrontation continued during the 1540s, the most notable being the 1542 rout in Tálaga of Sebastián de Benalcázar, founder of Popayán and of Quito (CDSB [*Colección de documentos inéditos relativos al Adelantado Capitán Don Sebastián de Benalcázar*] 1936 [1544]). From 1560 to 1589 a number of Spanish towns were founded and a series of battles for hegemony ensued, all of which the Páez won.[7] During this period of war, the Páez found their principal allies in the Pijao who had pushed into the cordillera from their center in the Magdalena Valley. With the Spanish defeat of the Pijao in the early seventeenth century, the Páez increasingly came under European influence.

The Spaniards penetrated indigenous communities by means of the *encomienda*, a royal grant given to conquerors in recognition of certain contributions they had made in the interests of the Crown. The *encomienda* gave its recipient rights to tribute from community members in exchange for a series of obligations, ranging from taking responsibility for converting them to Christianity, to defending the region militarily. *Encomienda* grants were made among the Páez early on, beginning with the 1538 contacts in Timaná. Nevertheless, tribute censuses or *visitas* indicate that although *encomiendas* were awarded, their fruits were never reaped, due to the high level of conflict in the area (AGI/S 1558; ACC/P 1583–89; Earle n.d.a). It was not until the 1640s that the Spaniards began to penetrate Tierradentro effectively, using the *encomienda* (Sevilla 1976a).

Although the *encomienda* was late in becoming a direct vehicle for European penetration of the Páez, indirectly it had already been very effective. The neighboring Guambiano were integrated early on within the *encomienda* system. In return for certain benefits, including land-grants and the opportunity to continue to develop their own political authority, Guambiano *caciques* became active allies of the Spaniards in their wars against the Páez (Earle n.d.a).

Stinging from the blow of military defeat, the Páez continued to resist the Spaniards, planning attacks on Spanish towns and also avoiding European hegemony on an individual basis. Many Indians reacted to the Spaniards by leaving Tierradentro, refusing to plant crops or by hiding in the mountains:

They hardly plant crops, even for their own sustenance, and most of the year they suffer from hunger due to their own laziness. Also, they have little stability in the places in which they live [and] they leave when they so desire and go to the Valley of Neiva and thus there is no *encomendero* who has been able to compel them or make use of them...   (ACC/P 1684: 6r)

and

There are more than six thousand Indians who have taken up arms and although many of them have been granted in *encomienda* to different persons according to their *parcialidad*, they have not reduced them to town life but let them live in the mountains and crags...   (ANH/Q 1663: 107r)

Abandoning their settlements, dying in warfare and from disease, the indigenous population of Tierradentro declined during the early colonial period (AGI/S 1673). Depopulation was heavy in the Popayán region, where a 1560 population of approximately 25,000 persons was halved by 1582 (Padilla *et al.* 1977: 55). It had halved again by 1600, and declined to a low of 2,500 by 1667 (Colmenares 1979: 178), primarily due to epidemics, war, family disintegration and the abuses of the *encomenderos* (Padilla *et al.* 1977). According to Sevilla (1976a), the population of Tierradentro plummeted from a precolumbian level of 7,000 to 10,000, to 4,000 by the beginning of the eighteenth century.[8]

Colonial Popayán

For much of its early colonial history Tierradentro fell within the jurisdiction of the Province of Popayán and the Royal Court (*Audiencia*) of Quito. Popayán was a frontier region, bounded by tribes hostile to the Spaniards, such as the Páez and their Pijao, Timaná and Yalcón allies. The Spaniards conquered the Valley of Pubén, where Popayán is located, and the western slopes of the Central Cordillera by the mid-1530s, but were not successful in bringing the border tribes under European supervision. The Crown disbursed land grants measuring in the thousands of hectares along the length of this border, thus creating frontier haciendas whose boundaries were not always clear, and which suffered from a continuous labor shortage; hence the *hacendados* preferred to concentrate on the raising of what were almost wild cattle (Colmenares 1979: 178–81). It was not until the mid-seventeenth century that these extensive landholdings were institutionalized and validated. Throughout the seventeenth century they remained in the hands of the families of the conquerors who had been granted them (ibid.: 181–90).

By the eighteenth century Popayán became a mining center with rich gold deposits around Caloto, which bordered on Páez territory, as well as in the western Chocó jungles. Cattle haciendas were converted into productive farms providing foodstuffs for the mining centers. The *hacienda de campo* or country plantation of the Popayán region supplied cereals to the mines. Lacking a substantial local labor pool, Indians were brought in from surrounding areas to raise wheat and corn. In the Caloto area and in the Cauca Valley *haciendas de trapiche* or sugar-processing plantations were established on former frontier lands. Most of these eighteenth-century grain and sugar haciendas developed out of the frontier haciendas of the earlier period, which were sold to businessmen and mining entrepreneurs and carved up into smaller pieces (ibid.: 186–206). Thus, the final defeat of the Páez coincided with the development of the hacienda system and the conquered Indians of Tierradentro, newly consolidated within working *encomiendas*, were fed into these enterprises.

The creation of new population centers

Much of the labor brought in to man the *haciendas de campo* was Páez in origin, precipitating a large migration of Páez to the western slopes of the cordillera. But western migration had its origins well before the mining boom, with the passage of Indians to the western slopes as war refugees. The records of the *cabildo* (council) of Popayán include references to 700 or 800 Páez settled in Guambía since 1572, most probably displaced by the Lozano encounter (ACC/P 1583–89, cited in Findji and Rojas 1985: 23). As the aboriginal population lost its possessions in the Valley of La Plata to the east, it was forced up the cordillera.[9]

The mining boom and the privatization of lands on the western slopes of the cordillera coincided with the conquest of the Páez. The seventeenth and eighteenth centuries were a period of dispersion and of forced relocation in the haciendas of Popayán. Many were plucked out of their territories by the *encomenderos* who received grants from 1640 to 1730. The most well-known was Don Cristóbal de Mosquera y Figueroa, *encomendero* of Vitoncó, who had also been awarded *encomiendas* on the western slopes, in Paniquitá and Timbío. In 1679 the *cacica* of Timbío complained that Mosquera

had placed there...heathen Indians with their families, from whom we receive notable harm and offense because they are barbarians without law and without god and they have tyrannized our lands.

(AJC/Q [Archivo Jijón y Caamaño, Quito] 1679: 113r)

The tribe closest to Timbío that had most stubbornly resisted both European invaders and Church influence was the Páez, many of whose communities were granted in *encomienda* to Mosquera. His grants provided him with a mandate to transfer his indigenous serfs from one region to another. Thus, the "heathen Indians" who caused so much trouble in Timbío were probably Páez from another of Mosquera's *encomiendas*. In fact, a large number of the eighteenth-century tributaries of Vitoncó were absent, working on Mosquera holdings near Popayán, and many never returned home, having either disappeared or acquired lands on the western slopes of the cordillera (ACC/P 1684, 1719a, 1733, 1745, 1757). This was as true in other parts of Tierradentro as it was of Mosquera's holdings, and indigenous subjects were forcibly separated from their *caciques* throughout the period (Colmenares 1979; Findji and Rojas 1985). Tributary lists from eighteenth-century Tierradentro indicate that as much as 10 percent of the population was absent from the area; in some *encomiendas*, this figure was as high as 24 percent (Sevilla 1976a: 3: 23–28). These Indians could be found on the haciendas of the western slopes, working as farm laborers, weavers, masons, "scarecrows" and harvesters (ibid.).

But not all movements to the western slopes were forced by the Europeans. Entire Páez towns were established during the colonial era in the Popayán area, including Paniquitá, Jambaló, Pitayó, Quichaya and Toribío-Tacueyó (AGI/S 1717; ANC/B 1768). Mid-seventeenth-century tributary records indicate that some of these populations had travelled to the western slopes along with their *caciques* (ANH/Q 1703). As was mentioned above, some of this migration probably resulted from the natural fission of communities into new ones that followed the sons of *caciques* into exile. This was in fact the case in what appears to have been a reverse-migration from the eastern Gobernación de Neiva to Tierradentro, as stated in a dispute over the colonial *cacicazgo* of Togoima:

The oldest Indians...said that they had known Don Pedro Chuvis [Subix, cf. Fig. 1] with one of his brothers (the said Don Pio [?]), [and] he held the title of *cacique* "nominatim" with his followers. And as in those days they were vagabonds and pilgrims, all the Indians of this province, [there occurred] the death of the brother of the said Don Pio who was conquered with all his followers... I also declare that another Spanish-speaking Indian woman [said that] Jasinto Huyumusa [Gueyomuse] "+allio" modo Chuvis, told her that he wanted to come to this, his town, from San Juan Baptista del Hobo because they wanted to conquer him, having other brothers...[illegible] who, in order to be *caciques*, had to be first-born, originally from, and native to the towns, and not intruders and useless subjects.

(AHT/B 1729: f.128r)

Similar evidence is lacking for chiefly colonization of the western slopes of the cordillera, but it can be assumed that this was probably a pan-Páez practice. It is also possible that there were some solid ecological reasons for the movement to the western slopes: seasons are reversed on the two slopes of the cordillera, so that when it rains on the eastern slopes, it is dry in the west; a westerly migration would have provided communities with a broader range of growing seasons. Nevertheless, these migrations increased in response to Spanish pressures.[10] Notwithstanding indigenous reasons for creating new communities on the western slopes, it is evident that people were also displaced from their own communities in the face of European expansion.

The *resguardo*

By the late seventeenth century, then, the Páez were militarily defeated and had suffered considerable population losses through death and forced migration, the consequences being a deterioration of community identity and of political authority. Nelly Arvelo Jiménez (1973) has studied how the political structure of the Ye'cuana of Venezuela changed as a result of invasions both by other indigenous peoples and the Europeans. She notes that invasion led to an increase in the number of villages created through internal migration. New patterns of community division developed, creating heterogeneous villages not defined by extended families. Arvelo sees these periods of fragmentation and anarchy as signs of political crisis, but not as evidence of disintegration; instead, they were defense mechanisms which assured Ye'cuana survival through dispersion. The early colonial break-down in the temporary unity that had been created in Tierradentro at the time of the Spanish invasion can be understood in the same light: dispersion ensured Páez survival better than a submission to the *encomienda* would have.

But as in the case of the modern Venezuelan invasion of Ye'cuana lands, the Spanish conquest of Tierradentro proved all too immutable. The European invaders established permanent control over indigenous territory, unlike earlier non-European invaders whose conquests had been short-lived. Thus, traditional defense mechanisms focusing on short-term dispersion would no longer work under European domination. In Venezuela and in Tierradentro regions of refuge became more and more scarce, since foreign settlement extended to surrounding areas and monolingual Indians were more easily exploited in Spanish-speaking zones beyond the boundaries of their traditional lands. Arvelo Jiménez suggests political unification and legal struggle as possibilities for continued Ye'cuana survival, political cohesion moving beyond the local community to the entire tribe (ibid.: 19–20). This is what occurred in Tierradentro in the late seventeenth and early eighteenth centuries, when fragmentation and escape no longer proved feasible or useful. By the late colonial period a new type of *cacique* emerged on the scene in Tierradentro, promising to restore a different but recognizable form of political unity to the fragmented Páez.

Averting the threatened break-down in the Páez nation entailed alterations in the character of the Páez polity. Throughout what is today southwestern Colombia indigenous communities chose an identical solution to these pressing problems: the consolidation of rule by *caciques* whose dominion was legitimized through both indigenous and Spanish channels. Firm territorial rights were acquired through native efforts to establish the *resguardo* (reservation) system, an institution that was formerly a vehicle of exploitation in lands to the north, and adapt it to their own purposes.

In Tierradentro the *resguardo* was established at the end of the seventeenth and beginnings of the eighteenth centuries. It did not arise earlier because the Páez were still recovering from their wars with the Spanish. At the inception of the Páez *resguardo*, the natives of Tierradentro were marginal to the Popayán economy and their rugged lands not particularly coveted. Hence the formation of *resguardos* was not resisted by the local Spanish elite, which was more concerned with Indian labor than lands. Moreover, indigenous attempts to consolidate political and territorial autonomy came at a time when the elite had more pressing concerns: the late seventeenth century was a period of meat shortage in the area and it is possible that the Spaniards saw the formation of the *resguardo* as a means of relieving what they perceived as native threats against their cattle-ranches along the frontiers (Findji and Rojas 1985: 36).

The new form of political leadership that developed a century and a half after the Spanish invasion was an innovation in political organization for the Páez. The new *caciques* based their power on the trappings of the earlier *cacicazgo*, but at the same time transformed it. They consolidated broader *cacicazgos* encompassing wide stretches of territory. This period is key to any analysis of the Páez vision of history because it is in the documents issued during the development of the "new *cacicazgo*" that we find the first detailed information regarding Páez ideas about the past. All subsequent attempts by the Páez to write their own history center around both the *resguardo* as a political unit and its founders, especially Don Juan Tama.

The origins of the *resguardo* system

The *resguardo* system, which was established during the second half of the sixteenth century in the Nuevo Reino de Granada (Bogotá), grew out of the transition from a conquest to a colonial administration and the subsequent need for the establishment of an Indian policy that would allow the Crown a wider range of control over indigenous populations. A direct outgrowth of the *encomienda* system, the *resguardo* was devised as a means of limiting *encomendero* influence, returning the benefits accrued by *encomenderos* to the Crown. The *resguardo* converted indigenous tribute into a State patrimony by isolating the Indians from Spanish and mestizo elements, including their *encomenderos*, by granting the Indians some measure of self-government so as to be able to live peacefully in sedentary communities, and by awarding *encomiendas* by virtue of participation in the colonial administration instead of as recognition of conquest activities (González 1979). In other words, the *resguardo* was part of the Crown's attempt to centralize and increase control of its overseas possessions.

The *resguardo* was comprised of an aboriginal community living within designated lands that were not always delimited in a strict fashion (Colmenares 1970: 195; González 1979: 27), but frequently included the terrain lying within the radius of a league from the town center. *Resguardo* lands differed in character from other holdings in the Nuevo Reino in that they could not be bought or sold (ibid.: 28). Although they were established on traditional aboriginal lands, Indians from different regions were often forced to come together into a single *resguardo* (ibid.: 29). Within the *resguardo* the terrain was subdivided into communal lands, forests and pastures, individual parcels to which community members held usufruct rights, and an urban center with a church. In the Nuevo Reino they were destined for agricultural exploitation, producing foodstuffs to be consumed within the Nuevo Reino itself (ibid.: 50). They also served as a labor pool for neighboring haciendas (ibid.: 76). But their primary purpose was to establish firm Crown control over indigenous communities.

Title to *resguardo* lands was vested in a *cabildo* or council, made up of the *cacique* and his *principales*. Land rights were administered by the *cacique* and *cabildo*, who consequently enjoyed certain privileges, such as private lands, the right to consume articles otherwise limited to the European population, the right to wear European clothing and the privilege of being called by the noble titles of *Don* and *Doña* (ibid.: 45–48).

The original *resguardo* developed as a form of increased and more efficient penetration and exploitation of aboriginal communities by the Crown, at a time when only 10 percent of the original population had survived the ravages of the conquest. The concentration of this small number of Indians into more central communities also left larger extensions of land free for use by the Spanish (Colmenares 1975: 226–27). Thus, it is doubly interesting that the Páez appropriated this uniquely Colombian institution and transformed it to suit their own purposes of territorial defense.

The Páez *resguardo*

Among the Páez the *resguardo* took on quite a different shape than it had assumed in Bogotá. The Páez *resguardos* were not forced on communities by the Crown, but arose through the efforts of the Indians themselves, as is clear in the title drawn up in 1708 which established the *resguardo* of Vitoncó:

Whereas by choice of the *naturales* [Indians], to be effected through statutes by the lords, captains and *encomenderos* of the Indians of this province of Tierra Adentro, Pais [Páez] and by the grace of the King our Lord... I give this title of *resguardo* to them, who are of the nation, of pure blood and pure sons and daughters of the stars... (ACC/P 1883 [1708]: 2182v and 2184r)

By choosing to form *resguardos*, the Páez hoped to validate their territorial autonomy over lands that they considered theirs by right, whether as a result of precolumbian occupation or post-Conquest settlement. This motivation was stated in the title drawn up in 1700 by the *cacique* Don Manuel de Quilo y Sicos for the *resguardo* of Tacueyó, located on the western slopes of the cordillera:

Until now, there has been no other owner of these lands under my dominion, and to us, the *caciques*, each with clear boundaries to our lands, and as we do not recognize any owners of the lands apart from Your Majesty, I approach you [in solicitation] of that which corresponds principally to me, and I wish to assure my successors, through sufficient titles, [that] our rights and property will not be disturbed... (Title to Tacueyó in Sendoya n.d.: 29)

Don Manuel's reasons for seeking *resguardo* title are instructive:

I believe that only Your Majesty has the right to cede lands to white individuals, and that only without injury to the Indian tributaries, because furthermore we have the right and preference because we are dependents of, and we are legitimate Americans and we are not originally from other foreign lands... (ibid.)

And so, Don Manuel, who was a relative newcomer to Tacueyó, globalized his demands and his legitimacy in a colonized territory by citing his rights as one of the first Americans. This document shows that the Páez rationale behind the drive to create *resguardos* was to assure dominion over lands which they already felt were theirs by a more ancient right. The Spanish *resguardo* was foreign to the Páez, but it provided a vehicle for attaining indigenous ends. This was possible under Spanish colonial rule, because the Crown was willing to recognize certain levels of political autonomy – *fueros* – so long as recipients complied with tributary arrangements, thus recognizing the ultimate authority of the King (Bonilla 1979: 331).

The same story arose time and again in southwestern Colombia, as much among Páez as among neighboring groups, where *caciques* sought to establish authority over lands which they had traditionally held.[11] The new *cacicazgos* were very different from earlier forms of government, legalizing and delimiting a specific extension of territory and vesting permanent authority in the person of the *cacique*. In order to comprehend how the Páez could put to use this new concept and transform it into Páez tradition, we must now consider the individuals who set this institution in motion, the new *caciques*.

The new *caciques*

Sometime around the mid-seventeenth century the *caciques* of Tierradentro began to consolidate their dominions and to create strong political units out of the diversity of small *cacicazgos* in the region (Map 5). This was accomplished in southern Tierradentro by the Gueyomuse family, *caciques* of Togoima, who consolidated Togoima, Santa Rosa, Avirama, Calderas, Cuetando, Itaibe, Yaquivá and Pisimbalá into a single *cacicazgo* (AHT/B 1729 [1667]: 9ʳ–16ʳ). In the Moras Basin, Don Juan Tama de la Estrella formed the Vitoncó *resguardo* by bringing together Vitoncó, Lame, Chinas, Suin and the very large Mosoco community under a single *cacicazgo* (ACC/P 1883). Tama also created a broader alliance of *cacicazgos* by linking his own chiefdom of Vitoncó with that of Pitayó. Located on the western slopes of the cordillera, the *cacicazgo* of Pitayó included Pitayó, Jambaló, Quichaya, Pueblo Nuevo and Caldono, a chiefdom that Tama had inherited from his uncle, Don Jacinto Muscay (ACC/P 1881 [1700]). The Tacueyó *cacicazgo* included Tacueyó, San Francisco and Cuetayuc under the leadership of Don Manuel de

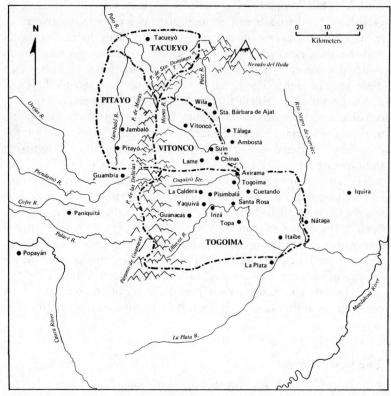

Map 5   Colonial Páez *cacicazgos*

Quilo y Sicos, a *compadre* (ritual coparent) of Tama. Quilo y Sicos, bound by fictive kinship to the *cacique* of Vitoncó, entered into an alliance with him (in Sendoya n.d.: 29–31; NC/S 1914).

Only the *cacicazgo* of Wila, which possibly also included Tálaga, maintained itself outside of the process of polity-building. Located on the upper Páez River, Wila had as its *cacica* Doña Mariana Mondiguagua, Don Juan Tama's wife (ACC/P 1883: 2184r). It has been impossible to locate Wila's reservation title, although the Páez of modern-day Vitoncó claim to have seen it. Neither has an oral tradition been recorded regarding the territorial limits of the *resguardo*, and we can surmise that it was an example of the older form of a Páez chiefdom, small and with little administrative legitimization. It is even possible that Wila's title was obtained after Tama married Mondiguagua, and that his input into Wila's political process brought about the entry of her *cacicazgo* into the new *cacique* movement.

Thus, the entire Páez nation at the beginning of the eighteenth century was composed of four major polities under the direction of three *caciques*, and a smaller autonomous political unit linked to the larger units through marital ties.[12] From the point of view of the Spanish administration these polities were legitimized by dint of land titles that formed *resguardos*, administered by *caciques* whose authority and nobility had been approved by the European overlords.

Although the net effect of the new *cacique* movement was the establishment of a series of strong political units on Páez territory, their founders enjoyed differing degrees of power with regard to the colonial administration. On the basis of a comparison of the various *resguardo* titles, Findji and Rojas (1985: 43–44) suggest that Quilo y Sicos (Tacueyó) and the Gueyomuses (Togoima) did not achieve such far-ranging political changes as did the *cacique* of Pitayó, Don Juan Tama:

> The *cacique* Quilo y Sicos chose the approach of requesting that colonial authorities demarcate his lands and this is what occurred: a delegate from the Royal Court travelled from Quito to Tacueyó, specifically to mark the limits. In contrast, what Juan Tama achieved through his title was that the capacity to distribute *resguardos* to the different villages under his authority be granted to him, Don Juan Tama de la Estrella, Principal *Cacique*, and this is what he did later. (ibid.: 43)

In other words, Tama first established his supreme authority over his dominions before delimiting his lands in his own name, while the other *caciques* relied upon Spanish colonial authority to establish the boundaries of their domains:

> Evidently, no autonomy in administering their dominions would accrue to the *caciques* if the internal delimitations or distribution [of lands] to the different villages were to have been subject to the Royal Court or other colonial authorities. For this reason Don Juan Tama requested that the Royal Court legalize his own authority to effect this [delimitation]; and he began to do this in Jambaló... From this moment on, the authority of the Principal *Cacique* was affirmed. (ibid.: 44)[13]

The net result was that the Páez *resguardo* acquired a special character in comparison to other indigenous communities, because a broad expanse of land was vested in the community by virtue of its residents' rights as the first Americans, and the indigenous leadership itself was granted the right to distribute the territory according to its own needs and specifications.[14]

Although the Crown granted the new *caciques* political authority, the chiefs would have to legitimize their power in a distinct manner

within their own communities. This was accomplished in part by the
de facto power given to the new *caciques* by their *encomenderos*: the
chiefs were active in the various tribute censuses conducted during
the colonial period, as is clear in seventeenth- and eighteenth-century
documents, and at least in one case, *caciques* actually served as tribute-
collectors for the Crown (AHT/B 1729: 170r). But the new *caciques*
also cemented their authority by modeling their political rule at least
in part, upon those patterns traditional to the area. This was
especially clear in Togoima (ANC/B 1791).

In the late eighteenth century Doña Angelina Gueyomuse, *cacica*
of Togoima, entered into a dispute over coca lands with the
hacendados of neighboring Segovia. She claimed that Segovia was
located within the limits of the *resguardo* of Santa Rosa de la Cañada
and that therefore, occupation of these lands by Spanish *hacendados*
was in violation of the territorial sovereignty of Santa Rosa and of
the *resguardo* of Togoima, to which Santa Rosa belonged. Her
opponents, who eventually won the suit, disagreed, claiming that
Santa Rosa was established as a colony of Togoima and did not in
itself constitute an independent political or territorial entity.
According to Don Pedro Gutiérrez, former parish priest of Santa
Rosa:

> As in the past, they lived disputing, this *cacique* [from Santa Rosa] with the *principal*
> of Togoima, they assigned him lands in which they could make their village, and this
> is affirmed by an Indian who lives at the confluence of the Páez and the Ríonegro,
> [stating that] the Togoimas claim that this land belongs to them... (ibid.: 683r)

By declaring that Santa Rosa was part of Togoima, the Spaniards
hoped to retain their claim over Segovia. In other regions *resguardos*
were limited in size to one league in radius measured from the village
church; in the case of Togoima they maintained that Segovia lay well
beyond the league from Togoima and therefore could not be claimed
as *resguardo* land. Countering these assertions, the *cacica* of Togoima
claimed that Santa Rosa was independent and that Segovia was
located within a league of the village of Santa Rosa.

Before beginning to analyze this political strategy, it must be
mentioned that for the Páez there was probably no contradiction at
all when they stated that Santa Rosa was both independent and at the
same time a part of Togoima. After all, territory was not static but
fluid in their eyes. Hence, Santa Rosa could at one point have
depended upon Togoima and subsequently split off from it to form
its own community. Moreover, under the *resguardo* titles forged a

century before, the new *caciques* maintained the right to subdivide their domains as they saw fit.[15]

Fr. Gutiérrez' allegation of fission presents a clear case of the Gueyomuse *caciques'* use of traditional concepts in forging a new brand of authority. As we remember, at the time of the Conquest, minor *caciques* were autonomous from the supreme chiefs. They came together in broad units only at time of war and those who wished at any point to transfer their allegiance to another supreme *cacique* were entirely within their rights to do so. In eighteenth-century Santa Rosa, the *cacique* exerted his independence from the Gueyomuse *caciques* by moving to another location. Nevertheless, given that the late colonial period was a time of political unification in the face of Spanish threat, it would have served both the Gueyomuse and the chief of Santa Rosa if the two communities were to remain linked through some sort of loose confederation. Within the colonial context these affiliations were more appropriately established in the course of legal battles, instead of the military encounters of the precolonial and Conquest eras. This is precisely what was accomplished by the new *caciques* when they created broad *cacicazgos* out of the union of several communities or *resguardos*.

Chiefly hierarchy is clearer in the documentary record of the new *cacique* period than it was at the time of the Spanish invasion. Colonial tribute censuses indicate that each community had its own *cacique*, many of whom inherited title to their *cacicazgos*. For instance, the *caciques* of Avirama, who belonged to the *cacicazgo* of Togoima, also maintained political hegemony over their own lands and inherited the title *Momosque*.

Lower-level *caciques* were required to submit to their new superiors. In a 1745 tribute list from Suin, we find two subjects of local *cacique* Don Sebastián Güeya working in the cane field of Don Martín Guagua Tombé y Calambás, the principal *cacique* of Vitoncó within whose jurisdiction Suin lay (ACC/P 1745: 40r). A good indication of the hegemony of the new *caciques* is that most legal papers arising from land disputes mention only the principal chief. For Tierradentro and the western slopes of the cordillera there were no instances of lower-level *caciques* initiating such judicial proceedings. It can therefore be assumed that the principal *caciques* of the four major subdivisions of the Páez area were not only permitted to extract labor from the subjects of their inferiors, but were required to represent their interests to the broader society. Lesser chiefs only appeared in tribute lists and seem to have exerted authority only on a local and internal level. This authority might have been further subdivided, as individual villages had multiple *caciques*, sometimes ruling "upper" and "lower" sections of communities (ACC/P 1745: 70r–v), but the documentary record supplies no further information on the lower levels of the colonial *cacique* hierarchy.[16] In addition, the data on Santa Rosa as well as other minor *cacicazgos* in Togoima illustrate that the principal *caciques* created new towns during the period of their rule (AHT/B 1729; ANC/B 1766). Their authority was therefore constituted over a constellation of lower-level *cacicazgos*, some of which were survivals of an earlier era while others were established by the principal *caciques* themselves.

Although the new *caciques* were able to expand their political authority to include peacetime, they still did not exert complete control over their subject chiefs. The Gueyomuse *caciques* lost their claim to the lands of Itaibe because the *caciques* of Nátaga, who were subject to the Gueyomuse, testified against them (AHT/B 1729: 19v). Moreover, although the principal *caciques* established an overarching political authority which encompassed the lesser chiefs, at times minor *caciques* from different *cacicazgos* married each other, thus cementing political alliances that crosscut broader political jurisdictions.[17]

A final important consideration with regard to the new *caciques* is their mode of succession to the chiefdom. Some chroniclers claimed that the chiefdoms of the Popayán area followed a matrilineal line of succession (Anonymous 1938 [n.d.]), a theme taken up by a number of contemporary scholars (for example, Hernández de Alba 1963). Nevertheless, there is ample evidence of sixteenth-century *cacicazgos* passing from father to son (Earle n.d.b). With little evidence to substantiate their claims, some have suggested that colonial Páez *cacicazgos* also followed a matrilineal line of succession (Findji and Rojas 1985). Nevertheless, the documentary evidence points to a far different state of affairs, both in terms of the Páez succession itself, as well as of the Spanish influences that impinged on the *cacicazgo*.

In the title to Pitayó we find a clear description of the nature of chiefly succession as stipulated by the colonial administration. *Caciques* were required to be succeeded by their sons, and if this were not possible, by the next oldest brother and as a final choice, by a nephew (ACC/P 1881: 1138r). In many cases, very different rules of succession were followed by the chiefly families of Tierradentro.

Let us examine, for instance, the *cacicazgo* of Togoima (Figure 1). The earliest occupants of the chiefly position were two pairs of *caciques*: Don Lázaro and Don Pedro Gueyomuse, and Don Carlos and Don Thomás Gueyomuse. The relationship between the members of each pair is unclear, but it is evident that they were all principal *caciques* who carried the same title and participated to the same extent in external matters. Don Carlos had at least two children, Juan and Doña Pascuala. Although colonial regulations would not have permitted the assumption by Doña Pascuala of the *cacicazgo*, she in fact became the next occupant. Similarly, her own children did not inherit the *cacicazgo*: instead, it passed to Don Luis Ñaqui, her nephew, and then to Don Jacinto Subix, who was either her son-in-law or her grandson; Don Jacinto Subix, we will remember, migrated to Togoima from the east, where he had been unable to assume the *cacicazgo* of El Hobo (see p. 42). From Don Jacinto, the chiefdom passed to two individuals, Don Andrés, who was Don Luis' illegitimate son, and to Doña Clara, who was Doña Pascuala's granddaughter. From there the *cacicazgo* fell to Doña Angelina Gueyomuse, Doña Clara's illegitimate daughter, irrespective of the fact that Doña Clara also had a son, Don Joseph.

In a number of chiefly successions some siblings held chiefly titles, although they were not chiefs. Thus for example, in 1745 Don Martín Guagua Tombé y Calambás, *cacique* of Vitoncó, had at least three siblings, two of whom were male. Nevertheless, the only other member of the sibling group to carry a chiefly surname was his sister, Doña Pascuala Tombé Calambás.

No simple principle explains this maze of chiefly successions. Only in some cases were *cacicazgos* passed from father to son, brother to brother, or uncle to nephew, as stipulated in Spanish law. Sometimes, the chiefdom was transferred from mother to daughter or from a woman to her nephew. Evidently, there was no single line of succession in Páez colonial chiefdoms. If anything, title was inherited bilaterally, as can be noted in the shifting of chiefly status from one line to another. This type of succession has been demonstrated by Earle (n.d.a) for pre-columbian Popayán, and suggests that although the new *caciques* embraced useful colonial institutions, they did not follow all the rules and regulations associated with them, but instead, adapted these administrative arrangements to their own political projects.

The sixteenth-century society of resistance, organized around *caciques* whose authority was strictly military in character, was thus transformed through interaction with the Spanish colonial administration. By the eighteenth century *caciques* had achieved hegemony in

TOGOIMA

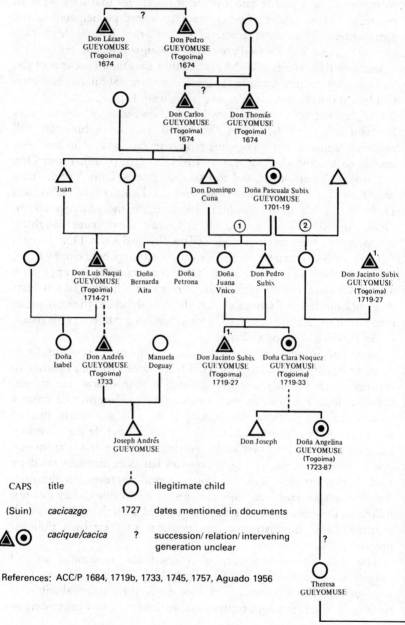

Figure 1 Genealogies of the new *caciques*

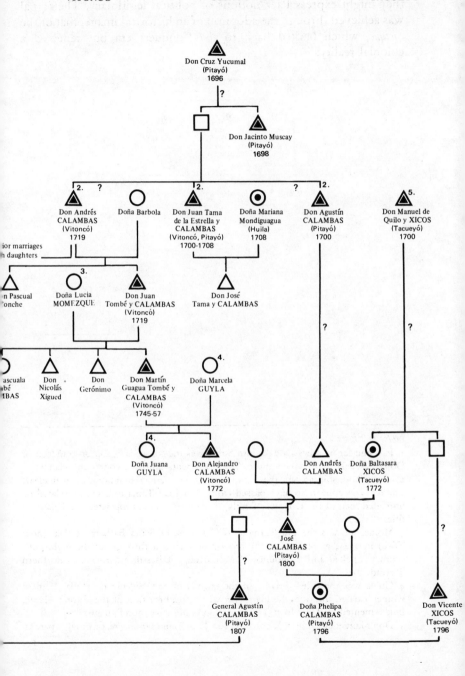

peacetime as well, altering European institutions in such a way as they might express Páez notions of political legitimacy. Their goal was achieved through the adoption of an historical image, that of the *cacique*, which harked back to the Conquest era but reflected a colonial reality.

Notes to Figure 1

1 It is unclear whether Don Jacinto Subix was the son-in-law, son or grandson of Doña Pascuala Subix Gueyomuse. The documents illustrate conflicting claims.

2 The relationship among these three men, who were contemporaries, is unclear. The *cacicazgo* appears to have passed from Don Juan Tama to distantly related or unrelated men of the Calambás family, or to men who appropriated the Calambás title.

3 Momezque was the title/surname of the *cacica* of Santa Bárbara de Ajat (now Tóez) in 1745, as well as of the *caciques* of Avirama throughout the eighteenth century. Spelled and pronounced "Mumucué," it is still a surname in northern Tierradentro.

4 Guyla was the title/surname of the *caciques* of San Vicente de Huila. If these women carried the title, the marriages were a reaffirmation of the Vitoncó–Huila link cemented by Don Juan Tama and Doña Mariana Mondiguagua.

5 Don Manuel de Quilo y Xicos was Don Juan Tama's *compadre*, or ritual coparent.

3

The birth of the myth: Don Juan Tama y Calambás

SOURCES FOR PÁEZ HISTORICAL CONSCIOUSNESS

Sources documenting the nature of precolumbian and colonial Páez historical consciousness are scarce. Until the mid-seventeenth century the Páez were in a constant state of war, and chroniclers were unable to describe their lifeways in any detail. After coming under the supervision of the Spanish colonial state they were exploited as a heathen labor source, and there is no evidence to suggest that their chiefs were educated or taught to read and write. Only late into the eighteenth century did *ladino caciques*, that is chiefs conversant with the Spanish language, appear in Tierradentro. Thus, there were no Páez capable of producing a written chronicle in Spanish. Knowledge of Páez was virtually nonexistent among Spaniards, and so there was little possibility of the emergence of a European-authored chronicle in Páez.

Nor did the Spanish overlords take a great interest in delving into Páez thought. Chronicles of the Páez were for the most part descriptions of battles. Quite simply, the Páez were not perceived as being worth the effort: unlike the Incas, they were simple savages meant to be worked, and not an object of study or speculation. Only the missionaries, who took an interest in Páez souls and therefore in the Páez language, give us even the briefest description of indigenous lifeways or cosmology.

In contrast, students of central and southern Andean society have produced a number of significant contributions to our knowledge of Andean historical thought (Zuidema 1964, 1982; Ossio 1970, 1973, 1977; López Baralt 1979; Adorno 1982, 1986; Salomon 1982), based principally on a corpus of chronicle sources which not only provides a detailed rendering of Inca cosmology, but also includes a number of works written by Indians themselves.[1] Through indigenous chronicles we can acquire a clear understanding of the differences between Andean and European visions of the past during the colonial period.

The colonial Páez Guaman Poma has yet to be uncovered, and probably never existed. But sometimes disadvantage can be turned to gain under such circumstances. While there are no full-blown chronicles that provide evidence for Páez historical thought, there are more modest documents that illuminate the nature of Páez ideas about the past. These documents were written by Spaniards and not by Indians, their form and purpose corresponding for the most part to the needs of the colonial administration. Nevertheless, in them we can deduce elements of Páez thought. Dictionaries written by missionaries, testimonies of idolatries committed by the Indians, *resguardo* titles and tributary lists do not provide full texts of Páez history, but they clearly reveal how the past was used to forge the present. We get little that looks like "myth," but we do encounter brief references to history used to bolster political and territorial claims, and even more fleeting references to chiefly lines, expressed principally through the use of chiefly titles. That is, the paucity of "texts" allows us to turn our attention toward the forms in which historical knowledge was operationalized in everyday life.

By necessity, we must concentrate on history as it was used instead of history as it was formally recounted. What we shall see in the documentary record is a series of images that are fleetingly recalled and linked to the present, historical referents whose contents cannot be analyzed in isolation as a text and whose structure is determined by such factors as the political needs of the narrator, his skill in making the contents understandable to the Spanish scribe and the limitations imposed by the nature of Spanish legal documents. In other words, the form of these narrations is as much determined by the conditions they seek to ameliorate, as it is a reflection of the structure of Páez cosmology.

THE SOCIOPOLITICAL CONTEXT OF COLONIAL HISTORICAL THOUGHT

The writing of history in colonial Colombia

Spanish colonial historiography was profoundly affected by the social tensions of the period. State and Church confronted individual conquerors, and also found themselves at odds with each other. Conquerors clashed with Indians; the latter looked to religious and political institutions for support. During the course of the sixteenth century the Crown consolidated its rule over these rival sectors by consolidating its administrative apparatus; it similarly found it necessary to control historiography, limiting discussion of such sensitive issues as justice in conquest and the rights and obligations of the different parties in the empire. Crown control was also aimed at acquiring extensive information of use to the administration in governing its overseas possessions. To these ends the Crown established a bureaucratic position, the "Chronicler of the Indies," charged with preparing a "true and official history" for the King (Tovar 1984: 19–25).

All of the histories written in this period were chronological narratives that focused on the actions of individuals, principally in an heroic vein (ibid.: 36–37). Chroniclers conducted bibliographic research, but did not cite their sources; often sections of two chronicles are almost identical because one writer copied from the other. Adapting to the new environment of the Americas, many of these writers incorporated indigenous voices into their accounts, voices which are frequently confused and ambiguous.

Writing

The Spanish colonial empire was highly centralized, with Crown supervision penetrating all aspects of daily life, from the appointment of officials to the clothes worn on one's back. Such deep centralization necessitated production of a huge volume of written documentation, all of which was duly notarized to acknowledge its authenticity. All evidence submitted to courts was accepted only in written form, thus fostering the development of a layer of notaries or scribes whose primary responsibility was the penning of documents that followed strict formulas governing the presentation of evidence (Phelan 1967: 142; Lockhart 1968: 68–71). Scribes, whose license required only minimal qualifications and whose positions were often purchased, were thus central actors converting evidence, complaints or requests into the acceptable discourse of the bureaucracy and legal establishment.

Colonial standards of legal evidence were quite different from our own. In addition to being written, evidence was only valid when signed by a notary. The legal system required extensive written testimony, and the contents of legal documents were influenced by highly manipulative questions with little cross-examination of witnesses, juridical procedure taking place according to a secret, inquisitorial pattern of dispensing justice (Phelan 1967: 198–201). Although Indians were encouraged to participate in the judicial process and were provided with translators to this effect, there was, as Phelan (ibid: 213) states, no equality before the law:

> The individual was not the common denominator of society. The rights, the privileges, and the obligations of each person came from the functional corporations and the estate to which he belonged. And there were built-in inequalities between those corporations and estates. The social status of a culprit influenced the nature of his punishment.

Finally, the exclusively written nature of the legal system, coupled with the state of erratic communications with Spain and the bureaucratic corruption that this bred, led to a fetishizing of the written word, whereby legal documents became the vehicle of governance (Vidal 1985: 31).

Writing, history and Indians

Spanish historical canons and the fetishizing of the written word would have profound implications for the development of a distinct colonial Páez historical vision. Since approved history was the province of the Spanish few, Páez history would have to take a different, non-narrative and fragmentary form if it were to be included within the discourse of the broader colonial society. And given the nature of the colonial documents in which it appeared, the parties to a dispute were treated more as corporate entities than as individuals. Under these conditions the representative *par excellence* of the indigenous community, the *cacique*, became the prime interpreter and communicator of the indigenous past; except for a few isolated instances in which indigenous commoners came into direct contact with the colonial bureaucracy, as was the case in the prosecution of the leaders of messianic movements, history expressed in oral form within the Páez community itself did not survive the centuries. Differential access to written modes of communication determined the future chain of transmission of Páez history, assuring the survival well into the 1980s of an eighteenth-century chiefly ideology. At the same time, the ambiguity of this ideology, which comes to us in fragments, fostered a reinterpretation and elaboration upon its contents over the years.

We must also look within the indigenous community to understand how its relationship to the colonial state and its emissaries could influence the aboriginal view of the past. Having suffered a demographic upset and having created new settlements, these communities were in need of a history to bolster their new-found identity. This identity, unlike that of the less-centralized precolumbian chiefdoms, was not defined entirely by allegiance to a particular chief, but through membership in a political unit which was subservient to a larger entity, the colonial state. The new Páez communities were, moreover, more rigid in the regulation of their membership, with periodic census listings of tributaries who were required to maintain a fixed allegiance to their chiefs to ensure a steady flow of tribute to the Crown. Finally, the *caciques* themselves were operating under a new definition of the chiefdom and were in need of a new past to legitimize their authority. Under these circumstances, a new theory of history had to be developed.

The eighteenth-century historical vision was not a simple rendering of earlier historical traditions, but involved the acceptance of new definitions of historical narration. Páez historiography was colored in part by the nature of the medium in which it was expressed, but it was also influenced by Catholic missionaries who had begun to teach the Christian doctrine to the Páez in the early seventeenth century (Pacheco n.d.; Arcila 1951, 1954; Mantilla 1980). Christian doctrine played an important role in altering the Páez vision of historical causation, as well as the place of the group within the unfolding of a cosmic history. It placed them within the more universal context of the struggle between good and evil, linking them to universal historico-mythical heroes and messiahs (Castillo 1987). Moreover, Christian history was written and linear in nature.

PÁEZ HISTORY IN THE COLONIAL PERIOD

The eighteenth century traces of historical thought that we will examine do not recount "what really happened," but instead, "what should have occurred." That is to say, according to our own cultural definition of historical truth, Páez history is not entirely accurate in its interpretation of evidence. Instead, past events are used to explain present concerns, and if this necessitates some alterations in, or omissions of, details or plot structure, the narration appears to depart from historical truth. Thus for example, eighteenth-century chiefly titles established a moral continuity between a contemporary chiefly line and the distant past. Such is the case of the *caciques* of

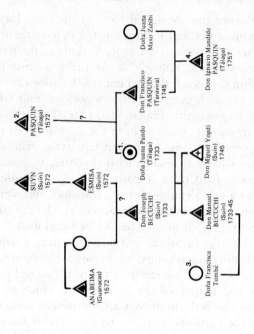

GUANACAS, TARAVIRA, TALAGA AND SUIN

AVIRAMA

CAPS   title
(Suin)   cacicazgo
◉   cacique/cacica
⚐   gobernador

○-̇   illegitimate child
1727   dates mentioned in documents
?   succession/relation/intervening
            generation unclear

References: ACC/P, 1719a, 1719b, 1719c, 1721, 1733, 1745, 1792, 1881, 1883;
AHT/B 1729; NC/S 1914; Gonzalez n.d.; Roldan 1974

Figure 2   Genealogies of minor caciques

Tálaga and Taravira, who took on the title Pasquín, linking them to the Conquest-era *cacique* and thus correcting gaps in the line of chiefly succession by recourse to the notion of moral continuity (see Figure 2). Similarly, the name Nuesga, attached in the sixteenth century to one of the group of siblings within the regional *cacicazgo* of the chief Páez, appeared once again in the mid-seventeenth century, linked to another chief in the general area (ANC/B 1699: 859r; ANH/Q 1699: 3r).

The colonial Páez were forced to provide a time-depth to their communities that would probably not have been important in pre-Conquest times, since they had only recently colonized Tierradentro. Thus, the *caciques* of Togoima called their *resguardo* "ancestral lands" (AHT/B 1729: 11r), that "belonged to our ancestors" (ibid.: 9v). This formula was forced upon them by the Spaniards but soon began to color their own territorial claims, as we shall see in nineteenth- and twentieth-century histories.[2]

Notions of the past were applied to the present and to the future in the form of millenarian ideas and movements. Messianism was an important component of the Páez world view even before the Spaniards, clearly expressed in Hazañero's account of the advent of a culture hero before the Spanish invasion:

As it is said and as is tradition [passing from] fathers to sons, even before the Spaniards came, there came a man who dressed like them, and wanting to preach to them like an Indian, seeing their stubbornness and divisions, he left without doing it. He must have been one of the Apostles of the Lord, of whom there is in these parts some news of their having passed through, preaching to the inhabitants.
(1645: 214)[3]

The same personage was alluded to in an eighteenth-century myth:

Guequiáu, the name of he who gave the Indians of this province of Páez the laws of false observance (disseminating them for posterity through the shamans), making

---

Notes to Figure 2

1 The relationship between Doña Josefa, *cacica* of Tálaga, and Doña Juana Pando, *cacica* of Tálaga, both in 1733, is unclear in the documents. They were probably the leaders of two different small *cacicazgos*.

2 Pasquin was not a principal *cacique*, according to Aguado (1956). More closely related to the principal chief of the area, Páez, were Taravira and Tálaga, all of whom were siblings.

3 Doña Francisca Tombé's relationship to the *caciques* of Vitoncó is unclear.

4 Taravira was attached to the town of Tálaga and since the Spanish invasion, the two *cacicazgos* have been interrelated.

them believe that he killed those who died naturally, telling them that he would turn them into stone and take them away if they cursed him or did not observe the laws, so that they feared him for his power and adored him... Although nowadays they believe that this legislator was the devil, and that he was not powerful, yet there was another more powerful than he (whom they now say is the true god) who, when he found him on the banks of this Páez River, wanting to ford [it], offered to help him across, and in the middle let go of him and of two other companions; and he ordered two trees on the riverbanks not to help him, and so he floated down river and had he not drowned, he might have reached the sea.   (Castillo 1877: 53)

In the pre-Conquest era knowledge was disseminated by shamans who, as those who implemented historical knowledge in practice, might be thought of as the historians of the community. Modes of recounting the past and of determining the future came together in the person of the shaman, who was also responsible for divination (Castillo 1877: 58–59).

During the colonial era messianism was adapted and transformed in practice through millenarian movements which attempted to throw off the yoke of Spanish domination. Most well-known was a 1706 movement based somewhere near Itaibe, atop a tall mountain called the Alto de la Quebrada de las Cuevas (AHT/B 1729; Rappaport 1980–81). A church was erected here to house a cult whose leader claimed to have had contact with God; the deity was said to descend weekly, dressed as a Franciscan friar. The messianic leader, Undachi, taught his followers that the world would be destroyed through fire or through earthquakes (AHT/B 1729: 156v, 158r, 160v). He thus alluded to some notion of a series of ages or creations of the world, a concept not mentioned for the precolumbian Páez, although it was for the people of the neighboring Cauca Valley (Andagoya 1892: 117). Undachi's prophecies could be taken to convey a belief in the reversal of the post-Conquest world order, a notion important throughout the Andean region (Wachtel 1973: 120), as well as a further indication of the centrality of knowledge of the future in the interpretation of the past.

DON JUAN TAMA AND THE IMPLEMENTATION OF HISTORICAL KNOWLEDGE

History and chiefly succession

It is within the context of political adaptation to colonial rule that we can most clearly note the nature of colonial Páez historical thought, in particular, in documents by Don Juan Tama, *cacique* of Vitoncó and Pitayó. Tama's histories employed images of previous chiefs in order to assert a new style of governance. The *cacique* of Vitoncó is key to an understanding of the Páez historical vision because his *resguardo* titles are the largest single corpus of historical information available for this period, providing indications of how historical knowledge was used in political practice.

Don Juan Tama created the *resguardo* of Pitayó in 1700 and that of Vitoncó in 1708. In the Pitayó title he claimed to have acquired the *cacicazgo* by virtue of inheritance, as was stated in an earlier testimony by his predecessor, Don Jacinto Muscay:

> [While] it is true that no one is disturbing or upsetting our rights, it is my duty to ensure [the territory of] my villages, so that when I expire or die no intruders will wish to take our lands from us... For this reason I appear, asking for the security of the lands of the abovementioned villages and so I am granted the faculty, if it is necessary, to divide the lands among my Indians in each village, because to me it is very clear that each one of them should know what belongs to him, but with the understanding that although the villages be divided, they will recognize no other *cacique* and my successor, who will inherit from me in the succession and rule, [is] Don Juan de Tama y Estrellas, my nephew.
>
> (ACC/P 1881 [1696]: 1140v–1141r)

Nevertheless, in the title to Vitoncó Tama did not trace his descent to any human chief, but to the supernatural, calling himself, "the son of the star of the Tama Stream" (ACC/P 1883: 2182v): hence, the surname Estrella, or "Star," which appeared also in the Pitayó title and in the demarcation of the lands of Jambaló (NC/S 1914). Moreover, he claimed to have acquired the Vitoncó *cacicazgo* by dint of conquest:

> Don Juan Tama has told me that within the jurisdiction of this village: there have been many Indians of tongues other than mine. And he says that they made war on him and caused harm to Don Juan Tama's other Indians who rose up in war. And Don Juan Tama's Indians defended themselves and he won the head of Calambás. And they were without Calambás. Don Juan Tama says that hoping to conquer him, they rose up against Don Juan Tama [who] defended himself and won the war. Calambás' Indians were without a *cacique* and Don Juan Tama exiled them. They retreated to this side of the *páramo* [highland swampy plain] to make their homes along the stream called the Piendamo Stream... They are to be granted to me in *encomienda* and subject to the *cacique* Don Juan Tama y Calambás, who is called Calambás in recognition of his having won the war against the said Calambás...
>
> (ibid.: 2163v–2164r)

Tama's *cacicazgos* were established at two different periods. In the title to Vitoncó Tama consolidated his dominions:

> On the road that leaves this City toward the said village of Vitoncó... at about a league at the foot of the *páramo*, on this side of Popayán, for three years there has

been a village called Pitayó and Quichaya in the same lands as Vitoncó, and they want to inhabit these lands of Pitayó and Quichaya with the consent of my *encomendados* and *encomendero*, and according to the said *cacique* Don Juan Tama this is fine because the Indians of my *encomienda* have their own lands... And I give to them this title so that they serve the *cacique* Don Juan Tama, for their *resguardo*... so that no one upsets them because they are on their own lands.

(ibid.: 2184v)

Tama could unify the two *resguardos* into a single *cacicazgo* because title to Pitayó had been vested in him by virtue of his role as chief:

Ending the task of demarcation I cause the *cacique* to recognize himself first, as the head of the villages and second, as the landowner...   (ACC/P 1881: 1135v)

The subdivision of the lands of Jambaló within the larger *cacicazgo* of Pitayó took place in the company of Don Manuel de Quilo y Sicos, *cacique* of Tacueyó, whose lands bordered those of Jambaló (NC/S 1914). Thus Tama consolidated a vast territory under his own dominion or influence.

In the Pitayó title Don Juan Tama stated that he did not have a son, and so he established a different line of succession for the *cacicazgo* (see Figure 1):

And from me [the succession] will fall to the Calambás family, as it is the straightest line and the most eminent family. Because there is no succession nor children, neither man nor woman, this is the reason that Don Agustín Calambás will inherit rule, and it will continue in his line without falling from the Calambás family, and he who is not of this illustrious family will not be valid nor taken as such and he who is will not lose the title and will be the only legitimate *cacique*...

(ACC/P 1881: 1133r)

He ordered that the *cacicazgo* continue in the Calambás line until the fifth generation (ibid.: 1141r).

But in Vitoncó, Tama claimed to have taken on the Calambás title in recognition of his victory over Calambás' forces. By this time he had a son, José, who was eight years old (Tama was 70 in 1708 [ACC/P 1883: 2164r]). José does not reappear in the documentary record; the next news of a *cacique* for Vitoncó was of Don Andrés Calambás, who was *reservado*, that is, over 50 years of age and exempt from tribute payment. The remainder of the chiefly line descended from him (ACC/P 1719a). Don Andrés could not have been less than 39 years old in 1708 when the Vitoncó title was drawn up if he was *reservado* in 1719. Tama's own son was only eight at the signing of the title. Hence, the succession cannot have passed directly in Don Juan Tama's line. Nevertheless, Tama ordered that successors *in his own line* take on the Calambás title: "Don Juan Tama y Calambás will always be titled Calambás up to his great-grandchildren who will not lose the title of Calambás" (ACC/P 1881: 2164r).

Although transmission of the two *cacicazgos* remains unclear, it is evident that Don Juan Tama's successors retained the Calambás title for over a century: the *cacique* of Pitayó in 1807 (and a hero of Colombian Independence) was General Agustín Calambás; in 1836 a copy of the Vitoncó title was requested by its then *cacique*, José Calambás (ibid.: 2181v, 2182r).

Moral continuity

The only true surnames in eighteenth-century Tierradentro were attached to chiefly lines, names such as Gueyomuse, Calambás, Pasquín, etc. These were passed from *cacique* to *cacique*, it appears, upon assumption of the *cacicazgo*, and occasionally were also adopted by siblings. Castillo (1877: 75) defined surname as *quigueyace*, or "place-name," and it is not accidental that the new *caciques* utilized names as a means of consolidating territory under their rule.

Commoners did not inherit names. They carried Páez given names and Spanish baptismal names; given names were chosen by their mothers, and often referred to topographic features (ibid.). Only chiefly surnames were passed from generation to generation. The historical record demonstrates that even these were not true surnames, but titles. *Caciques* were sometimes referred to by their own names, for example, Doña Clara Subix (of Togoima) and on other occasions, called by their titles: Doña Clara Gueyomuse. Moreover, chiefly titles were only affixed to baptismal names after the individual had officially assumed the *cacicazgo*. Thus, Doña Angelina Gueyomuse was called "Angelina without a surname" as a child, and Doña Angelina Gueyomuse once she became *cacica* of Togoima.

One of the clearest indicators of the titular nature of chiefly surnames appears in the documentation pertaining to the *cacicazgos* of Vitoncó and Pitayó, where the choice of names was validated by Don Juan Tama Estrella, who subsequently passed them on to his successors. The choice of the title "Calambás" lends an insight into the historical value of chiefly titles for the Páez.

Remember that at the time of the Spanish invasion of the Popayán area, two chiefs shared the supreme rulership, one of whom was Calambás. Forty years later, Aguado (1956) speaks extensively of the *cacique* of Guambía, Don Diego Calambar. The *cacica* of nearby

Timbío in 1679 was Doña Beatriz Timbío Calambás (AJC/Q 1679). When the new *cacique* Don Juan Tama, who supposedly triumphed over Calambás in order to extend his dominion, established title to his lands, he took for himself and his descendants that *cacique*'s name. For the remainder of the document, he was called Don Juan Tama y Calambás.

If it were not for Don Juan Tama y Calambás' proclamation that he took on the name Calambás in recognition of his triumph over his rival, all other data would lend itself to a simple interpretation of Calambás as an inherited surname. But the *cacique* of Vitoncó adopted this name in a fashion that obliges us to consider it from another point of view. Given that Tama conquered – or said he conquered – Calambás, we can compare his use of this surname to analogous practices in Peru. There, in order to acquire the lands of a conquered lord, he who triumphed had to take possession of that lord's mummy and keep it in his house, marry his wife (Polo 1917 [1567]: 117), or take his name (Urioste 1983: 2: 190–91). Thus, when Tama conquered Calambás, he might have been obliged to take on his name. Although this comparison explains the particular case of Don Juan Tama y Calambás and his descendants, it does not clarify for us the use of the name Calambás in the other cases mentioned.

Perhaps it would be best to consider Calambás as a title that accompanied political leadership. This interpretation accords with the precolumbian case of the Guambiano *caciques*, as well as with Tama's efforts to acquire the surname in order to control a territory. One indication that this was a title and not a surname was its short duration in Tama's family: in Vitoncó Tama ordered that Calambás continue as a family title through his great-grandchildren. In the title to Pitayó, his specifications also extended for five generations, but this time maintaining the *cacicazgo* in the Calambás family itself.

Within the Inca hierarchical system, there was a classificatory unit composed of four generations governing lines of descent. Named groups called *ayllus*, composed of brothers and sisters descended from a common ancestor, were organized in two parallel lines continuing over four generations (Zuidema 1977: 256). Including the genitors, these groups had a duration of five generations; after that time had elapsed it was possible for great-grandchildren to marry each other (ibid.: 258). This same multi-level model is reproduced in the Inca political hierarchy (ibid.: 269), in the origin myth (ibid.: 271) and in the concept of a cosmic or universal hierarchy (ibid.: 264). The general model stressed parallel transmission along matrilineal and patrilineal lines, in other words, bilateral descent.

Among the Páez there were similar indications of some type of parallel transmission of names. As was remarked above, in many cases two individuals in each generation of a chiefly line adopted the chiefly title; the two were generally siblings although sometimes cousins, and frequently were a male–female pair. At the commoner level there was also some evidence for the treatment of men and women in parallel lines. Although both men and women could use the same names, there were suffixes which served to distinguish men from women:

> If one calls the child *Táquiene*, this will be his name until puberty, from whence until old age [he will be] *Táquipiz*; in old age he will be called *Táqui-tee*; this is what occurs when they do not change their surname for a different one. In women there is generally not this mutation, although they acquire [their names] in the same way as do the men. Ordinarily they place after their surnames the word *oi* (woman).
>
> (Castillo 1877: 75–76)

Although the writer did not supply translations in his definition, *piz*, which was added to a grown man's name, can be translated as "man," and *tee*, which indicated old age, means "grandfather." Thus, although they carried similar names, the Páez distinguished the sex and generation of the holder by adding suffixes signalling gender. This could indicate some notion of parallel lines organized according to sex among the Páez.

The Inca applied their model of the patriline to their political hierarchy: the names for the four grades of relationship or the four generations, were also applied to the royal dynasty (Zuidema 1977: 269). Here was an ego-centered system, governed by rules of relativity: as each new generation was added, the focus for the nomenclature changed. I believe that Don Juan Tama's orders that Calambás be his surname/title until the fifth generation reflected a similar principle. Among the Páez it was used in the political domain, although authorities also often continued to use their own surnames and were apparently free to take on titles under certain circumstances: this is what Don Juan Tama did, tacking both Calambás and Estrella onto his name to justify his pretensions to the *cacicazgo*. According to Castillo (1877: 75–76), the changing or adding-on of names was common among adult Páez, so Juan Tama's appropriation of the title Calambás was probably accepted by his people.

What was the utility for Don Juan Tama Estrella of assuming the title Calambás? It was a way for him to legitimize his leadership role through the use of a title that at the time was synonymous with the notion of *cacicazgo*. By taking on this title – and pretending to assume it in a native manner – Tama created a new dynasty in the region. Although the title was not Páez in origin, the people of Tierradentro had certainly come into contact with the Calambás dynasty at the time of the Spanish invasion if not before, and it held meaning for them.

What does his use of names indicate about Juan Tama's vision of history? First, it demonstrates the use of historical knowledge for creating a moral continuity between past and present. Although Juan Tama's *cacicazgo* was a departure from the chiefdoms of the precolumbian period and although the Páez had never belonged to the *cacicazgo* of Calambás, his choice of a title was a link to the past, and a glorious one at that. Moreover, as Tama's chiefdom was under Spanish law less fluid and more stratified than those of the precolumbian Páez *caciques*, it was in fact more comparable to that of Calambás. Finally, the creation of the *resguardos* of Vitoncó and Pitayó incorporated the lands on both sides of the cordillera into a single dominion, territory that had once belonged to the Guambiano. Tama thus recognized the non-Páez roots of the chiefdom. What he created was new, born within a colonial context and developed according to an incipient pan-Indian ideology which stressed the importance of being the first Americans and claiming land rights for that reason. His new approach to *cacicazgo*-building encompassed both Páez and Guambiano; hence the acceptability of the new title.

We can only guess as to what the title Calambás elicited in the minds of Don Juan Tama's subjects and his Guambiano neighbors. It was a multivocal symbol which at one and the same time invited thoughts about the precolumbian past, the strengths of the autochthonous *cacicazgo*, the power of the new holder of the title, the shame of the Guambiano who had, in some way, fallen from power. The title was a potent historical referent, no less captivating because it was non-narrative.

The passing of the *cacicazgo* to the Calambás line in Pitayó and the adoption of the title in Vitoncó are also salient in that they point to the temporal parameters of Páez historical thought. In both cases we are talking of a five-generational model which provided a conceptual point in the past at which historical process was seen to begin, and a hypothetical time in the future toward which prophecy could be directed. It is irrelevant that the title remained an essential part of the *cacicazgos* way beyond the stipulated five generations; what is significant is that the time-frame was chosen in the first place.

From whence did this five-generational model arise? It was prevalent in sixteenth-century Peru among Quechua-speakers. Quechua influence was substantial in colonial Colombia: there was a Quechua-speaking population near Popayán and much Spanish–Indian communication was at least attempted in Quechua, or with Quechua intermediaries. Don Jacinto Muscay, the occupant of the Pitayó *cacicazgo* before Don Juan Tama, had travelled to Quito to assure his successor and he was the first to stipulate the five generation succession (ACC/P 1881: 1140r–1141r). It is quite possible that the concept was first made known to him during that trip. I would venture to guess that he learned it from the Spaniards who, lacking knowledge of Páez lifeways, consistently transported Incaic ideas and terminology to the Páez landscape, imposing a new indigenous, but quite foreign, ideology upon the people of Tierradentro.

Aside from any conjecture regarding the origins of the five-generational model, it is evident that it was important to Don Juan Tama: it was not only applied in the 1700 Pitayó title, but was adopted again, eight years later, in his stipulations regarding the *cacicazgo* of Vitoncó. Regardless of whether or not it was an autochthonous temporal model, it quickly became tradition for the Páez, and will arise time and again in our analysis of subsequent indigenous historians.

History as "What should have happened"

A number of contradictions and inconsistencies appear if we compare the texts of the two *resguardo* titles. There is a lack of factual agreement between them, although both documents were written with the input of Don Juan Tama. In them the *cacique* of Vitoncó articulated much deeper ideas about history than can be found in the "facts" he laid out.

According to the Pitayó title Don Juan Tama assumed leadership by virtue of inheritance: the *cacicazgo* passed to him from his uncle, Don Jacinto Muscay. On Tama's death it would pass to the Calambás family, since the *cacique* claimed to have no heirs. Both Muscay and Calambás were most probably Guambiano: Muscay is a Guambiano surname and the Calambás family had controlled the

Guambiano chiefdom for at least two centuries. As Muscay's nephew, Don Juan Tama might have even regarded himself as Guambiano as well, although it is clear that since Tama's time, the Calambás of Pitayó came to identify themselves as Páez, and the Páez themselves regard Tama as one of their own. As a result of the smooth succession laid out in the title, the colonial *cacicazgo* of Pitayó was forged under peaceful circumstances.

In contrast, Don Juan Tama's account of his acquisition of Vitoncó was steeped in a more fabulous and militaristic imagery. He gave no indication of his parentage; in fact, he alluded to a supernatural birth, calling himself the "son of the star of the Tama Stream," even assuming the surname Estrella, or Star, to reinforce his supernatural ties. Thus he labelled himself a divine emissary, a messianic figure. He claimed to have assumed the *cacicazgo* through military triumph, killing the rival Guambiano *cacique*, Calambás. Contradicting what he ordered in the Pitayó title – that the Calambás family retain the *cacicazgo* at his death, since at that time he had no heirs – as *cacique* of Vitoncó Tama stipulated that his *own* descendants assume the Calambás title and that, moreover, he himself also adopt it in recognition of his victory over the Guambiano. In effect, he altered the evidence he had previously offered, given that the title of Vitoncó establishes control over both *cacicazgos*.

What was the significance of such political maneuvers recounted by Don Juan Tama? Why such obvious disparities between the two titles? In 1700 Tama inherited through the collateral line a chiefdom belonging to one ethnic group. Eight years later he consolidated dominion over a different community, repudiating any relation he might have had with the former and defining himself and his territory as Páez. Traditionally the Páez and Guambiano were enemies; this is clear in Don Diego Calambar's collaboration in the Spanish conquest of Tierradentro. So Tama manipulated the sentiments of his people, reinterpreting history, making it his own and basing his claim to leadership on military conquest. In this way, using the alien but more permanent medium of the administrative document, he defined himself as Páez, legitimized his authority and linked the two *cacicazgos* into a single territorial unit.

The sort of history used by the *cacique* of Vitoncó was not quite that which we as Euroamericans recognize as objective. Tama *was* telling the truth when he claimed that the Páez conquered the Guambiano and thus gained control over the western slopes of the cordillera. After all, at the time of the Spanish invasion the Páez forces resisted Lozano's army and banished Calambar from Tierradentro. What makes Tama's account ambiguous is that the events recounted occurred at least 75 years before their main protagonist was even born, over 130 years before he set them in writing!

Condensation of time-periods in oral narration, frequently called telescoping (Henige 1974), takes on a special nature in the Vitoncó document, since its author was well aware that he had not killed Calambás, nor banished the Guambiano to the banks of the Piendamó. This was clearly not a case of a confusion of time-frames, but a very conscious effort at revising history. How, then, was it accepted by Tama's followers, who would have known had a major battle taken place on their soil? It could have been understood metaphorically since over the century and a quarter since the battle with Calambar, the Páez had effectively banished the Guambiano to Guambía by colonizing their lands. Moreover, Vitoncó's new *cacique* cemented the Guambiano exile by capturing – albeit pacifically and legally – Pitayó, formerly Guambiano territory.

At the same time, Tama's use of evidence established a moral continuity with the Páez militaristic past. His pretensions were most probably accepted for quite traditional reasons, namely, that the Páez defined history as what "should have occurred," and not "what happened." For them, history was the living past, part of the present and a road to the future, intimately linked with divination. Don Juan Tama embedded his claims within a traditional model of historical time by drawing a connection to the past and to the future: to the past by claiming to have defeated Calambás, and to the future by appropriating his name for five generations. Thus situated in a comprehensible and acceptable notion of historical time, what appear to us as jarring and contradictory assertions would not have been taken as such by his followers.

The implementation of historical knowledge

Don Juan Tama both drew upon and created Páez history in his two *resguardo* titles. He did not do this as a mere intellectual exercise, but to press a political claim in a non-traditional context. It is to this legitimizing effort that we will now turn, in order to see how historical knowledge was implemented by the eighteenth-century Páez.

No one in modern Tierradentro would ever admit that Juan Tama

was not Páez. But Tama's claim of having been born in a stream, the
son of the star, points to another conclusion. Why would he wish to
legitimize himself in such a manner, emphasizing the fact that he was
not Páez at all?

Evidence from several documentary sources suggests that Don
Juan Tama might have been Guambiano or at least, a native of the
western slopes of the cordillera. According to the Pitayó title, he was
the nephew of Don Jacinto Muscay, a Guambiano himself. In 1683
there was another mention of a *cacique* named Tama from the same
general area, this time in Toribío. His name is found in a list of
repartimientos associated with the Páez Province, including Páez
communities on the western slope of the cordillera (ANH/Q 1703:
5v). In most of these western entries, communities of migrants
from Tierradentro were mentioned as such. Tama of Toribío was
not classed in this category. We could venture to guess that Don
Juan Tama was somehow associated with this *cacique*, if not the same
person; since the list of *encomiendas* did not supply the ages of the
caciques, it is difficult to substantiate this claim, and since most of
these *caciques* were unbaptized and had no Christian names, the two
leaders cannot be compared on that basis. Nevertheless, that Juan
Tama was foreign to Tierradentro is clear: there were no others
called Tama appearing in Tierradentro tributary lists, and the
surname is absent among the modern Páez.

Don Juan Tama could also have hailed from a group located to
the east of Tierradentro. Throughout the multiethnic communities
which sprang up in the colonial period in the Gobernación de Neiva,
settlements inhabited by Páez, Andakí and others, we find mention
of the surname Tama with much more frequency than in the tribute
lists of the villages on the western slope of the cordillera (ANC/B
1784). The Tama, frequently known as the "orphans," hailed from
the Upper Amazon. As early as the second half of the sixteenth
century they were already being enslaved by the Spaniards, and by
the late seventeenth century they were settled throughout the
Gobernación de Neiva, in many of the same towns inhabited by
Páez; in fact, some Páez *caciques* in the area controlled Tama slaves
themselves (ANC/B 1739: 67v–68r). By that time many Tama had
become totally hispanicized (Pineda 1980–81: 352). The Tama were
not a single tribe, but originated in an indigenous form of slavery
that produced a host of "orphans," isolated from their own ethnic
communities. The Spanish were able to take advantage of this
institution in their search for a labor pool. Although we cannot

define the Tama as a single ethnic group, they were frequently distinguished in tribute lists by the surname Tama (ANC/B 1629).

Slaves in Amazonian societies were not condemned to a life among strangers, but could, if they were not killed, be adopted into their new ethnic group by achieving the status of warrior. Nevertheless, their children continued to belong to the original ethnic group of the parents (Pineda 1980–81: 345–55).

It seems quite plausible that Don Juan Tama was in fact, a kind of "Tama." As a foreigner, and a subordinate one at that, Don Juan Tama would have done well to claim a supernatural birth. Furthermore, given that Tamas could alter their ethnic identity by becoming warriors, we have another explanation of Don Juan Tama's story of having killed Calambás and taken over his dominion. By telling this tale Tama could prove himself a warrior and thus integrate himself into the Páez ethnic unit. It also explains why Don Juan Tama y Calambás was so adamant about assuming the title of Calambás, in whose name the Pitayó chiefdom was already lodged. By passing his title on to his children, his line would be assured membership in the Páez nation, whereas normally the children of Tamas-turned-warriors would belong to the father's original ethnic group. The supposition that Don Juan Tama was a Tama does not conflict with Don Jacinto Muscay's statement that he was his nephew: as an "orphan," Tama could integrate himself or be adopted into any group, including the Guambiano.

The convention of welcoming *caciques* from other ethnic groups was known in the area. The Andakí, who were neighbors of the Páez, frequently had foreign chiefs (Friede 1953: 89–90). Hence, it is entirely possible that the Páez, who have always lived in a multiethnic situation, followed the same practice and were thus able to accept foreign *caciques* like Don Juan Tama. In at least one case, the *cacique* of Ambostá, part of the Gueyomuse *cacicazgo* of Togoima, was himself a descendant of the *caciques* of Wila (ANC/B 1766): if not from a different ethnic group, he was certainly from a different *cacicazgo*. But in the case of Vitoncó, Don Juan Tama, who carried the stigma of the Tama identity, would have had to achieve some degree of legitimacy in order to be accepted into the Páez nation. This he accomplished through recourse to history.

A Tama *cacique* would have been a boon for the Páez of the early eighteenth century. The Tama spoke Spanish and were more experienced in dealing with Europeans than were the monolingual Páez. Moreover, the Tama were already versed in the tradition of the *resguardo*, having fought for one as early as 1646 in Timaná (Pineda 1980–81). The nature of the region and of the wanderers in it suggests that many of the strategies which characterize the new *cacique* period in Tierradentro were actually attempts by foreigners from the lowlands to acquire dominion in the sierra, while at the same time strengthening Tierradentro, Pitayó and Tacueyó against the foreigners from over the sea.

The writing of history

In the long term, the fact that Don Juan Tama set his historical interpretations in writing assured him a place in posterity. This was not an option for the anonymous many, whose narratives remained in oral form. It could only result from Tama's political position as a *cacique* at the juncture in which he forged his *resguardos*, when the Páez were not perceived as a threat and were permitted to develop their own modes of political authority. In other words, the survival of Tama's memory is a product of events unfolding in the wider Spanish colonial arena.

But if Tama was skilled in establishing contacts that facilitated the setting down of his thoughts in an alien medium, his followers were not as knowledgeable of the mysteries of writing. Undachi, Tama's contemporary, and a messianic leader in Togoima, belied his mastery of the written word when he justified his movement in the following manner:

While in said prison, said Indian stated in an unsolicited declaration while talking with this witness and the rest of those who had accompanied Your Honor, that if they did not want to believe that God had spoken to him, he would show them a letter that God had written and left for him and if they would free him, he would bring it. The Governor informed Your Honor, who sent for him to be taken from prison and, accompanying Your Honor, to deliver the aforementioned letter. Going with said Indian to the other building he ordered that they take down a small woven bag which was hanging on the wall. When the aforementioned bag was opened, in it they found some sheets of white paper. When said Indian took hold of one of the sheets he said that this was the letter that God had left him on the altar in the chapel, and that they should look at what was written in the letter, because he could not understand it. Once inspected by Your Honor, it was seen to be simply one of the several sheets of white paper. When he was told that there was nothing written on said sheet, he asked for it and examined it and spoke in his own language, pointing to the water-mark [and saying] that that was what had been written.

(AHT/B 1729: 160r–v)

Undachi's lack of experience with the written word was probably the rule among the Páez. Bolstered by European tradition which juxtaposed ritual with the production of written documents (Clanchy 1979), *resguardo* titles were validated by Spanish ceremony:

Finding all together and in agreement, I took the hand of the governor Luis Dagua, Inocencio (—?) and asked them and all if they found themselves in peaceful proprietorship, and scattering water I had branches pulled and spread around, signalling possession.   (NC/S 1914: no pagination)

The contents of the titles, unread by commoners, were expressed to them in oral form during the formal walk around *resguardo* boundaries that preceded approval of the title. Thus, the historical knowledge included in the documents was codified in topographic space and ritual time, strengthening the impact of the geographic medium for transmitting and interpreting history.

Don Juan Tama did not write the titles himself; this is clear from their language, since Tama's contributions were phrased in the form of quotations. His historical digressions were extremely brief and somewhat cryptic, requiring background knowledge if they were to be understood. The cryptic nature of Andean narration has been emphasized by Poole (n.d.), who suggests that the lack of clarity of oral accounts is dispelled by explanatory material present in other, non-narrative forms, such as dance and pilgrimage, both related to space. Juan Tama's history reflected other knowledge which his own followers possessed, some of which was probably articulated in the ceremonies accompanying the ratification of the title. Surviving fragments of historical interpretation were fragmentary to begin with: unlike linear narratives, these were images that invited participation and interpretation, they existed because they were ambiguous, and they were useful in practice for precisely this reason.

II

From colony to Republic: *cacique* and *caudillo*

4

The chiefdom transformed: the nineteenth-century Páez

The late colonial period was an era of empowerment for the Páez. Extensive landholdings were legitimized and protected through *resguardo* titles. Political authority was cemented under the new *caciques*. The colonial state accepted and even encouraged the creation of semi-autonomous political units, so long as they continued to provide a source of tributary revenue for the Crown. But during the nineteenth-century rise of the Colombian Republic the nature of the relationship between community and state was profoundly altered and indigenous communities found themselves confronting a new political system that denied them autonomy in the interests of forging national unity and accommodating the capitalist expansion which would benefit the ruling elite. Among the Páez, loss of autonomy resulted from a number of developments, including Republican legislation that sought to destroy or at least weaken the *resguardo* system; the utilization of the Páez landscape and of indigenous leaders and soldiers in the civil wars which were fought to define which sector of the elite would maintain hegemony; the rape of Tierradentro's resources for the new extractive economy which focused on quinine; and the loss of community lands to the hacienda system in the name of freeing unexploited holdings for commercial development (Bonilla 1979; Rojas and Findji 1985). The result in Tierradentro was the carving up of the landscape into smaller and weaker *resguardos* headed by indigenous political intermediaries working in concert with the emerging Colombian elites. Colombians struggled to define their own territory and nationality at the expense of the autonomy of the indigenous communities living within their borders.

INDIANS THROUGH COLOMBIAN EYES

We now have 300,000 Indians born in this country. Given that not all of them are male, nor are all of them able to work, let us say that they are only worth one hundred dollars, a tenth of a European immigrant. I am sure that as we learn to take advantage of Indian labor we will earn interest on an appreciating capital. Thus the Indian population is worth a minimum of 300 million gold pesos.

(Uribe Uribe 1907: 37–38)

In his 1907 pamphlet entitled *Reducción de salvajes* (The Reduction of Savages to Civilization), Rafael Uribe Uribe made what was then a strong case for the incorporation of Colombia's indigenous population into the labor market. Colombia found it difficult to attract European immigrants to settle as homesteaders in its vast hinterlands; nevertheless, there was a pressing need to relieve what had become a serious labor shortage in order to bolster Colombia's export economy. Uribe Uribe's solution was to civilize the Indians: teach them to speak Spanish, slowly rid them of their "savage" culture, convert them into mestizo laborers, in short, make citizens of them. His opinions regarding the fate of Indians grew out of nineteenth-century dreams of transforming Colombia into a nation of mestizos.

The issue of citizenship was central to the nascent Colombia's policy toward its Indian population. Upon assuming Colombian citizenship the Indian would no longer swear allegiance toward a semi-independent unit, such as the *resguardo*. He would speak Spanish, would engage in useful wage labor and would till his own privately-owned plot. That is, he would live within Colombia and would become an active agent in developing the national territory. At the same time as it civilized the Indian, the ideal of citizenship encouraged the expansion of both small and large individual landowners onto communal lands: mestizo settlers hoping to acquire *resguardo* lands leaned on their own rights as citizens to these territories (LeGrand 1986).[1]

Although national citizenship was a principal component of Republican policy towards Indians, it was never denied that foreigners could play an important role in both civilizing savages and in developing their lands. Thus, at mid-century a solution was proposed to the problem of the warlike Páez who battled government forces in the War of 1859–1862:

[We should] either give an English or North American speculatory company part of the land, on condition that they found and maintain a settlement there; or mount a strong expedition against the Indians, by which, destroying their houses and crops, we would capture men and women of all ages and transport them to another location where an abundant population would restrain them. The first of these measures is more feasible, all the more so as in these lands there is a multitude of exportable substances, such as laurel wax which is very abundant. And a foreign settlement would be like a colony and would impede, as in other countries, all sorts of upheavals and excesses.

(BLAA/B [Biblioteca Luis Angel Arango, Bogotá] 1863 : 12v)

But alongside national society's hopes for civilizing the Indians and integrating them into the national economy, they also opted to harness the Indians' savagery, especially that of the Páez, who were remembered as fierce warriors. Thus, in an account of the November 1860 battle between Páez and government forces at Segovia, Tierradentro, the contemporary Páez were compared to their Conquest-era ancestors :

The war that the Indians waged with us was unyielding and exhausting. It is enough to know that this is the famous Páez tribe, so feared by the Spaniards who defeated the troops sent by Pedro Anazco and by Juan de Ampúdia in 1540; who resisted the conquest attempted by the Jesuit missionaries in 1620; and whose reduction to town life was not begun until the year 1634, so that you can guess how they must be, now that they have firearms and use them with skill, now that they are disciplined and directed by expert leaders. (ibid.: 7r)

Even as late as 1910, in the first edition of their history of Colombia, Henao and Arrubla (1938) treat Indians almost exclusively as savage warriors, confining them to chapters on the Conquest and the colonial period. The Páez are only mentioned with regard to their resistance to the Spanish invaders and are not accorded a role in the growth of the nation (ibid.: 1 : 60, 66, 68–69, 106). Thus, the savage Indian was conceptually banished to the pre-Independence era, remaining invisible to the Republican mind.

Indian legislation in the Republican era

Nineteenth-century Colombia was the union of a number of autonomous states only partially subservient to the central government. In contrast to the centralized colonial administration, there was no real post-Independence administrative unity, no national coherence binding these regions, the largest of which was Cauca (Map 6). Colombia was only beginning to define its national territory and the process was initiated at the regional level by local elites whose economic and ideological interests were sometimes at variance with those of the elites of other regions (Tirado 1982 : 346–47). Lack

Map 6   Nineteenth-century Colombia: political divisions

of political homogeneity would have a profound influence on the developing Republican policy toward Indians.

At the time of Independence, the founding fathers saw Indians as among the prime recipients of the fruits of the birth of the Colombian nation. It was believed that the war had been fought to free the Indians from Spanish oppression (Bushnell 1954: 175). Early Republican legislation gave the Indians legal equality by freeing them from tribute obligations (although these were substituted with personal contributions, which played the same role as tribute) and by attempting to replace communal *resguardo* lands with the private property that came along with full citizenship. Thus, in the first year of Independence Indians were declared full citizens and the dismantling of the *resguardo* system was proclaimed; but the desired effect did not come to fruition, due to resistance by *resguardo* members (ibid.: 176–77; Friede 1972: 106).

The first 60 years of Republican rule were administered for the most part by Liberal politicians, who represented the interests of exporters of agricultural products and importers of foreign goods. Liberal rule promoted the expansion of private property and the growth of competition and free trade. In terms of its Indian policy, it advocated the dissolution of the *resguardos* through a series of national laws (cf. Friede 1972: 106–15).[2]

But the very federalism that characterized Colombia politically also blocked the implementation of anti-*resguardo* legislation. Local elites continually disregarded national law: an 1834 bill requiring that states dissolve *resguardos* was disputed by the provincial legislature of Cauca on the grounds that the process of surveying communal lands was too costly for both communities and the State, and because Indians were actively resisting the process by destroying the boundary-markers laid down by surveyors (Helguera 1983 [1835]).

By mid-century local governments were given new options for implementing national Indian legislation. An 1850 law decentralized the *resguardo* liquidation process, placing it in the hands of individual states (Friede 1972: 115). In Cauca, a long-term alliance between Indians and politicians forced local elites to meet the needs of their indigenous population, instead of following national policy. Such alliances were generally military in nature. For example, in 1861, lands belonging to the *latifundista* and politician Julio Arboleda were ceded to the *resguardos* of Pitayó and Jambaló in recognition of their participation in the War of 1859–62, in which Tomás Cipriano de

Mosquera took up the reins of national government, aided in Cauca by Páez armies (*Registro Oficial*, Popayán, 24 February 1863; *La Opinión*, 8 February 1865; Roldán 1974: 22).[3]

Colombian Liberalism met its downfall in the 1880s, poor economic policy and conditions forcing the establishment of a stronger central government with a less markedly *laissez-faire* policy. This period, called "The Regeneration," was the product of an alliance of independent Liberals and the Conservative Party. The Regeneration renewed relations with the Church, established a protective tariff and founded a national bank to stimulate economic growth (Bergquist 1986). During the Regeneration Colombian Indian policy shifted emphasis and began to consider Indians as only part-citizens, legal minors who would need to be civilized by the Church (Bonilla 1979: 333–34; Castillo 1987: 28–29). Central to the turn toward a more gradual process of integration was Law 89 of 1890 (Colombia 1970 [1890]: 19–31), which included protectionist measures safeguarding the *resguardo*, but also stipulated a period of 50 years within which the communal holdings must be prepared for privatization. Building upon earlier nineteenth-century legislation, Law 89 also defined the *resguardo* as a much smaller and weaker unit. In the Páez area colonial *cacicazgos* were broken into a number of independent *resguardos* which, deprived of political autonomy and broader unity, could no longer resist the advances of the state as effectively as they had before. Moreover, by dividing the colonial chiefdoms into smaller units, discord was sowed between contiguous *resguardos*, and new titles were drawn up to mitigate tensions arising from border disputes (N/S [Notaría de Silvia, Cauca] 1941). Law 89 was given more teeth in 1905, when regional authorities were accorded the right to initiate the process of alienating unused portions of *resguardos* for colonization by non-Indians (areas called *zonas de población*).

PÁEZ POLITICAL ORGANIZATION IN THE NINETEENTH CENTURY

While evidence for colonial Páez history is contained in numerous documents that give voice to indigenous actors, the nineteenth-century historical record is notorious for ignoring the Indians' existence.[4] Given the paucity of direct evidence, it is tempting to concentrate more on nineteenth-century Colombia than on the nineteenth-century Páez; to date only one analysis of Republican

Páez history has been written (Findji and Rojas 1985). The following analysis will build upon that earlier contribution.

Cabildo vs. *cacicazgo*

Republican Páez communities were considerably less unified than were their colonial forebears. While in the eighteenth century there were four large *cacicazgos*, by the late nineteenth century political hegemony was distributed across a landscape composed of multiple centers of power. At the close of his 1877–78 voyage to Cauca the English botanist Robert Cross wrote:

Until of late years every village had a *cacique*, or chief, whose dispositions, however, were always guided by the counsels of a few of the older and more experienced inhabitants. In this way the whole tribe was composed of a multitude of communities, possessing more or less a municipal character, all of whom combined to attack the hostile tribes by which they were surrounded. (1879: 32)

Colombian mining entrepreneur and amateur ethnologist Carlos Cuervo Márquez, writing in 1887, described the Páez region as a patchwork of communities, some administered by elected *cabildos* and others ruled by hereditary *caciques*:

Internal administration of the tribe's interests over and above the authority of the *cabildo*, is vested in the *cacique*, when he exists. The *cacique* is able to exercise his dominion over a single *parcialidad* or over several. The *cacique* of Pitayó, for example, whose ancestors led the occupation of the territory on the western slope of the cordillera, probably in the last third of the fifteenth century, still exercises his authority over four of the *parcialidades* there; but this title is disappearing all through Tierra Adentro; and there are many *parcialidades* which we might call free, such as Toribío, Tacueyó, Huila [Wila], etc., who do not recognize any *cacique* nowadays (1956[1887]: 284).

Some of these communities were more powerful than others. When a group of white entrepreneurs in search of quinine encroached on Pitayó lands, they were met by the *cabildo*, which was sufficiently strong to repel their advances:

The Indian governor of Pitayó, having learned that we had begun to cut quinine bark, presented himself before us, armed and accompanied by many other Indians, in order to prevent us continuing our work and to embargo what quinine we had already harvested. (*El Tiempo*, 4 May 1858)

In contrast, the *cabildo* of Wila was duped into signing a document ceding its control over vast quinine forests to another group of white entrepreneurs (ACC/P 1871).

Cacicazgos were officially liquidated after Independence. In 1825, when a Guambiano requested that he be awarded the office of *cacique*, his petition was rejected on the grounds that the government no longer recognized the existence of hereditary leaders in indigenous communities (ANC/B 1825). Nevertheless, travellers continued to cite the existence of *cacicazgos* among the Páez. It is plausible that nineteenth-century hereditary chiefs were recognized by Indians, but not by the Colombian government. That Indians continued to look toward *caciques* well beyond their official demise is indicated in a 1920 law enacted by the Caucan legislature abolishing the practice of re-electing Indian governors, so that they could not be transformed into *de facto caciques* (Findji and Rojas 1985: 76).

In the following pages we will examine the history of indigenous participation in the civil wars that ravaged the countryside during the nineteenth century, seeking out the basis of Republican chiefly power. But before this, let us dwell briefly on the disparities between indigenous political authority on the western slopes of the cordillera and in Tierradentro itself. As the quotations cited above illustrate, it is in such areas as Pitayó that we find strong *cabildos*, while in Tierradentro *resguardo* councils were prey to influential individuals, both Indian and white, who usurped their authority from them, thereby laying claim to their lands. The Páez of the western slopes lived in closer proximity to white settlements, continually invaded by land-grabbers and sharing borders with large, well-established haciendas. In contrast, Tierradentro's lands remained distant, inaccessible and, in general, less appealing. The territory was only beginning to be colonized by non-Indians during the Republican era. Thus, the communities of Pitayó and Jambaló, living under continuous attack, were forced to empower themselves by appropriating as their own the very limited political authority that the Republican legislators vested in their *cabildos*. Tierradentro was more of a no-man's land, a battleground, where Republican law had not yet taken root and where *latifundistas* had only begun to venture; its Indian communities, in turn, were not forced to develop political institutions for self-defense until the end of the century.

Caciques without *cacicazgos*

Nineteenth-century transformations in the nature of Páez political power were the product of a merging of non-Indian military, political and economic interests with a revitalized aboriginal memory of precolumbian and colonial forms of political organization. The *cacicazgo* took on a new character influenced by developments in the broader society, including the nine civil wars that raged during 30 years of the century, in which the Páez area was a major battleground. Findji and Rojas (1985) point out that nineteenth-century Páez political leaders weakened the indigenous colonial political system by utilizing precisely those characteristics that had been its strength during the previous century. Where colonial *caciques* asserted their political autonomy by ruling over large, semi-independent *resguardos*, the Republican self-styled *caciques* accomplished this by commanding independent Páez military units during the civil wars. Through their military activities and their participation in the Colombian political party system they were able to assert influence over a territory much wider than a single *resguardo*, corresponding more closely to the extensive *resguardos* of the colonial era. Although the Colombian state did not recognize *caciques* and sought to abolish the *cacicazgo* in favor of small elected councils or *cabildos* that served as intermediaries between smallholders and the government and not as authorities in themselves, the nineteenth-century indigenous *caudillos*, or politico-military leaders, operated as *de facto caciques* and were even called such, although the title had no basis in Republican law.[5]

Throughout the nineteenth century indigenous *caudillos* derived their stature from presumed links to colonial or even pre-columbian chiefs. As early as 1820 we learn that the *cacique* of Vitoncó was targeted by the pro-Independence forces as a potential leader because as a nephew of the *cacique* Calambar, he commanded a special authority (Caycedo 1942: 96–97). Agustín Calambás, a direct descendant of the colonial *caciques* of Pitayó, became a powerful military commander and ultimately, a national hero (González n.d.: 121; Sendoya n.d.: 28). The Guainás "dynasty" of politico-military leaders also derived its influence from presumed precolumbian links:

Less than 30 years ago the 21 Páez villages, especially those situated on the eastern slopes [in the region] called Tierra adentro, recognized the authority of a single *sath* [Páez for *cacique*] named Guainás, the brother-in-law of the last *cacique* who was, himself, descended directly from Calambás, a famous chief at the time of the Conquest. (Douay 1890: 785–86)

The Guainás family was more than a line of Colombian *caudillos*; it was a Páez phenomenon, as can be ascertained from Robert Cross' (1871: 36) narration of the death of one of its members:

The Páez Indians were then brought together by a chief, called Waynass, who was popular about Huihla, where there are sixteen towns and villages. Waynass was himself a Páez Indian. His family must have been wealthy, as he was sent when young to Popayan, where he was taught to read and write, a most uncommon thing for an Indian in these parts, but which may have been beneficial to him, as he was the only Indian leader who did not practise cruelty toward the whites. Some time after the commencement of the war, when crossing a rushing stream which unites with the river Páez near the volcano of Huihla, the bridge broke down and he was carried away and drowned. His body, brought down by the current, was afterwards found near the city of La Plata, which, calculating the numerous tortuous windings of the river Páez, will be seventy miles from the spot where Waynass lost his life.

This account can only be taken as an attempt by the Páez to situate Guainás within their own ideological mold as a culture hero. In this same area in the mid-eighteenth century Father Castillo y Orozco (1877: 53) was told a strikingly similar story regarding the disappearance of the culture hero, Guequiáu. Hence, Guainás may not have died in the Páez torrent, but as a *"cacique"* he was undoubtedly better remembered as having perished in this way.

Ties to earlier *cacicazgos* determined both the power of self-styled *caudillos* and the election of *cabildo* members, according to Cuervo Márquez (1956: 6) who, writing about the *resguardo* councils of San Francisco and Toribío, noted:

To achieve these offices more notice is taken of birth than of age, since the Páez, even though they have lost almost all their historical and cosmogonic traditions, carefully preserve those that refer to the importance of [certain] families.

Thus, the *capitán* of Toribío in 1887, Vicente Vitonás, was believed to be descended from the *cacique* Cayaimas, founder of the community in the mid-eighteenth century (ibid.: 8).

These self-styled *caciques* hailed from the small and autonomous communities of the nineteenth century, but cemented their dominion over broad expanses of territory, reproducing colonial *cacicazgos* by forging marital ties. Take, for example, General Guainás:

The general, who is one of the *caciques* of Lame in Tierra Adentro, is also recognized as such by the Indians of Toribío and San Francisco, by virtue of his marriage to the daughter of the *cacique* of the latter village... Today he is a General of the Republic, but it is not from here that his influence over Tierra Adentro stems; he is recognized by dint of the rights which by inheritance correspond to him and the virtues that adorn him.
                                                                              (ibid.: 4)

Guainás was a *cabildo* member in San Francisco and at the same time wielded influence over the *cabildos* of Tierradentro, among them, Wila (ibid.: 5, 32; ACC/P 1871). Findji and Rojas (1985: 72) associate his marital strategy with the perpetuation of colonial modes of territorial consolidation, suggesting that both Don Juan Tama and the Guainás *caudillos* managed their affairs through the careful establishment of kin ties.

Nineteenth-century *caciques* influenced their subjects in many spheres, coercing them into permitting mining exploration on their territory (Cuervo 1956), and actively recruited Indians to political parties (ACC/P 1888). But their primary link to political power derived from their participation in the civil wars.

From the Wars of Independence onward the Páez collaborated with Colombian armies as carriers, spies, messengers and trail-blazers (Caycedo 1943: 40, 52–53, 104–107). Nevertheless, they were never respected as disciplined soldiers, capable of carrying out the orders of non-Indian officers. An 1826 report laid out the rationale behind excluding Indians from the Caucan militia:

> Although Indians are not excluded under the law of militias since as citizens they are required to take on ordinary duties, I believe it necessary to show the government that the Indians of this department are not yet in a state to follow military discipline, because most of them are so rough that they do not even know our language and they are so afraid of arms that when we try to recruit them, they will flee into the forests, persuaded that we come to take them from their homes, and no one can persuade them to the contrary. Such desertions will prove to be of great harm to the public and even to the troops themselves, because they trade their products with the settlers and they are the best labor there is in agriculture. For these reasons, as much as because the militia drawn from the departmental population can excel without the Indians, I believe it would be to the common good to exempt them from this law until they are a bit more civilized.
>
> (ANC/B 1826: 390r-v)

Nevertheless, Indians continued to be recruited to civil war armies, some forcibly conscripted at festival time (Tirado 1976: 38), but many hid in the forests to avoid military recruitment (ibid.: 39; Mollien 1944 [1823]: 252, 256). To a certain extent, the Indian rank and file was involuntarily incorporated into Republican armies. Nevertheless, a number of indigenous recruits were undoubtedly attracted by the charisma of the *caciques*-turned-*caudillos*. Perhaps only a minority understood and agreed with the political aims of their leaders.

Lack of European-style military discipline did not keep Páez *caudillos* from turning the civil wars to their own ends. Cross (1879: 31) suggested that they used the pretext of civil war to attack neighboring non-Indians:

> Since the establishment of the Republic they have generally sided with the Government, especially during revolutions, but their employment in a military way

does not seem to have been of much benefit, since they devoted themselves chiefly to robbing farmhouses and plantations in remote districts.

Accounts from almost all of the civil wars fought on Páez soil point to the fact that indigenous *caudillos* used the battleground to acquire ascendancy within their own communities (Findji and Rojas 1985). Thus, in the War of the Convents (1839–41) we hear of the independent forces led by the indigenous *caudillo* Ibito (*El Día*, 17 June 1841). During the War of 1859–62, 600 Páez under the leadership of Peteví attacked government forces (*Gaceta Oficial*, 9 November 1860; *Boletín Oficial*, 13 January 1862); other indigenous units numbered up to 1,000 warriors (BLAA/B 1863: 11v). Independent native forces were created by the rebel armies of Tomás Cipriano de Mosquera and José Hilario López (*Boletín Oficial*, 17 December 1860 and 6 November 1861) and were used in ambushes against government battalions (*El Colombiano*, 5 July 1862); the Indians of Pitayó occupied the town of Silvia during the war (Cross 1871: 20).

The political centralization of the Regeneration began with the War of 1885–86. The Páez participated to some extent in actions led by non-Indians (*El Comercio*, 22 March 1885), but many refused to participate in the uprising, claiming that:

What they want is to take us [*sic*] out of Cauca and Tolima so that the cavalry will kill them and so that they can take over their lands, kill the Priests and demolish the temples. (*El Comercio*, 1 February 1885)

Nevertheless, we hear in 1885 of 2,000 Indians rebelling in Tierradentro (*El Comercio*, 28 March 1885). During this conflict the government used the Guainás family to lead indigenous forces in Jambaló and Pitayó (*El Comercio*, 20 April 1885). Operating independently of the rival white armies, Indian bands sowed confusion in Pitayó:

In Pitayó there are still small bands of armed Indians who are a terror and a menace to those towns in the cordillera and enough to interrupt communication with those towns. (ACC/P 1888)

Throughout these reports we read of the actions of "the Indians," with no reference to any non-Indian supervision or orders (Findji and Rojas 1985). We are witness to independent actions, led and fought by the Páez for their own unstated reasons, probably related to the acquisition of political power, the protection and reclamation of aboriginal lands, and the infliction of punishment on local non-

Indians. This is the hearth in which nineteenth-century *caciques* without *cacicazgos* were forged, enabling them to move across a territory as though it were a single, broad *cacicazgo*.

The last civil war of the nineteenth century was the War of the Thousand Days, which lasted from 1899 to 1902 and was prolonged beyond this date by the operation of guerrilla bands. Findji and Rojas (ibid.: 85) maintain that it differed from its predecessors in that its Páez participants were active in each of the warring armies, at times fighting each other. Thus, at La Ovejera the Páez General Francisco Guainás fought a band of 400 Indian rebels (Navia 1908: 53); a similar battle took place between Indians from Tierradentro and from the Jambaló area (AACH/B [Archivo Academia Colombiana de Historia, Bogotá] n.d.: 116–17, 181). Nevertheless, there are also reports of indigenous guerrilla bands from Tierradentro (AFCN/C 1971b), of wholly native battalions led by such *caudillos* as Guainás (*Boletín Militar, Pasto*, 24 August 1901), as well as by lesser-known officers, such as Captain Juan Yonda, who led 105 Indian soldiers from Quichaya (Navia 1908: 109). As was the case among precolumbian chiefs and for the new *caciques* of the colonial era, the image of a unified political leadership inherent in the symbol of the *cacique*, conflicted in practice with the decentralized character of nineteenth-century Páez politics. On the ground, a broad range of *caudillos* with conflicting party allegiances organized military units independently of one another.

Although the War of the Thousand Days pitted Páez against Páez, it continued to provide a context within which native *caudillos* could wield their influence over widely-dispersed communities. Some of these actions took on a distinctly ritual nature. One Páez revolutionary leader, for example, led a column of Indians from Vitoncó on an expedition into the neighboring department of Huila, where they attacked a farm and took prisoners. The captives were marched back to Vitoncó and were thrown into the Moras River at a place called Tarpeya (González n.d.: 122), following a pattern that was also noted in previous wars (ibid.: 121).

LAND AND LABOR

Public lands vs. *resguardo* lands

Rafael Uribe Uribe's proposal to civilize Colombia's Indians for inclusion into the labor force as an alternative to the promotion of

European immigration accords with the nation's nineteenth-century policy for developing frontier lands. Colombia and Costa Rica were the two Latin American countries that most strenuously encouraged homesteading by their own citizens. Public lands – in Colombia called *baldíos* – were distributed with increasing intensity during the Republican era, the intent behind this policy being the desire to create a rural middle class where one did not exist. In addition, the distribution of *baldíos* was hoped to increase governmental revenues, fostering economic growth and feeding Colombian products into the agricultural export economy (LeGrand 1986: 11).

Legislation set maximum extensions for individual recipients of *baldío* lands. For most of the century there was no limit on the amount of land encompassed by any individual grant. After 1882, a limit of 5,000 hectares was set, falling to a maximum of 2,500 by 1912 (ibid.: 16). Instead of creating a rural middle class, Colombian homesteading was a major force in the formation of landed estates in what were once undeveloped areas.

Catherine LeGrand (ibid.; 1980) has conducted the most extensive research on Colombian homesteading, documenting the consolidation of great estates out of individual homesteads, a process that gained impetus as the agricultural export economy grew in the second half of the century. LeGrand demonstrates that entrepreneurs availed themselves of lands already developed by small homesteaders, already linked to population centers and markets and thus suitable for the production on a larger scale of export produce. The bulk of these lands was not so much usurped for their intrinsic value, but because once small homesteaders lost access to it they would be more likely to work as tenant farmers or wage laborers for the large entrepreneurs (1986: 56–59), providing a solution to the acute labor shortage which continued to beset rural areas. The Colombian government had few records of the dimensions of the individual grants. Moreover, most small homesteaders were unable to follow through with the complex process of obtaining title to their holdings due to illiteracy, lack of funds with which to pay surveyors and poor communications with more populated areas (ibid.: 30–31). Entrepreneurs managed to gain influence over local authorities, monopolize water resources to starve out small settlers, produce fraudulent bills of sale for already-developed lands, force homesteaders into signing tenancy contracts and sometimes even usurp the lands by brute force (ibid.: 50–56). Already-existing valley haciendas also expanded up mountain slopes, creating private property from *baldíos* (ibid.: 53).

Although Cauca was by no means the prime center of *baldío* expansion, nor of the consolidation of large estates on once public lands, *resguardos* were a target of the entrepreneurs, who frequently claimed that communal lands were in fact *baldíos*. As a result, Indians who had formerly enjoyed usufruct rights to communal lands were converted into a rural labor force:

In Cauca, the majority of the *hacendados* have taken over vast zones of public lands and even parts of the Indian *resguardos* which they neither work themselves nor allow others to work. By monopolizing the land they aim only to undermine the position of the independent cultivators so as to form out of their ranks groups of dependent laborers. This trend is inhibiting agricultural production in the region.
(LeGrand 1980: 192)[6]

Resguardos were also threatened by earlier encroachments that were further consolidated during the course of the Republican era. Most notorious were the haciendas of the Arboleda family, located between Pitayó and Jambaló. These had been purchased by the Arboledas from other *hacendados*, and the claims raised by neighboring *resguardos* had been carried over from the colonial era (Roldán 1974; also ACC/P 1888). Indigenous sharecroppers formed the center of the workforce of these estates and as early as 1865 they were refusing to work for, or to pay rent to, the Arboleda family (AINCORA/B [Archivo del Instituto Colombiano de la Reforma Agraria, Bogotá] 1865). By 1905, moreover, there were at least eleven large haciendas in the vicinity of Silvia, with as many as 1,000 Indian sharecroppers attached to these estates (*El Trabajo*, Popayán, 23 September 1905). But in the later years of the nineteenth century the primary threat to indigenous landholdings came through the *baldío* system, spurring communities to revalidate already-existing colonial *resguardo* titles (ACC/P 1881, 1883) or to draft new ones based on knowledge of boundaries, handed down orally from generation to generation (ACC/P 1897, 1898a, 1898b, 1898c), in an attempt to stave off the expansion of estates onto their communal properties. The worst threat to indigenous territorial and political autonomy and the greatest impulse to the increase in *baldío* claims came at mid-century with the expansion of extractive industries into the Páez area.

Quinine extraction and the Páez

Latin America's nineteenth-century economy was organized around the export of raw materials to the industrialized world, including plant products extracted from marginal, unsettled or frontier areas. Among the more well-known plant products harvested in Latin America and sold to the developed world were the chicle of the Yucatán peninsula and the rubber of the Amazon forests. Rubber, in particular, was essential for industrial development in Europe and the United States after the discovery of the vulcanization process in 1836.

But industrial development was not the sole motor behind the development of extractive economies in Latin America. The expansion of European empires also required large-scale extraction of products that facilitated the establishment and maintenance of new colonies. As the British, Dutch, French and later, the Americans acquired control over tropical areas, of utmost concern to these powers was the protection of colonial officials, soldiers and dependents against malaria. Until the development of synthetic anti-malaria drugs in the twentieth century, natural quinine was the greatest weapon that existed against this disease. Quinine-based medications were derived from the bark of approximately 30 species of trees of the Cinchona family, growing exclusively in the eastern forests of Colombia, Ecuador, Bolivia and Peru at altitudes ranging from 800 to 3,400 meters above sea level. European and North American demand for cinchona bark stimulated the growth of an intense and short-lived extractive industry during the latter half of the nineteenth century, a demand met largely by Colombia, whose best cinchona (*Cinchonae pitayensis*) was located in the vicinity of Pitayó.

The medicinal benefits of cinchona bark had been discovered in the eighteenth century and the product studied, extracted and transported to Spain through colonial channels.[7] But it was with the chemical isolation between 1820 and 1847 of the various alkaloids present in the bark that demand for quinine grew beyond the Spanish empire (Ocampo 1980–81: 27). Reports of cinchona being extracted from the Pitayó forests date from the first years of Independence (Mollien 1944 [1823]: 288). Nevertheless, it was not until the 1850s that quinidine, the principal alkaloid of Pitayó bark, was considered a medicinal substance. Subsequently, the quinine industry boomed in Pitayó (Ocampo 1980–81: 35, 42).

Like the other extractive economies of Latin America, the quinine industry operated on a boom–bust cycle. The Colombian economy was dependent on fluctuations in international demand for the plant, with peaks occurring in 1849–52, 1867–73 and 1877–82 (ibid.: 37). As with rubber in Brazil, Colombians reaped a wild resource. The more efficient method of establishing cinchona plantations never really took hold in Colombia. Although the concept was promoted by a number of entrepreneurs (Osorio 1880; Ocampo 1980–81: 39), the population density necessary to maintain a labor force to work plantations was lacking in the principal quinine areas (on related problems in the Brazilian rubber boom, see Bunker 1985: 69). High prices and inconsistent supply led the Europeans, principally the Dutch and the British, to invest substantial effort in the discovery, classification and evaluation of Colombian plants (Markham 1867; Cross 1871, 1879) that were subsequently transferred to Europe where strains were developed for the creation of massive plantations in Java, India and Ceylon (Brockway 1979); Colombians decried this policy, but were unable to halt its progress (*Diario Oficial*, 13 December 1869; Camacho Roldán 1983 [1878]: 640). By the 1880s international demand was satisifed by the lower-price cinchona of Asian plantations and Colombia's quinine boom came to a close.

The extraction of the wild product in Colombia was never conducted with conservation in mind. The quinine boom moved like a wave across the cinchona forests, leaving behind a wake of destroyed and dead plants. The pillage of the Pitayó forests was documented by Robert Cross of Kew, who found few trees during his 1868 voyage:

Returning again to Silvia, I spent several days in searching and travelling to the westward of the Piñon, in the direction of the farms called Chiman and Ambalo, both of which, but especially the latter, at one time furnished a large amount of a yellow kind of bark of very fine quality. Throughout all this district I did not find a single seed. (Cross 1871: 15)

As regards those of Pitayo, there appears to be three distinct and prominent kinds, one of which yields the "yellow barks," another the "red Piñon" bark considered so valuable by Mr. Howard, while a small lanceolate leaved variety gives the *Amarilla fina* of the Piñon. At present it is not possible to examine a developed healthy tree, as those from which I collected seeds were mere bushes from barking or ill-treatment, so that the natural habit of the plants were much injured. The quinine trees of Pitayo are being rapidly extirpated. (ibid.: 46)

Pitayó bark was extracted from the roots of mature trees or from immature seedlings, condemning the forest to extinction (Ocampo 1980–81: 43; Saffray 1984 [1869]: 270).

After the extinction of the Pitayó forests in the 1860s the quinine frontier moved east into Tierradentro. But Cross' 1877 trip found many of the forests of southern Tierradentro already devoid of cinchona trees:

This locality [Corales] for some time past has been well searched by collectors, and, besides the first gatherings obtained by cutting down all trees met with, there has since been three "re-collectings," when the bark of every stump, root, or sapling met with has been pared off. The bark of the Coralis and Inza district, and southward about Pedregal and Tulmina, has been wrought for a long time. At present it is being collected to the northward about four or five miles distant, adjacent to some Páez villages, where, until of late years, the forests, owing to the hostility of the Indians, remained wholly untouched. The trees, however, in this locality, are not so massive, because the country is more open, and the climate is certainly drier than that of Coralis.   (Cross 1879: 28)

The frontier had once again been displaced, this time northward to the Moras Basin where, in Lame, Cross found a new center for the extraction of cinchona bark (ibid.: 31); at that time, cinchona harvesting was also moving out of the Páez area and into Tolima and what is now the department of Huila. By 1887, when Cuervo Márquez visited the Moras Basin, there was no quinine left in the area and attention had shifted to a new extractive industry, laurel wax (Cuervo 1956: 24).

The quinine boom affected the Páez in a number of ways. First, it provided the stimulus for the growth of the town of Silvia, which thrived for some 30 years as a marketing center (Comisión Corográfica 1959 [1859]: 158; Otero 1968). By the turn of the century there were 4,000 mestizo residents in the town, including traders, *hacendados* and small farmers (*El Trabajo*, Popayán, 23 September 1905). The boom would convert the town into a major center for the Páez of both the western slopes of the cordillera and the Moras Basin.

According to Ocampo (1980–81: 31) the relationship between the harvester and the quinine merchant was one of mutual distrust. The trader was never sure that the laborer was selling him bark of consistent quality. Prices were only finally fixed once the bark had reached its final destination. Nevertheless, there is no evidence that the quinine extraction process entailed the development of a relationship of debt servitude for the harvester, at least, for the Indian harvester. In contrast, several sources indicate that cinchona collectors were paid several times more than other agricultural laborers or industrial workers (Cross 1879: 20; Ocampo 1980–81: 44), although prices of trade goods were also somewhat higher in the quinine centers (1980–81: ibid.).

The labor process associated with cinchona extraction affected community organization. Cinchona was harvested by an overwhelmingly indigenous labor force (Cross 1866: 263) that sold the dried bark to Silvia's merchants. French traveller Charles Saffray described the extraction process as follows:

The Indians of the province of Popayán are very skilled at searching out and exploiting cinchona. Those who engage in this activity are called *cascarilleros*, because cinchona is commonly called *cascarilla*, or bark, in this country, just as the Peruvians called it *quina* or *quinaquina*, bark *por excelencia*.

The *cascarillero*'s occupation is a rough one: after having agreed upon a price for the bark with a trader, and having asked for a small payment up front, the Indian goes into the deep forest with a week's worth of food, armed with an ax and a machete. He advances without benefit of a compass, laboriously breaking a trail through the unknown. He examines the bark and fallen leaves; occasionally he climbs a tall tree to look over the green ocean surrounding him, for the reflection of foliage, a flowery peak, indicating to him the presence of cinchona.

Having discovered the tree, he must use an ax to make a clearing around it, for it is not enough to cut it down at its base, because it would remain suspended by the vines and neighboring branches. If the Indian decides that it will be a good harvest, he erects a temporary hut for himself and the bark, and immediately afterward begins his work. The tree felled, he rubs the trunk with dry and rough grasses to purge the cryptogams,; then he detaches the bark with his machete and begins forthwith the process of drying it.

After a week, if the weather has been good, he packs up his harvest and returns to the village. (Saffray 1984 [1869]: 269–70)

Harvested bark was dried above constantly-burning fires in special structures built for this purpose at the collection site (Cross 1879: 19–20). Extraction was conducted year-round, with less work done in the rainy season in July and August (ibid.: 21; see also Markham 1867: 106–107). As the quinine frontier migrated eastward into less-populated areas, the *cascarillero* was forced to intern himself deeper and deeper in the forest.

The process of cinchona harvesting and sale had a number of effects among the Páez, especially but not exclusively on those of Pitayó, who were associated with the trade for a longer period of time. First, collecting trips plucked individuals from their communities and from community life, isolating them for several weeks in the forest. Occurring concurrently with the civil wars of 1854, 1859–62, 1876–77, the boom thus provided further impetus to the break-down in community solidarity as well as diminishing the intensity of agricultural work on *resguardo* lands. In particular, communities were weakened by the development of relations with traders, associations that encroached on the traditional role played by community leaders, who had always served as intermediaries with the non-Indian world. The *cascarilleros* dealt more directly with whites, without the protective buffer of *cacique* or *cabildo*, both of whom were more skilled at communication with outsiders. Thus on the one hand, the bark collector was laid open to an exploitative relationship that he could not handle well, while on the other hand, the *cabildo*'s legitimacy as an intermediary broke down.

Both civil wars and the quinine boom separated individuals from their communities in the long run as well. In his travels to the Caquetá River in the lowlands to the southeast of Tierradentro, Cross discovered "Páez families, speaking their own language, occupying a little cluster of houses in a rural district surrounded by Indians of another tribe, who employed a totally different language" (1871: 31). Thus, as the quinine frontier moved east, so did Páez *cascarilleros*. Of those bark collectors who remained in their communities, Cross notes that they spent their time gambling and drinking for the most part (1879: 35–6; also Otero 1968: 33); this was also true of Indian ex-guerrillas and government militia members (Cross 1879). Former *cascarilleros* had earned good money in the bark trade, more than they would have as agricultural laborers, and certainly more than as subsistence agriculturalists.

By the end of the quinine boom, the Páez began to cultivate cinchona trees in their household gardens (Cross 1866, 1871: 12, 14, 46; Osorio 1880: 7). During civil wars, when the trade was slowed down by the dangers of transportation and a scarcity of traders in the area, the Indians occasionally forcibly obliged merchants to buy bark:

During a civil war, the village of Silvia, abandoned by its inhabitants, was occupied by the Páez among whom we found ourselves alone. An Indian of Pitayó, who had entered our house with many other of his armed compatriots, attempted to sell us quinine at a fixed price, which we refused. An Indian from Tierra Adentro wanted to force us to buy it – seeing us being pushed towards the Páez who were threatening us, his compatriot, who had tried to trick us, came to our assistance, believing that we were right, and helped us to expel the intruder...

(Douay 1890: 785)

But the greatest danger that the quinine boom presented to the Páez was that it laid communities open to land loss, because it was often difficult to define where *resguardos* ended and where *baldíos* began. The problem was addressed by the government in 1869:

Indian *resguardos* are, generally, passing into private hands for quinine extraction, with the consequent freeing from all fiscal obligations. But the Government should know that few *resguardos* have written title; instead actual possession gives indefinite extension to the imagined properties of Indians in the high regions of the cordillera. It would be convenient and just to require the small Indian *cabildos* to present their property titles, in order to set boundaries between their *resguardos* and the *baldíos*. In the event of their being unable to present such titles, possession should be recognized; but there should be no corresponding guarantee of their ownership of the quinine forests and other precious substances, ripe for exploitation.

(Diario Oficial, 13 December 1869)

The distinction between *baldíos* and *resguardos* was imperative by the 1860s, when entrepreneurs began to apply for land grants specifically for cinchona extraction (LeGrand 1986: 35).[8]

In addition to indigenous extraction of quinine from their own forests, a variety of arrangements permitted exploitation of the product by other individuals and entities. Peasants applied for small *baldío* grants in order to gain access to forests (ANC/B 1881). Entrepreneurs frequently attempted to usurp homesteads from their peasant occupants (ibid.). Other entrepreneurs drew up rental agreements on cinchona forests (ACC/P 1871), sometimes leasing forests from the government itself; rental was preferable to ownership, as the extractive process swiftly left the forests barren (Catherine LeGrand, personal communication). Existing *hacendados* and their agents extracted quinine from forests that they claimed were theirs, and even extended their search onto nearby *resguardos*.[9] And in some areas to the east of Tierradentro, Colombian and foreign companies set up extraction operations, employing a large number of laborers.[10]

The rape of the cinchona forests is brought vividly to life in the dispute between Julio Arboleda's agents and the Indians of Pitayó over quinine extraction in the vicinity of Asnenga. Arboleda's properties had been placed under embargo as a result of his participation in the 1851 civil war and were being administered by Francisco José Chaux. In 1852 Chaux drew up a contract with Carlos Michelsen and Miguel Arroyo, permitting them to extract quinine from the Asnenga forests, "for as long as there are cinchonas in the forests of the hacienda" (*El Tiempo*, 2 February 1858). Arroyo was obliged to turn over 800 *arrobas* (20,000 lbs.) of quinine a month and was permitted to extract it from Asnenga, as well as to purchase it from neighboring Indians (ibid.). According to the testimony of the Indians of Jambaló, there were supposedly $7\frac{1}{2}$ million cinchona trees in Asnenga, which could produce 60 million *arrobas* of dried quinine (*El Tiempo*, 20 April 1858). One hundred laborers were contracted to extract the quinine from Asnenga (*El Tiempo*, 4 May 1858); whether or not these were Páez laborers is not specified. Nevertheless, no quinine was discovered on the hacienda (*El Tiempo*, 2 February 1858) and the search was extended to the neighboring *resguardo* of Pitayó (*El Tiempo*, 4 May 1858).

Asnenga itself was under dispute during this period. According to one account the hacienda had been purchased without demarcating clear boundaries between it and neighboring *resguardos*:

These forests were purchased two or three years before [1851, when the property was embargoed] for 1,800 pesos... without specifying its boundaries with the Indian *resguardos* of Quichaya and Pitayó; and now it has been proved that the Salado mine and the hamlet of Asnenga are located within the lands of those Indians, the hacienda only reserving the right to cut wood for the salt mine. The quinine they are claiming was not theirs, even though, as has been claimed, the administrator contracted Mssrs. Miguel Arroyo and Francisco Urrutia in 1852, to harvest it. (*El Tiempo*, 14 September 1859)

When the harvesters entered the forests belonging to the *resguardo* of Pitayó they were met by an armed band led by the *cabildo* and were not permitted to continue operations there (*El Tiempo*, 4 May 1858).

Similar entries into embargoed lands bordering the *resguardos* of Toribío, Tacueyó and San Francisco were also documented at this time (*El Tiempo*, 14 September 1859). In fact, numerous *baldío* requests and disputes are documented for the Páez area and surrounding regions during the quinine boom (AINCORA/B 1855a, 1855b). Frequently, the testimony of the parties in dispute reads like a political history of the Colombian nation, including not only Arboleda (AINCORA/B 1865), but also José Hilario López (AINCORA/B 1873, 1875), Tomás Cipriano de Mosquera (AINCORA/B 1872, 1875) and Elías Reyes (AINCORA/B 1874), concerning lands of Coconuco, La Plata, San Agustín, Timaná, Páez and Inzá; the Reyes family ran a trading company that purchased quinine in the area (Eder 1959: 403).

QUINTÍN LAME

Cauca at the turn of the century

By the turn of the century other events on the national plane began to affect the Indians of Cauca. Gran Cauca, the massive state within the nineteenth-century United States of Colombia that extended from the southernmost boundaries with Ecuador through the northern coastal Chocó, was dismembered and transformed into a series of departments within the more centralized Colombian nation. Cauca's capital city of Popayán and its ruling elite lost the Chocó mines, the fertile lands of Nariño, the cattle and cane haciendas of the Cauca Valley, the growing urban center of Cali, as well as the political authority and prestige they had enjoyed during the colonial era. In response to these conditions, the Caucan elite turned in upon itself, sucking dry its Indian and peasant populations, expanding coffee- and sugarcane-producing landholdings and cattle pasturage at the expense of the *resguardos*. The multiplicity of sharecropping arrangements which characterize twentieth-century Cauca became more and more widespread (Castrillón 1973; Earle 1985; Findji and Rojas 1985; Sevilla 1976b; Tello 1982).

During the first few decades of the twentieth century a large influx of colonists entered the *resguardos* of the western slopes of the cordillera and *hacendados*, employing sharecropper Indians, consolidated their estates (Findji and Rojas 1985). In Tierradentro the Vicentian Fathers established their mission, also consolidating landholdings in Wila and Tálaga (González n.d.); the Vicentians, particularly Father David González, were also active in promoting the privatization of *resguardo* lands (ibid.) and in the early part of their stay in Tierradentro, worked together with the Guainás family to gain acceptance in the region (APVC/B 1905–06: 57). During the first three decades of the century, the search for baldíos continued, with public lands discovered in Belalcázar and Yaquivá (ANC/B 1917), Jambaló and Nátaga (ANC/B 1921) and in the *páramos* at the peak of the Central Cordillera (ANC/B 1922a). Indian activists teamed with existing *cabildos* to dispute many of these *baldío* claims, as is documented in the collaboration of José Gonzalo Sánchez with the *resguardos* of Topa and La Laguna to reclaim the lands of Yarumal (ANC/B 1922b); Sánchez, an Indian from Totoró, later became an important leader of the Communist Party.

The consolidation of estates beyond Páez borders also affected the *resguardo* system. In the Coconuco area Ignacio Muñoz cleared 10,000 hectares of forest, using Páez laborers from Tierradentro. Contingents of 300 Indians, contracted by intermediaries who were at the same time *cabildo* members, spent four months a year working for Muñóz at Calaguala:

Listen, my dear friends, in those days no one around here paid even five centavos. So I too, when I was not even old enough to start working in the fields, in 1913 and 1914, I went twice to Calaguala and I was working on the Patogó hacienda opposite Calaguala. But damn it, you went to work at 6.00 and left at 5.30, starving hungry. And as I told you, they paid twenty centavos. Captain Dicue, he sure earned money. He was the only Indian who earned more. In those days he earned a peso and all he did was watch the peons... (AFCN/C 1972b)

Thus, Tierradentro's communities were deprived of a significant number of their inhabitants for long stretches of time. Local *cabildo* members became mini-*caudillos*, supervising the workforce. Participation of *cabildantes* as labor contractors further undermined the indigenous governments already weakened during the course of the nineteenth century.

La Quintinada

From 1910 until 1918 a growing confrontation arose between the elite of Cauca and its dispossessed Indians, who fought to maintain *resguardos* or to re-establish them in the face of white encroachment on their lands. By the early twenties the movement had established firm roots in the neighboring departments of Huila and Tolima. Although this was a regional movement, its reverberations were felt nationally. Non-Indian inhabitants of small towns, hacienda owners and local politicians sent a never-ending stream of messages to Bogotá, labeling the confrontation a "race war" which would need military intervention to be quelled (ANC/B 1916: 317r). In response, the movement's leaders were frequent visitors to the ministries of the Colombian capital and became the subject of many a newspaper article.

The leaders of the *Quintinada* were, on the whole, dispossessed Indians. Manuel Quintín Lame himself was a sharecropper from Polindara, near Popayán. He was a Páez who did not speak Páez (AFCN/C 1971a),[11] whose family had migrated to the Popayán area from Tierradentro (Lame 1971: 87). A staunch Conservative for many years, Lame's name appeared in a 1901 proclamation signed in Puracé, in support of the Conservative government (*Boletín Militar del Cauca*, 9 November 1910). He served as a government soldier in Panama in the War of the Thousand Days (Castrillón 1973: 45–46) and in 1902 was transferred to Tierradentro to help maintain the public order there (ibid.: 49). His major collaborator was José Gonzalo Sánchez, from the acculturated Guambiano-Coconuco area of Totoró. These two men had lived long on the outside, were at least nominally literate and claimed familiarity with Colombian institutions and history. Not formally attached to *resguardos*, they spearheaded a multiethnic movement of Páez, Guambiano, Coconuco and Indians from Tolima and Huila. For the first time, communities pressed indigenous demands within the national arena, using Colombian political language.

Lame's demands as outlined by Gonzalo Castillo (1971: xviii) were as follows:

1	defense of the *resguardo* against attempts to divide it;
2	consolidation of the *cabildo* as a center of political authority and organizing;
3	the reclaiming of lands usurped by landlords and the rejection of titles not based on royal decrees;
4	refusal by sharecroppers to pay rent;
5	a reaffirmation of indigenous cultural values and a rejection of racial and cultural discrimination.

The Lamistas sought to further their goals through political organizing, generating legal documents, influencing public opinion by means of press interviews and, at least for a time, participating in national elections.[12]

Castillo (ibid.: ix–xxvii) outlines the most prominent moments in Quintín Lame's career, a trajectory fleshed out in considerable detail by Castrillón (1973) and later by Tello (1982). The following are the highlights of the *Quintinada*:

1910	Lame was elected "Chief, Representative and General Defender" by the *cabildos* of Pitayó, Jambaló, Toribío, Puracé, Poblazón, Cajibío and Pandiguando (*El Espectador* 12 July 1924).
1914–18	Organizing drive in Cauca. Lame was imprisoned for a year from 1915 to 1916. In November 1916, when Lame and his followers attended a baptism in the town of Inzá, local defense brigades headed by another Páez *caudillo*, Pío Collo, attacked the Lamistas and a massacre ensued. The area was militarized by police and troops from Popayán, Neiva and Cali. Lame fled, although several of his followers were arrested. Ultimately, he was arrested and spent 1917 to 1920 in prison.
1920–45	Lame moved his operations to the neighboring departments of Huila and Tolima. In 1938 he succeeded in reconstituting the *resguardo* of Ortega, Tolima. At this time he also completed his treatise.

1945–53   Severe repression was unleashed against the Lamista
           movement which cracked under the pressure.
1953–67   Until his death in 1967 Lame continued his struggle,
           working now within purely legalistic means and
           without a strong organizational base.

For our purposes, the period that will be followed in most detail
runs from 1910 to 1920, the decade most properly called the
Quintinada, when Lame dedicated most of his efforts to organizing
the Páez. Before beginning the analysis, it should be pointed out that
even within this short decade there are conflicting evaluations of the
nature of Lame's aims in Tierradentro. Some (for example, Castillo
1971) maintain that Lame's intent was entirely peaceful. Others (for
example, Castrillón 1973 and Tello 1982), following newspaper and
government reports from the period, emphasize the armed nature of
the Lamistas; the latter assertion is backed up by some of Lame's
former associates in Tierradentro, who describe in detail some of
Lame's military tactics (AFCN/C 1971a, 1971b, 1972a, 1972b).

As we shall see, the leaders of the *Quintinada* articulated a new
interpretation of Páez history derived from archival research and
expressed in both oral and written form. Manuel Quintín Lame and
his followers interpreted the eighteenth-century documents we have
already analyzed through nineteenth-century spectacles, their actions
underlining the importance of studying Páez historical thought as it
is transformed by events taking place in the broader society, as well
as among Indians themselves.

5

From sharecropper to *caudillo*: Manuel Quintín Lame

In 1939 the semi-literate sharecropper and activist Manuel Quintín Lame completed a 118-page manuscript entitled *Los pensamientos del indio que se educó dentro de las selvas colombianas* (The Thoughts of the Indian Educated in the Colombian Forests; henceforth to be referred to as *Los pensamientos* [Lame 1971; English translation in Castillo 1987: 97–151]).[1] Dictated to Florentino Moreno, his Indian secretary from the department of Tolima, the treatise was to be the culmination of three decades of struggle against the oppression of Colombia's Indians, laying out Lame's teachings so that future generations could take up where he left off.

Like his distant Peruvian cousin, Felipe Guaman Poma de Ayala, Quintín Lame did not live to see his treatise published. And like Guaman Poma's *Nueva Corónica*, *Los pensamientos* provides us with one of the richest known mines for indigenous historical consciousness in Colombia. But unlike Guaman Poma's chronicle, Lame's manuscript need not stand on its own; there is also extensive documentation available regarding Lame's political activities, facilitating the task of studying the leader's implementation of his historical philosophy. By examining Lame's manuscript and his actions, we can identify the parameters of his historical thought, detecting how he combined a variety of symbols and rituals hailing from precolumbian Páez tradition, from the colonial heritage of the people of Tierradentro and from their experiences under Republican rule. He expressed these in a national idiom, employing ideas and symbols from the dominant society, concepts which on the one hand, had influenced Lame, and on the other, could be used to influence the power-wielders of Bogotá. In short, *Los pensamientos* and the activities of its author provide us with a crucible within which we can follow the process of Páez historical interpretation which, to use Hobsbawm's and Ranger's (1983) terminology, might be called the "reinvention" of tradition.

Although *Los pensamientos* remained hidden from non-Indian eyes for three decades, it was a fundamental source of teachings for the Indians of Ortega, Tolima, the community in which Lame passed the last 40 years of his life before he died in 1967. Castillo recalls his "discovery" of this source of inspiration to the Indians of Ortega:

Then Gabriel Yaima, one of the younger members of the inner group and the secretary of the Cabildo, read several pages filled with metaphors and poetic images, sprinkled here and there with poignant statements about "God the Supreme Judge of every human conscience," "the rights of the aboriginal race," "the destiny of the Indian people," and ending with a call to continue the struggle against "land grabbers" (*acaparadores*), "multimillionaires," "aristocrats," and "oligarchs," and to remember Quintín Lame's "doctrine and discipline"... The statements made at the cemetery had triggered in my mind the suspicion that subsequent visits and lengthier conversations would fully confirm that the "Lamista" peasants were in possession of a common body of teaching, which they referred to as "the doctrine and discipline," taught by Lame. Was it an oral tradition or perhaps a written document? For the following six months my empathy with the group increased...[and] one Sunday they produced before my eyes a handwritten document, half destroyed by time and moths, authored by Manuel Quintín Lame.

(Castillo 1987: 1–3)

Once published in 1971, the Indian movement began to employ *Los pensamientos* as an organizing tool. In coming years we can expect to witness among the Páez and other indigenous groups a process of reinterpretation of the manuscript, giving rise to a new oral tradition paralleling that of the Lamistas of Ortega.

HISTORICAL INTERPRETATION IN THE NINETEENTH CENTURY

To know the biographies of all the outstanding men of any period is to know the history of those times.   (Januário da Cunha Barbosa cited in Burns 1980: 40)

Once the Latin American creoles threw off the yoke of Spanish colonial rule and began the process of nation-building, historiography took on a new nature and purpose. Espoused by white male members of the Europeanized and educated elites, history became a vehicle for fashioning and perpetuating an ideology of "progress" within which societies were seen as developing toward the European ideal of "civilization" (Burns 1980: 35–36, 46). Nineteenth-century historians looked toward Europe for their models and for their evidence, and focused on great figures as the embodiments of the march of progress. They used history to justify their own national projects: it provided a vehicle for arousing citizenship and patriotism (ibid.: 41), an "ideological arsenal" supporting their political aims (ibid.: 43), an intellectual means of homogenizing society, mirroring Republican legislation and its emphasis on citizenship. The lovers of progress had much invested in the historical endeavor, for they were not unattached observers, but judges, legislators, even presidents (ibid.: 38–39).

The rise of nineteenth-century historiography occurred concurrently with the spread of the printed word in Latin America. While colonial historiography was meant for the use of the Crown, the writings of Republican historians became increasingly available to educated Latin American readers. The growth of a lively news industry fostered the transmission of many of their historical ideas in popularized form in the numerous newspapers of the day and the even more widespread broadsides. The development of educational institutions in city and country, themselves aimed at promoting the values of citizenship and patriotism, provided fertile ground in which such ideas could take root. In short, a more permissive atmosphere now existed in which ideas could be published and exchanged. Quite obviously, the authors of these ideas were overwhelmingly members of the elite, and the form in which they interpreted history corresponded to the nineteenth-century ideal. Nevertheless, as we shall see, a new opening had been created even for members of the non-elite classes, and this would be used by Indians like Quintín Lame.

Although the Liberal administrations rejected a political alliance with the Church, even to the extent of banning the existence of religious orders such as the Jesuits, Catholicism was the principal religion of the people of Latin America, including the Indians of the highlands. With the signing of the Concordat and the Missions Agreement between Rome and Colombia in the years of the Regeneration, Church influence was once again formalized in Colombia. Missionaries fostered the development of a popular form of Christian historical consciousness, emphasizing the "Angry God" who judged individuals on the basis of their good works and their transgressions (Castillo 1987: 25). Within their vision of the relationship with the deity, history was interpreted as the sum of the actions of individuals. In a secular context theology would bolster the "great men" theory of history.

Among the Indians of Cauca a number of traditional and invented histories continued to flourish. The memory of political boundaries was kept alive through a lively oral tradition:

Since childhood, his grandfather, the late José María Quilcué, told the present
informant the extent of the boundaries of the *resguardo* of Tálaga.

(ACC/P 1898c: no pagination)

Oral memory was transferred into the written record with the late
nineteenth-century registry of *reguardo* titles.

The Páez also retained the memory of the precolumbian *caciques*,
whose exploits were adapted to Republican needs by the indigenous
caudillos who traced their descent to the Calambás family. Although
copies of Juan Tama's titles were requested by communities
throughout the nineteenth century,[2] the absence of Tama's name in
the historical record is striking. While Calambás was mentioned by
many of the travellers who visited the Páez, these men did not hear
about the *cacique* of Pitayó and Vitoncó. The only references we have
to the Páez *cacique*'s exploits are allusions to the consequences of the
Guambiano exile from Tierradentro, in stories collected in Guambía
(*El Trabajo*, 23 September 1905). In other words, Tama was not
selected as a relevant historical figure, despite the fact that he appears
in documents available to the communities of the time.

LOS PENSAMIENTOS: THE MANUSCRIPT
Purpose

Quintín Lame wrote *Los pensamientos* to provide an example to
Colombia's Indians, a focus for their struggle:

This book will serve as a horizon in the midst of darkness for the generations of
Indians who sleep in those immense lands of Divine Nature... (Lame 1971: 5)

A light illuminating indigenous political action, the book would
outline Indian rights and the means of attaining them:

I will clearly demonstrate to the Colombian Indian people that their obligations and
rights still exist, as do their dissected dominions, and that the bite of the serpent of
ignorance, ineptitude or illiteracy has become gangrened. But the Indian who
interprets the thoughts of the six chapters of this work will rise up better equipped
to confront the "Colossus of Colombia" and reconquer his dominions just as I
reconquered the Indigenous *Resguardos* of Ortega and part of Chaparral in the
department of Tolima.   (ibid.: 39)[3]

The treatise was meant to play as transcendent a role as Lame
believed himself to be playing. He was an apostle who would sweep
away the darkness of ignorance in which the Colombian Indian was
wandering.

It was important for Lame that his thoughts be set down in writing, as he believed that illiteracy was one of the clouds causing the darkness of ignorance that imprisoned the Indians. Once the *cabildo* of Ortega was reconstituted on 21 December 1938, Lame created a registry in which family heads could sign their names, "...thus claiming their 'right' to the lands of the old *resguardo*" (Castillo 1987: 37). In other words, he saw writing as a means of empowerment, an extension of the potentialities harnessed by colonial *caciques* when they drew up *resguardo* titles. As a semi-literate living in a nation which fetishized the written word, Lame was driven to do the same in his activism and in his treatise (Rappaport 1987b).

But Lame also sought a second means of empowerment in his written treatise. Nineteenth-century historiography deprecated the Indian. In his manuscript Lame made multiple references to the faults of Colombian historians, who lacked the civic pride, honor (Lame 1971: 24) and morality (ibid.: 42) needed to write the history of the Indian. In contrast, most historical works reflected only "hate and envy" (ibid.: 70). The treatise would refute assertions of indigenous intellectual inferiority by displaying the written fruits of its author's intellectual efforts (Castillo 1987: 48).

Los pensamientos was written in Spanish. Linguistically accessible to the Indians of Ortega who carefully guarded the manuscript for 30 years, it would only have been understood with great difficulty by his Páez contemporaries, many of whom were monolingual and illiterate. That it was in written and not oral form was of little importance in its diffusion: the use of quotations by the *cabildo* of Ortega demonstrates that even illiterates could partake of its teachings, but only if they understood Spanish and only if their leaders had knowledge of its existence. *Los pensamientos* was not, then, destined for Lame's contemporaries, but for the Indian future, when the darkness of ignorance and illiteracy would be swept away.

Style

Los pensamientos is divided into two books with a total of 20 chapters that detail in an extremely cryptic style – perhaps due to his lack of experience with the written word – his prophetic philosophy, personal reminiscences, denunciations of specific abuses against Indians (Castillo 1987: 4–5), and his vision of Páez history. Some of Lame's historical material was culled from reading and archival research and related directly to the Indians of southwestern highland Colombia; other material defined a precolumbian golden age which was not territorially based and which was generic in nature. The four classes of information are interspersed throughout the length of the manuscript in varying combinations in each of the chapters. *Los pensamientos* is by no means a chronological narration. It is organized around philosophical concerns, with history employed in a fragmentary fashion to support philosophical assertions. Although Don Juan Tama's titles were political and not philosophical in nature, they also employed non-linear historical referents. For both Tama and Lame, the focal point of history lay in the present and not in the past; historical data was useful only as a support for current concerns.

THE NATURE OF LAME'S HISTORICAL THOUGHT

In Quintín Lame's theory of history, time is both a progression of ages and a means of judging the actions of human beings, it is both historical and philosophical (Castillo 1987: 75). This combination permitted Lame to situate the sufferings of his indigenous brothers and ancestors, the oppressive actions of non-Indians and his own struggle within a common messianic context. History is at once an individual and a social process, situated in the past and in the present, but bearing implications for the future.

Lame conceptualized history as the depository of individual actions over the course of time (Lame 1971: 7, 29, 122), as a vessel that collects deeds in anticipation of each individual's final judgment:

A sage said that time flies and never returns, but this is not true; time has a glove in which it deposits all of the evil actions of man, and slowly it punishes him, making his body as an archer's bow and taking from him all riches, at which time the man is submerged in material and civil calamity ...   (ibid.: 25)

Although judgment is ultimately divine, history is constructed by the individual, like a personal road that each person builds (ibid.: 59). Punishment does not take place in the afterlife, but before death, impoverishing man and creating havoc in his life. Nevertheless, history is larger than the individual human, because during its course a broader truth is crystallized out of action. For Lame, history is "time united with truth" (ibid.: 33).

Two parallel worlds participate in this history: the Indian and the European. While the Indian is of the natural world, the bearer of

supreme knowledge, the European spends his life storing up those
evil acts that will lead to his final judgment. For Lame, the most
basic law of history was what he called the "Law of Compensation."
His legal opponents in Cauca and Tolima would, he claimed, count
among this law's victims. But the clearest historical evidence he
provides for the innate evil of whites and the inevitability of their
final judgment is taken from the life of Christopher Columbus:

Why? The Law of Compensation answers this question. It condemned the
Conservatives to live in ruin by order of the Liberals, etc., and to die as did that man
who came to this land under the name of Conqueror on 12 October, 1492, because
nothing is stable in this world for us men.   (ibid.: 50–51)

Columbus died "in the city of Valladolid in the arms of misery and
hunger" (ibid.: 4).

Columbus and the Spanish invasion comprise one of two pivots
of Lame's temporal framework. *Los pensamientos* outlines three broad
periods in the history of Colombia's Indians: the precolumbian past,
a period of European oppression beginning in 1492, and future
salvation, first achieved with the completion of *Los pensamientos* in
1939. For example, man and woman were created by the sun god,
Mushca (ibid.: 24); the Páez word "muscha" means "mestizo" or
"white," and does not appear as the name of the Creator God in any
other book, document or oral tradition. In Lame's reading of
history, the news of the arrival of the white invaders came to the
Indians a century before 12 October 1492 in a meeting of sages at the
oracle of the sun (ibid.: 23). A period of anarchy followed, with
individual Indian sovereigns battling each other (ibid.).

Lame's precolumbian past is divided into three periods, the time
of creation and learning, the golden age and the period of anarchy
which gave way to the Spanish invasion. Evil, judgment, retribution
and Europeans were not a part of this glorious past, which was
closely in touch with nature. But Lame also believed that Christianity
touched the Indians before the Conquest, and that Indians were
present at Christ's birth (Castillo 1987: 76). In this sense, his treatise
is similar to the *Nueva Corónica* of Guaman Poma. Both intertwine
European and Indian histories, placing the indigenous world at
history's center (ibid.: 77).

Lame believed that evil came into the world with the Spanish
invasion. His vision of the Conquest is as generic as is his image of
the precolumbian past: the turning-point of Lame's history is 12
October 1492. From that date onward, Indians were oppressed by

whites. But his descriptions of abuses committed by the Spaniards are as general as is his emphasis on 1492. He cites few names of conquerors besides Columbus. The most vivid examples that Lame provides of white abuses against Indians come from his own experience of arrest, trial and imprisonment.

Although 12 October 1492 is emphasized as a pivotal day in almost every chapter of the manuscript, Lame did not employ a chronological dating scheme to sort out historical events. 12 October is not an historical date, but a mystical one, opposed to 1939, the year in which he completed his manuscript and, to Lame's mind, the year in which the salvation of the Indian became a reality. This period of 447 years, a number often mentioned by Lame, marks the general oppression of the Indian. At one end of these four and a half centuries stood Christopher Columbus and at the other end, Quintín Lame. In between these two pivotal points few dates and few personages are included.

That Lame did not utilize dates in the European sense is clear in his description of his own genealogy:

This is how he who writes this Work was born, legitimate son of Mariano Lame and Dolores Chantre; Mariano Lame, legitimate son of Angel Mariano Lame; Angel Mariano Lame, legitimate son of Jacobo Lame; Jacobo Lame was the one who fled the village of Lame, the highest mountaintop of Tierradentro, because he was punished by the Governor of the community of Lame for disobedience. Upon arriving in Silvia and presenting himself to the *cacique* of that area, he forgot his surname, which was Estrella and his mother's Cayapú; since he did not remember his surname the *cacique* named him Jacobo Lame.   (Lame 1971: 87–88)

Here we have a list of four generations, including Lame himself, traced back to the town of Lame in Tierradentro. It is significant that the author chose the surname Estrella as the name forgotten by his great-grandfather, for this was Don Juan Tama's surname. If we consult another passage it becomes clear that the occupant of the fifth generation of this genealogy is Juan Tama himself:

But after 447 years, among the descendants of the Indian race [there appears] the great-grandson of the Indian Juan Fama [*sic*] de Estrella and, why de Estrella? You'll find out in another book...   (ibid.: 24)

The years between 1492 and 1939 are thus divided into five generations, each approximately a century long, leading from Juan Tama to Manuel Quintín Lame. The chronology approximates Don Juan Tama's five-generational model as outlined in the Pitayó and Vitoncó titles. In fact, it is quite possible that Lame adapted his own genealogy from one of these documents, as he misspelled Tama's name, committing an error traceable to his lack of expertise in reading eighteenth-century script. The error also indicates that Tama was not an active part of the Páez historical consciousness at the time.

But although Lame's general temporal scheme is not strictly linear, chronology gives form to his own life and experiences as recounted in the manuscript. In fact, the only historical details he provides stem from his personal reminiscences. Here considerable care is given in providing the names of his opponents and the dates on which he confronted them. Thus, it cannot be said that Lame did not comprehend chronological dating schemes, but instead, that beyond the narration of his own personal experience he did not find this format to be meaningful. In Lame's scheme, time is a self-enclosed progression of five generations, much as it was for Don Juan Tama.

Don Juan Tama's five-generational unit did not originate in the past and move toward the present, but ran from his epoch toward the future. Quintín Lame also envisioned historical time as encompassing future events. His treatise is strongly messianic, with the salvation of the Indians stemming from his birth or, more correctly, from the completion of his manuscript. That is why 1939 is a pivotal date; it marks the point at which the millennium became a possibility, if only Indians would speed its coming through political activism (Castillo 1987: 78), inviting the Law of Compensation to take place on a cosmic level:

And so tomorrow a communion of Indians will be born, the legitimate descendants of our Guananí land, the descendants of those hated tribes persecuted by the non-Indian; but the Law of Compensation exists, gentlemen, and in itself it is avenging justice, because the deed of old Adam and the caprice of old Eve were paid for after four thousand years.   (Lame 1971: 19–20)

Lame's political activities and his treatise were meant to speed the coming of this indigenous millennium.

Historical evidence

It has been noted that Quintín Lame employed historical evidence to support his more philosophical or political points. In this sense, his treatise is similar to the histories written by his non-Indian elite contemporaries, works with which he was to some degree acquainted. Nevertheless, *Los pensamientos* contrasts with other contemporary historical writings in its treatment of evidence.

The primary "sources" cited in *Los pensamientos* come from Nature, which the author held as superior to books and universities. Although Nature surrounds us, the Indians have more immediate access to it because they live in closer proximity to the natural world:

Where is the cradle of Knowledge? The cradle of Knowledge is hidden under cruel mountains, as is told in the dreams of the Indian who ascended to visit the newborn in that straw cradle, who was a guest in one of the halls of the "House of Bethlehem," he who left the philosopher's stone, etc., that Indian who brought a gift of gold to the man and King of Kings.

Science has a large garden that few men have seen except from very far, [and] the little Indian has seen it up close, united with those disciples whom Nature has raised and raises in the Forest.   (ibid.: 13)

It is interesting that Lame refers to Jesus Christ as occupying the central place in the domain of knowledge. The white man's god, associated by Lame with American Indians at the moment of his birth, is a greater presence for those more proximate to Nature, that is, for indigenous peoples.

At the end of *Los pensamientos*, Lame lists those "books" of Nature which provided him with this education, likening himself to other historiographers who cite their sources:

But it is the thought of a highlander, whose inspiration comes from the mountains, who was educated in the mountains and learned to think there. He also entered the deep forest and then ascended to the treetops of the Cedar of Lebanon to extend his thoughts over the Meadows of Civilization. [These thoughts] may seem only to limp through this work, but one day they will take universal history by surprise, because they are not the work of an ignorant. Those who were educated in antiquity, in the middle ages and in the present day all speak of the schools in which they were educated. For this reason I must also speak, as I do, of the cloisters in which I was educated by Nature, my school.   (ibid.: 123)

Lame goes on to cite 15 "titles" through which he gained his knowledge (ibid.: 123–24), including the four winds of the earth and of the sky, the sun, the animal kingdom, and the babble of forest streams. By the mid-point of his list he incorporates more human themes: the idyll, love, agriculture, animal husbandry. Finally, he ends his register with a number of philosophical disciplines, including hygiene, metaphysics, ontology and logic.

Even though he places Christ at the center of the sphere of Knowledge, Lame questions whether there is adequate evidence available for the biblical creation story:

It is said that God created the world in six days; but there does not exist satisfactory proof of this, you Christian and pagan philosophers: because everything said regarding the creation of the world has come down to us from mouth to mouth and there is no evidence to prove that the world was created in six days.

(ibid.: 73–74)

In contrast, Lame finds satisfactory evidence for the indigenous creation story:

And what should I say of when the Nature of "*Mushca,*" the sun god, caused two sages, man and woman, to appear: the woman to learn to spin gold and to weave it, the man to carve rocks and make hieroglyphs on them, to make faces of men, of animals and birds; also, to make fetishes, crocodiles and birds of gold with their chicks, cicadas, toads, lizards, snakes, etc. The fury of the centuries could not erase those writings, nor could the ages destroy the clay fetishes that my ancestors prepared, kneaded with sap from the trees.   (ibid.: 24)

Petroglyphs and Indian cemeteries (ibid.: 76) provide Lame with evidence for the veracity of his own creation legend.

Nevertheless, Lame did find written evidence for the abuses committed by the European conquerors. His knowledge of Columbus' penance derives from book-learning. He even cites documents from the Archivo Nacional (ibid.: 69) and from court records (ibid.: 65). But his greatest sources of documentation are his personal and visionary experiences. At one point, for example, he refers to the brutal treatment he received from 1923 to 1930 under Conservative politicians. He addresses himself to the possibility of similar treatment in Liberal courts by stating: "I am not acquainted with their good intelligence in the city of Neiva, but very soon I will know it, in order to write another work" (ibid.).

Quintín Lame perceives his greatest wisdom as arising from the visionary experience, through which he became a messiah or a savior:

After almost five centuries there appears a being, like a pilgrim, in the midst of the shadows of the night, as I appear in the midst of the darkness of ignorance, [and] I have been able to see the valley of justice, and before arriving at the end of my life, I have reflected upon presenting myself privately and publicly before all those societies that constitute and guard this valuable treasure (justice), so that they will examine all of the abuses and attacks that they have violently and villainously committed, and so that they will punish them for their sins, and will give to each the rights that correspond to them.   (*El Espectador*, 23 January 1922)

The messianic vision came to Lame early in life:

A thought struck me, that my thoughts should be lodged among the Colombian people at a high level, when I would descend from the mountain to the valley to defend my Indian people, discriminated against, persecuted, insulted, robbed, murdered by non-Indians; because this is what the depository of actions indicates, and the witness from the past said so, the witness who came with the order that I should prepare myself for the defense of the coming generations of the Colombian Indian race. (Lame 1971: 6–7)

As an apostle chosen by Nature to educate Colombia's Indians and lead them on the path toward salvation, Quintín Lame took upon himself more than the historical vision of Don Juan Tama: he also bore his political inheritance.

THE USE OF IMAGES

Like his colonial forebear from Vitoncó, Quintín Lame articulated a series of images which expressed his historical vision in an abbreviated form. Fragmentary in nature, these images are not developed in any detail in his writings, nor in his political activities. They are left as images, meant to evoke thought and further action in the hearts of his followers. Some of them are of pre-columbian origin: an emphasis on high places and the animals that live and move there, on the rivers that flow from these mountains, on the thunder and storms that batter their peaks and on the sun. Others, such as the vision of himself as a *cacique*, were colonial images interpreted through a Republican filter. And still others were purely the product of the post-Independence era: the notion of patriotism and of belonging to a nation. In the remainder of this chapter, we will explore the images born from Lame's Páez past, his historical juncture and his fertile imagination.

Precolumbian symbols

The "Indian who descended from the mountain to the valley of civilization" derived his knowledge from his natural surroundings. But these were not the idyllic pastures of the nineteenth-century imagination, although they may have been expressed in this form. They stemmed from a Páez environment, made up of mountains, eagles and highland rivers. Lame descended from the mountain to the valley of civilization because as a Páez, the heights of the Andes were a source of inspiration and of knowledge.

If we turn for a moment to the precolumbian and early colonial eras, we will note that knowledge of the past and of the future, articulated by shamans, was lodged in high places: oracles of the sun located atop the high mountains that rise above the Páez River (Castillo 1877: 58–59). The power of knowledge was derived from these high places and looking down from them, one acquired wisdom.

Given this precolumbian heritage, it is not surprising that Lame descended from the mountain to the valley of civilization. Castillo (1987: 82–83) correctly notes that the mountain was associated with the "Indian way," while the valley, where non-Indians live, was seen as artificial and corrupt. But Lame did not only draw this contrast as a literary metaphor. The comparison between high and low places was born of a Páez vision of the acquisition of knowledge through the experience of geography.

The animals of the high places, evoked in Quechua because Lame did not speak Páez, indicate a continuation of the Páez notion that knowledge comes from on high:

Atallo cundulcunca, bird or condors' nest. That condor of my mind and that eagle of my psychology, an Indian psychology that was conceived when the condor or condors passed by, like a concert of swallows that visit the seasons. Those condors sought their abodes in the high peaks, and others in the shadows of the ancient oaks. They shout out in the midst of the immense solitude that accompanied me...

(Lame 1971: 65)

Lame's thought was like birds, descending from the peaks of Tierradentro's mountains.

Similarly, the power unleashed by storms was a source of knowing for Lame, as he cites in his description of his first numinary experience: "I met it in rapture even though it passed so swiftly, as when the lightning tears the majestic mantle which the gods wear in the late hours of the night" (ibid.: 15). Lame was not the first Páez messiah to have linked his own power to that of lightning and thunder. A divine emissary who visited Suin in 1833, exhorting the Indians to destroy their Church and saintly images, descended to earth in the midst of a din reminiscent of a tempest, and did not permit the people to view his face (Cuervo 1956: 288; Rappaport 1980–81). This pose was prefigured by *Chuquiylla yllapa* the Inca *huaca* of thunder and lightning (Molina 1959 [1573]: 54–55). Lame's allusions to natural phenomena are thus appropriate Páez forms of discourse on knowledge.

Similarly, in *Los pensamientos*, as well as in his political practice, Quintín Lame drew upon the sun and other heavenly bodies as vehicles of learning. We have observed this in his writings, where he describes the sun god as the divine creator. The same emphasis was also present in his actions and in those of his followers. For example, in a letter to the Ministry of Government, the *cabildos* of Tacueyó and Toribío called him: "A crystal in which dance the brilliant rays of the supreme star which on summer mornings peeks out in the east" (ANC/B 1915: 40v). Even more interesting were Lame's activities at Llanogrande, Tolima – whose name he changed to San José de Indias – where he established a religious and cultural center. Here he celebrated the saints' days with dances and representations of the ancient Indian legends he describes in *Los pensamientos*. He would awaken every morning before dawn to pray to the sun (Castillo 1987: 36–37). His actions were similar to modern Páez myths of St. Thomas, who also prayed to the sun (cf. Bernal 1953) and who was believed to have been a pre-columbian Christian emissary to the Americas (Rappaport 1980–81).

In his treatise, Lame also merges his own apostolic calling as a being of the high mountains with the more specific geography of Tierradentro. His vision of the Páez heartland paints a picture of powerful rivers and high mountains, more grandiose and powerful than those of the Polindara of his childhood. In chapter 8 of the second book of *Los pensamientos*, entitled "The Birth of the Source in the Darkness," he asks why he, a Páez Indian, was chosen as the apostle of his race:

Because in the midst of this vast cordillera there is born a large and swift river, called the Páez River. For now I will not develop its origins, nor its chronology, nor the chronology of my sovereigns, nor the chronology of the sages who lived before 12 October 1492, etc., etc.   (Lame 1971: 121)

The mountains streams' song is one of the 15 books that Lame cites in his "bibliography" (ibid.: 124). It is not at all surprising that he should evoke the image of the mountain stream, for the *cacique* of Vitoncó – whom Lame claimed as an ancestor – called himself the "son of the stars of the Tama Stream." And Lame saw himself originating in the same place that bore that mythical being: in his genealogy he indicates that his great-grandfather, Jacobo Lame, was from Lame, "the highest mountaintop of Tierradentro." True, Lame is located at an intermediate altitude in Tierradentro, where sugar cane still grows. But for Quintín, who only dreamed of his birth in those high mountains, they were the highest in Tierradentro, the source of the ultimate knowledge that would be the salvation of the Páez people.

From *caudillo* to *cacique*

In earlier chapters we traced the development of the image of the colonial *cacique*, that powerful personage who founded the *resguardos* and established a longstanding myth of his role as a savior of the Páez. We also examined his transformation into a nineteenth-century *caudillo*. Now, we must inquire into how Lame articulated this same historical referent with his own image as a political activist.

In their study of nineteenth-century Páez political history Findji and Rojas (1985) place Quintín Lame's movement as an outgrowth of the Republican *cacique* without a *cacicazgo*. Lame attempted to unite broad expanses of territory and the people living therein into a centralized political movement extending from Popayán to Tierradentro, and on to Tolima and Huila. That is to say, his "*cacicazgo*" was even larger than the traditional Páez area, spilling over into areas occupied at the time of the Spanish invasion by the Pijao. Lame presents similarities with the nineteenth-century *caudillos* in that he attempted to forge a political unit where it did not legally exist. In contrast to his nineteenth-century predecessors, Lame inverted their purposes, pressing for indigenous demands instead of seeking ends which would only benefit himself and the ruling elite.

Of great importance in understanding Lame's role as a Republican *caudillo* are the titles that he attributed to himself. Although he never called himself a *cacique*,[4] he did see himself as a chief whose position would be inherited by his son, Roberto (*El Espectador*, 12 July 1924), thus taking on the trappings of the traditional *cacicazgo*. Moreover, he traced his descent to the *caciques* of the colonial era by claiming that his great-grandfather's surname was Estrella ("Star"), as was that of the great colonial *cacique* Don Juan Tama de la Estrella. His elaborate signature included a picture of a man bearing two stars, again reminiscent of Don Juan Tama (cf. Castillo 1987: ii, for a reproduction of the signature).

Lame was able to diffuse the chiefly image among his followers by claiming descent from the culture hero, by emphasizing his heavenly visions and by cloaking himself in an aura of invincibility, disappearing from the hands of his white captors (Castrillón 1973: 156–9) and lauding himself for appearing as his own attorney against incredible odds (Lame 1971: 17, 48). That his followers accepted this superhuman picture is clear in the testimony of his contemporaries:

Plate 5 *Manuel Quintín Lame.* Lame is seen here at center, with long hair and a cigar in his mouth. The photo, from the collection of Diego Castrillón Arboleda of Popayán, was taken at his 1916 arrest at San Isidro.

Quintín said to us that we needed to arm each other until the entire population of the *parcialidad* was armed to the last man, to oppose the division of the *resguardos*. He told the women to earn respect for ourselves wielding kitchen knives if necessary! *I have never seen or heard any man like him*!

(Castillo 1987: 168; emphasis mine)

Similarly, when the ceremonial center of San José de Indias was destroyed by the army on 1 February 1931, his followers believed that his escape from the arms of repression was due to his supernatural power to become invisible (ibid.: 172).

The special image that Lame created for himself was reinforced by some of the novelties of his physical appearance: unlike most Páez, Lame had long hair, and thus looked like an ideal Indian (Plate 5).

But while Lame played upon traditional ideas of the *cacique* and the messiah, he interpreted them through a nineteenth-century filter and behaved as a nineteenth-century *caudillo*. Many of his Páez associates were *caudillos* in their own right, with their own followings. Rosalino Yajimbo from Tierradentro, for example, was a colonel in the War of the Thousand Days and was believed never to have suffered a wound during this conflict, making him invincible (AFCN/C 1972b). He was a hero in Tierradentro because he killed Captain Lorenzo Medina, a government officer who had killed many Páez. He was known for having led ritual sacrifices at the Puente Bejuco in the War of 1876 (*El Nuevo Tiempo*, 1 June 1917). In keeping with the *caudillo* image, Lame's followers were given military titles: Yajimbo was a General (Castrillón 1973: 151), and Lame called himself a Marshal (ANC/B 1919a: 292) and wore a military uniform given to him in Bogotá (ibid.: 294). As a *cacique* without a *cacicazgo* he battled others of similar position, including Pío Collo and Francisco Guainás, Páez military leaders at the head of indigenous troops (*El Tiempo*, 16 November 1916; ANC/B 1919b: 142). In his treatise, Lame even compares himself to one of these "*caciques without cacicazgos*":

There is the defense of Colombia that I offered the first Magistrate in the Palacio de la Carrera, Doctor Olaya Herrera, to come out at any time with 5,000 Indians to punish the invaders of the Amazonian frontiers, General Sánchez Cerro, and that I wanted to go there personally and use my sword against the invader, leading those 5,000 boys, heroically waving the tricolor flag, as I did in the invasions of the border of Ecuador and Colombia with General Avelino Rojas in the year 1903 to 1904.

(Lame 1971: 70)

Moreover, as has already been described, Lame conceived of himself as a "Representative" of the Indians, an intermediary like the nineteenth-century *caciques*, and not an autonomous ruler like the colonial chiefs.[5]

Although he behaved like a Republican *cacique* without a *cacicazgo*, Lame stressed the colonial roots of his movement, information he acquired through documentary research and historical reading. For example, in 1920 he established, together with a number of Páez and Guambiano *cabildos* from the Popayán area and Tierradentro, as well as *cabildos* from Huila and Tolima, a Supreme Council of the Indies whose President would be José Gonzalo Sánchez and whose members would include Lame and other associates (ANC/B 1920: 17r–v). The rationale behind this formation is interesting in terms of Lame's use of general historical information for grounding a very modern action:

This Council recollects the *Supreme Council of the Indies* which was a high *Court* of Justice that ruled in Spain in the fifteenth century, *under which all the interests of America were guarded and protected*; so the current *Council* that is formed refers to this and we recognize and respect it, because under it and through it our own *Rights*, which day by day they want to take from our hands [leaving us] no protection, will be respected and recognized.   (ibid.: 17v; emphasis in original)

Yet unlike any colonial Páez institution or the Council of the Indies in Spain, Lame's council was tied to a broad *cabildo* structure through the election of Sánchez as the "National Indian President or the Superior President of the *Cabildos*" (ibid.). This is a clear indication of telescoping in the implementation of historical knowledge.

From colony to state

While Lame emphasized the colonial roots of his movement, he also recognized that it operated within the Colombian nation. His offer to participate as a *caudillo* in defense of the motherland in its war for its Amazonian frontiers, quoted above, illustrates that he felt that he owed part of his loyalty to Colombia. Castillo (1987: 64) cogently explains Lame's dual loyalties toward his race and toward his country:

"The national conscience" is not, however, identical with white civilization or with the Colombian nation, but rather the adherence to a moral principle that has expressed itself through history in outstanding moral figures who have come out in open defense of Indian rights. Lame mentions at random a number of personalities from all centuries, including popes, presidents, and priests, and affirms that it was because of this "national conscience" that he has pledged allegiance not only to the Indians but also to Colombia as "the motherland." Thus, Lame sees himself as a citizen of two worlds: on the one hand, he is first and foremost the apostle and advocate of the Indians, and on the other, he is bound in loyalty to the national society based on the moral bond of "justice."

The importance of Lame's "national conscience" was very clear in the various rituals that accompanied his visits to indigenous communities. Most significant among these were his "teaching *mingas*," political meetings named to reflect on the traditional Andean communal work party, the *minga*:

Everything began then with a ritual. Quintín ceremoniously greeted those present and stood on a box or a table placed there especially for the occasion, in order to begin with a singing of the National Anthem. When all were singing, plunged into fanaticism, he would suddenly raise his hands asking for silence, and he would begin his speech in a solemn and stately tone.

"Everything that the National Anthem says is a lie, because liberty has not arrived among the Indians. I come to defend the dispossessed, weak, ignorant Indian tribes, abandoned by the whites who govern us with no [legal] right and who have taken the lands of America that Jesus Christ Our Lord gave us so that we would work them and defend them. I am writing a law to take to the government of Bogotá asking that it order the return of our lands to us, [lands] that the whites have. We Indians do not have to pay rent because Colombia is one big homestead that the King of Spain could not grant to the white conquerors who came to rob us and murder us."   (Castrillón 1973: 91–92)

The *minga* continued with a discussion of law or of the Constitution, a meal and finally the preparation of legal documents.

The teaching *minga* was a combination of Andean concepts of labor exchange, traditional means of forging a communal identity through community-based work parties, and references to highly-charged national symbols, such as the Constitution and the National Anthem. The *minga* was, in fact, a work meeting at which legal documents were drawn up and people were taught the essence of the Lamista philosophy. In this way, the national context of the movement was made apparent to its members through a ritual which was novel in content but familiar in form.

From Tama to Lame

Manuel Quintín Lame demonstrated the Páez preoccupation with a moral continuity from the times of the beginnings to the present, from Juan Tama to the context of contemporary action. Many of the concepts articulated in Lame's writings and in his political activity were in evidence at the end of the nineteenth century: the importance of high places, the messianic ideal, the persona of the *cacique*. But until Lame broke onto the scene in Tierradentro, there was little mention of Don Juan Tama as an historical actor, no reference to the relationship between political power and topographical features, no documented allusion to a five-generational model of history. These themes arise again once Quintín Lame's presence was felt among the Páez, most certainly communicated to the Indians through brief images and not through the text of *Los pensamientos*, which was only made known to the Páez after its publication in 1971.

We shall see in Part III that the modern Páez have reinterpreted the *resguardo* titles, forging a complex oral tradition whose continuity with the past owes much to the intervention of Quintín Lame. Nevertheless, his stature as a folk-hero is not apparent in modern-day Tierradentro. His own image has given way to the more ancient one of Juan Tama. More than achieving his political demands among the Páez, a venture in which he was unsuccessful, Lame succeeded in reinforcing a moral continuity with Tama, reinstating the concept of the colonial *cacique*, who was so much more successful in achieving his goals and who began the process that Lame only continued. Moreover, Lame sparked a renewed interest in written documents and, ironically, left few of his own in Tierradentro. Finally, Lame's actions, which were based on nineteenth-century methods and institutions, placed a new value on colonial institutions and philosophies that had permitted a greater autonomy for minority communities than did their Republican counterparts. His efforts to revive the *resguardo* succeeded in the long run because he forced Indians to recognize their moral continuity with the colonial past, even though the *resguardo* existed within the Colombian state. Thus, the colonial *cacique* who created the original *resguardo* became more important than the sharecropper *cacique* without a *cacicazgo*.

III

Contemporary historical voices

6

The *cacique* reborn: the twentieth-century Páez

The twentieth-century Páez have continued to confront many of the same problems they faced during the nineteenth century. Civil war and violence have endured, particularly at mid-century. *Resguardos* cling to their communal identity under the unremitting threat of extinction. New latifundia have been established and an influx of settlers has resulted in the further annexation of communal lands. An indigenous resistance has grown to counter these pressures, but has thus far been unable to coalesce the population under a single leadership. Historical consciousness continues to provide an important tool for transcending the limits of the political juncture, but divorced from a unitary organizational reality, it has not been used to its full potential.

Up to this point, we have analyzed the works of Páez historians within their political and historical contexts. Given the paucity of documentary data, we could not detail the nature of the historical ideas known to the followers of Don Juan Tama or of Quintín Lame. The situation is quite different in the twentieth century. Here, we can read Julio Niquinás' histories within both their political and their intellectual contexts: an analysis of contemporary storytelling provides more than a glimpse at the ideological substratum of his accounts. Therefore, in this final section, the political backdrop of Páez historymaking will not only consider the actions of contemporary leaders, but also the ideology upon which they structure their activities and the oral traditions that inform their ideology.

Land and labor in the twentieth century

Nineteenth-century land-loss among the Páez was directly related to the expansion of great estates by the elite of Popayán. In the twentieth century, Páez lands continued to be expropriated, now by a mixed group, including entrepreneurs from Cali and peasant colonists from the outskirts of Popayán. Cauca was in a period of economic and political flux. The construction of railway lines, coupled with the administrative changes that carved several departments out of the old provincial boundaries, broke the dependence of local producers upon the provincial capital Popayán; they now turned to Cali to sell their products. Until the Great Depression, coffee boomed on the western slopes of the cordillera, with northern Cauca and the region around Jambaló planted in the lucrative crop. The introduction of artificial pasture and of barbed wire fostered more intensive developments in cattle-ranching. Caleño entrepreneurs engaged in commercial farming in the north, around Toribío and Caloto, while peasants from the Popayán area, where soils were exhausted, encroached upon Páez lands in the vicinity of Jambaló. By the late twenties, colonists had climbed the cordillera and begun to plant coffee in Tierradentro, provoking outbreaks of violence between Indians and outsiders (Earle 1985). A new social configuration arose in the Páez area: where once Indians stood in opposition to the Popayán elite, they now constituted barriers to the expansion of landholdings by other peasants, as poor as themselves (Findji and Rojas 1985).

Sharecropping arrangements continued to be the rule on the western slopes of the cordillera, although the wealthy Popayán *hacendados* were replaced by new mestizo patrons. Tenant farming provided a convenient way of shifting risk and responsibility from the shoulders of the landowner to those of Indian semi-serfs (Earle 1985). As we have seen, tenant farmers, always on the brink of dispossession and overexploited by their patrons, were also a fertile medium for the growth of political dissent: they were the most important sector organized by Quintín Lame. In 1936, new legislation regarding land ownership was interpreted by local landowners as recognizing the rights of tenant farmers to the lands they tilled. As a result, sharecroppers were dislodged from their lands, which were then planted in pasture for cattle-raising (ibid.). Evicted tenant farmers settled in neighboring *resguardos* on the western slopes, forming colonies that submitted to *cabildo* authority (Findji and Rojas 1985); other disenfranchised sharecroppers sought public lands in Tierradentro, further exacerbating Indian–colonist conflict (ibid.; Earle 1985).

1941 marked a turning-point for the continued existence of the *resguardo* system. By this time, Law 89 of 1890 had been in existence for 50 years, and communal land tenure was slated to be phased out under the law's provisions. Privatization of *resguardo* lands – known as *parcelación*, or the division of a territory into private lots – was bitterly resisted by the Páez, as is evident in the testimony of a man who campaigned for the renewal of Law 89:

In those days the whites were the only ones who wanted to privatize the land; no, the Indians didn't want it. The Indians were the enemies of private plots. So my Uncle Víctor and Captain Dicue,[1] since he was such a friend of the late poet Guillermo Valencia[2]... they availed themselves of him and they went to the departmental government [saying] that the Indians wanted [the *resguardo*] and that they would have to leave it as is. That is what they said, but [they were told that privatization] is national law, so they would have to have individual plots and the *cabildo* would have to distribute them. So they gave them ten years' extension and look, since then, they haven't said anything.   (AFCN/C 1972b)

Although the *resguardo* acquired a new lease on life when the liquidation clause of Law 89 was postponed, zones of non-Indian settlement (*zonas de población*) were nevertheless expanded: mestizo colonists attempted to wrest a further 100 hectares from the *cabildo* of Mosoco, for example, eliciting fierce resistance on the part of the Indians (ibid.).

But while some *cabildos* effectively staved off privatization, others embraced government-sponsored propaganda efforts and relinquished their rights to communal lands and autonomous government; not by accident, many of these communities were located in southern Tierradentro, where the greatest influx of peasant colonists had occurred in previous years.[3] Beginning in 1945, five of Tierradentro's *resguardos* were privatized. Even the communities most resistant to privatization lost some lands to private property. For instance, a number of indigenous *latifundistas* emerged in Pitayó, gobbling up vast dominions that had once been *resguardo* (AFCN/C 1973). Interestingly, the most prominent indigenous landlord in Pitayó was Calambás, believed to be descended from the chiefly family of the same name. Indigenous landlords were only building upon the inequalities already inherent in the distribution of *resguardo* lands by local *caudillo*-run *cabildos*:

In some *resguardos*, there is true injustice in the distribution of lands among members, because while some individuals possess extensive lots, generally uncultivated, others hold such small lots that they cannot produce enough to subsist.   (Lugari 1936: 703)

Political organizing after the *Quintinada*

Once Quintín Lame abandoned Tierradentro for new political vistas in Tolima a political vacuum developed among the Páez. Multiple individuals and organizations courted the allegiance of the Indians, none of them achieving the regional hegemony they sought.

Depression-era Cauca, haunted by the dislocation of tenant farmers and the expansion of commercial landholdings and colonization, was a fertile ground for political organizing. The Communist Party established Peasant Leagues among the Páez in the 1930s and 1940s. Aimed primarily at ending sharecropping and *hacendado* abuses (AFCN/C n.d.a), the Leagues also hit out against forced labor levies for public works (*El Bolchevique*, 18 August 1934) and the dissolution of *resguardos* (*El Bolchevique*, 29 September 1934). Communist cells, each numbering a dozen or more Indians, were created in a number of communities, especially on the western slopes of the cordillera (*El Bolchevique*, 9 February 1935), and numerous regional meetings were held with Indians in attendance. The overwhelming majority of indigenous League members were sharecroppers, who thus stood in political opposition to the *resguardo* Páez who owned land and whose leaders received favors from politicians of the traditional parties: the result was the polarization of the Páez into two bands (Findji and Rojas 1985).

The Communist party was able to effectively incorporate Indian demands into their program, thus introducing indigenist ideas into the politics of the dominant society. This was accomplished through the active participation of such Páez leaders as Quintín Lame and his associate from Totoró, José Gonzalo Sánchez, in national meetings and congresses, as well as through the frequent reporting of Indian news in the party press. On a local level, Communist organizing achieved the elevation of Indians to posts of authority: Sánchez was elected to the municipal council of Miraflores in 1937. Numerous strikes were organized ·to demand better working conditions for tenant farmers. A Communist-sponsored regional Indian and peasant federation was created (Earle 1985).

But the success of the Peasant Leagues was limited. Their emphasis on sharecroppers' demands left them with little to say to *resguardo* Indians. Moreover, the urban-based leaders of the peasant struggle took little account of the ideology of resistance that had grown among the Páez since the colonial era, and which had been cast in modern form by Quintín Lame. Some grassroots League members attempted to convert their organizations into *cabildos*, legitimizing their leadership through appeals to Juan Tama (Rappaport 1985). But they did not have time to recast the Communist Party within a Páez historical framework. Heightened tensions ensued as the Peasant Leagues fought to protect Indian rights and government authorities met the Leagues with violence, murdering Páez Communists, imprisoning hundreds of Indian sympathizers and assaulting villages (*El Bolchevique*, 18 August 1934, 6 October 1934, 4 May 1935; AFCN/C n.d.a). The Leagues did not survive the onslaught.

Violence

Violence has been a constant in Colombia's post-independence history. Some analysts suggest that violence lies at the heart of Colombia's political system, side by side with the restricted democracy that characterizes Colombian political process (Pécault 1987). For others, it has become an integral part of Colombian culture (Uribe 1988).

Violence is also a constant reality in the history of the Páez. The *resguardo* system was born of the violence of invasion and colonial *caciques* articulated their political claims by recourse to violent images. Nineteenth-century Indian leaders revived colonial chiefdoms by filtering contemporary violence through the memory of the *cacique*, converting the space of chiefly rule into the territory of politico-military leaders. Manuel Quintín Lame advocated violent tactics among the Indians he organized and on the spiritual plane, promised violent supernatural retribution against his enemies. The twentieth-century Páez continue to live in violent times. For anyone studying Tierradentro, a pertinent question to ask would be whether the Páez have effectively harnessed violence in the modern era, or whether it instead, controlled them. Sadly, the latter is more true.

After the 9 April 1949 assassination of the populist leader, Jorge Eliécer Gaitán, a spontaneous insurrection erupted in Bogotá and violence spread to the countryside. This period, called simply "La Violencia" lasted for at least a decade in most of Colombia, and for longer in some areas. It was a time of agrarian conflict, clashes between Liberal and Communist guerrillas and Conservative government troops, and the beginnings of a general war against the Colombian peasant, especially the Indian, who forfeited a great deal of territory during this era.

Certain areas developed into refuge regions where peasants cooperated in self-defense, although little social reform resulted. Gilhodès (1970: 433) characterizes the solidarity that grew in these areas as a "solidarity of misery." Some of these regions survived under Communist control well into the 1960s, among them Riochiquito, which lies within the confines of Tierradentro to the east of the Páez towns.

The Páez, especially those of Tierradentro, were hard hit by the Violencia. Overwhelmingly Liberal with a history of Communist Party membership, they were singled out by the Conservative government's military police as potential subversives. Entire villages were decimated, soldiers looted homes and harassed their inhabitants. Many were forced to flee, taking refuge in the communities of the western slopes or in the Valle del Cauca. A passage from my field diary conveys the feeling of terror and impotence during this era:

> During the Violencia, this family stayed in San José. They were the only ones who did. After the troops killed all the people in town, the survivors went to Valle. Don Vicente Yandy treated his son,[4] who had been wounded by the troops, and took him to Valle. They did not return for five years. Sebastián was an orphan and he had no brothers, nor any friends outside, so he had nowhere to go. His family took to the mountains, hiding from the troops who accused them of being guerrillas, and from the guerrillas who accused them of being friends of the troops. They lived in the bush for a year, eating food they had stored. The children were small: Laurentino was a toddler and Apolinar, an infant. Once the soldiers caught them, saying they were guerrillas, but luckily they were not killed. The soldiers burned all the houses in the village and left the plaza empty. His daughter became frightened and said that the soldiers were going to kill them for guerrillas, because they were in hiding. So they went to stay with some of Dionicia's relatives in Moras, where there was a hut in the *páramo* and they could work as peons. The military was not entering Moras, just San José. And they waited there until the Violencia was over. To this day, whenever soldiers pass by, even if they do not enter San José, the people become very frightened.[5]

The Violencia did not destroy all Páez towns to the extent that San José was decimated. But it touched everyone in Tierradentro and on the western slopes of the cordillera. Those towns not hard-hit gave refuge to the survivors of massacres; such was the case of the relatively peaceful San Andrés de Pisimbalá (Ortíz 1973: 32). Páez territory was overrun by the military police, disrupting community rhythms and depleting foodstuffs. *Cabildos* were forced to submit to new local political *caciques* and the Church, a bastion of the Conservative Party, gained a stranglehold over most towns. On the western slopes of the cordillera landowners established death squads made up of hired assassins (*pájaros*) who continue to operate against Indian leaders up to the present day.

The Violencia was a blow against independent Páez unity, which had begun to crystallize under Manuel Quintín Lame and which was reinterpreted by the Peasant Leagues. Civil war effectively dampened the political process for two decades, perpetuating the political fragmentation that had resulted from the legislation of small and isolated *resguardos* during the Regeneration. Violence exacerbated the *cabildos'* lack of authority, their hegemony questioned by the various political organizations which had erected political hierarchies parallel to the *cabildos*, instead of within them.

The last 20 years: violence and hope

Tierradentro was not untouched by the political radicalization that characterized Latin America, North America and Europe in the early 1970s. Although the *Quintinada* was disarmed among the Páez by 1920, and although Peasant Leagues met with little immediate success in the 1930s and 1940s, the survivors of these movements were influential in the more permissive political climate of 1970, when Indian ethnic demands were revived. Their tradition of struggle was embraced by a generation of younger Indians trained in peasant organizations in the 1960s. In 1971, young activists joined with old Lamistas and ex-Peasant League members to form a regional Indian federation, the Consejo Regional Indígena del Cauca, or CRIC (Regional Indian Council of Cauca). Organized primarily around *cabildos* from the western slopes of the cordillera, CRIC revived many of Quintín Lame's demands:

1 repossession of usurped lands belonging to *resguardos*;
2 enlargement of *resguardo* territories;
3 strengthening of *cabildos*;
4 an end to sharecropping;
5 broadening knowledge of Indian legislation and demanding its application;
6 defense of the history, language and customs of indigenous communities;
7 formation of Indian bilingual teachers. (CRIC 1973)

CRIC quickly spread through Páez territory. Many, although not all, the *cabildos* of Tierradentro embraced the pan-Indian organization. In some parts of the western cordillera, it effectively repossessed lands, incorporating them into communal farms sponsored by the Colombian Institute for Agrarian Reform. Its initial recognition of *cabildo* hegemony gave indigenous authorities a new lease on life. The movement became influential on the national and the international planes, founding a newspaper and ultimately, a national Indian organization.

But CRIC was unable to maintain its ascendancy in Tierradentro, where communities did not see land repossession as a primary objective: most of these villages are surrounded by neighboring *resguardos* and there are relatively few haciendas to repossess. Furthermore, the Church, through its bishopric in Belalcázar, maintained a strong ideological hold over the Páez and controlled Indian education. As a result, the Tierradentro of the 1980s is divided among pro-CRIC sectors, unorganized sectors, and groups affiliated with traditional political parties.

CRIC's influence has been stronger on the western slopes, where sharecropping arrangements persist, where *resguardo* lands remain in non-Indian hands, and where the Church does not function as efficiently as a paternalistic intermediary. Nevertheless, even here certain sectors have become dissatisfied with the growing bureaucratization of the Indian movement and with the control exerted over it by Spanish-speaking monolinguals from the Guambiano-Coconuco community of Coconuco and non-Indian advisors. They are also disturbed over the lack of active participation of *cabildos* in decision-making. Moreover, they are unhappy with CRIC's policy of creating communal farms in repossessed lands, as opposed to expanding *resguardos*. As an alternative to CRIC, the more traditionalist Movement of the Southwest was founded in the late 1970s, functioning with *cabildo* leadership instead of professional organizers divorced from their communities, and intent on reincorporating repossessed lands into the communal structure of the *resguardo*. Jambaló and several other communities near Popayán have been especially successful in expanding communal land tenure, in reconstructing devastated economies, and in reviving historical knowledge. Many of the aims of the two rival organizations have coincided in recent years, focusing on the creation and expansion of *resguardos* and on cultural revitalization.

The Violencia was not the last turbulent era lived by the Páez. During the Turbay administration (1978–82) the armed forces were authorized to attack a growing guerrilla movement. Most well-known of the guerrillas operating in Cauca were the Revolutionary

Armed Forces of Colombia (FARC), affiliated to the Colombian Communist Party and made up, for the most part, of peasant fighters initially organized in self-defense organizations during the Violencia; another important group was the 19 April Movement (M-19), which at one time had formed the left wing of the National Populist Alliance inspired by military dictator Rojas Pinilla, and whose membership is middle-class in origin. By the late 1970s, the guerrillas had arrived in Tierradentro.

The attacks sustained by the Páez on all fronts had taken their toll. Many of Tierradentro's communities were empty during the coffee harvest, the population converted into a rural proletariat; others were away, working in sugar cane plantations. In Jambaló, the ravages of the Violencia, the continued existence of landlord-sponsored assassins and labor migration gave rise to a population deficit and a consequent labor shortage; the Páez of Jambaló can no longer reproduce their population (Findji and Rojas 1985). Cash crops, such as hemp, left a badly eroded landscape. With the introduction of synthetic fibers in the 1980s, the lands dedicated to this product and the machinery used to process its fibers became almost useless. Conditions were ripe for guerrilla activity. The subhuman conditions endured by the Páez and the memory of fierce Páez warriors drew the guerrillas to Tierradentro; guerrillas attempted to channel violence according to their own stereotype of the Páez and their history. Violence flared. Rural areas were especially targeted by the government as presumed guerrilla hideouts and training camps (Americas Watch Committee 1986). Once again, Indian leaders were imprisoned, their villages looted and a climate of terror sown throughout the region. The steady stream of persecution has been a major factor in inhibiting the development of a unified political leadership in the 1980s. It has also dampened the *cabildo* political process because their administrative approach, guided by consensus and implemented through communal works, has been constrained by military occupation (Sánchez *et al.* 1988).

The massive repression under the Turbay administration was unable to quell the tide of social unrest in Colombia, fueled by an unemployment rate of over 20 percent, a foreign debt of $12 billion, rampant inflation, and a growing drugs trade. The interparty conflicts of the Violencia had been assuaged from 1957 to 1974 by the establishment of the National Front, whereby the two major political parties, Liberal and Conservative, shared power; although the Front was formally dissolved in 1974, other currents were not given a slice of the political pie, and a large number of Colombians felt they were politically disenfranchised. With Belisario Betancur's assumption of the presidency in 1982, a new approach to the guerrillas was charted. Betancur advocated the negotiation of a cease-fire with the major guerrilla organizations, coupled with the promotion of political and economic reforms and an extensive investigation of human rights violations on the part of the military. In 1984, peace accords were signed with four of Colombia's major guerrilla movements, including the M-19 and FARC. By June 1985, few reforms had been promulgated, the military continued to persecute those guerrillas who had signed the accords, and the President was increasingly receptive to the military and to powerful economic interests that opposed his peace policy. The M-19 withdrew from the peace process and returned to active warfare. The FARC, in contrast, continued to adhere to the accords, and participated under the rubric of the Patriotic Union in national and local elections, winning council seats and mayoral posts in several localities. The broad contours of the political juncture have been potently analyzed by the Americas Watch Committee (ibid.). What remains confused is the situation in Cauca.

In January 1986, 172 bodies of guerrillas were discovered in a mass grave in Tacueyó, Cauca. Further investigations revealed that the victims were members of the Ricardo Franco Front, an armed organization that had split from the FARC after disagreement over the signing of the peace accords. These 172 guerrillas were, it was reported, killed by their own leaders, who had accused them of being government agents.

The Tacueyó massacre conveys the confusion that has beset Cauca during most of the 1980s. All of Colombia's major guerrilla organizations maintain fronts here. The National Guerrilla Co-ordinating Committee (CNG), which groups all of the movements that reject the peace process, has established an international battalion in the Páez area. The indigenous regions of Cauca have come under continuous military occupation. The Páez find themselves caught between contending armies. Some Indians have been recruited to guerrilla armies, others forcibly conscripted into the government army, while still others forced to flee their homes. Once again, Páez villages are the theater for civil war.

In the midst of the violence, a new guerrilla movement arose, the Quintín Lame Command, whose members are primarily Indians. The Command grew out of a need guerrilla organizations perceived for an entirely indigenous army that would press Indian aims and relate more easily to Cauca's Indian population.

The Quintín Lame Command by no means enjoys the support of the majority of the Páez, nor of the majority of Cauca's organized Indians and has been accused of murdering a number of Indian activists. Nevertheless, it feeds upon the Páez historical memory in ways reminiscent of Don Juan Tama and of Quintín Lame. As in the past, the current period of war has given rise to a new mode of interpreting history, in which new images are incorporated into a familiar historical vision. The Quintín Lame Command explains its name in the following manner:

Who was Quintín Lame? MANUEL QUINTIN LAME was a great Indian fighter who, following in the footsteps of his ancestors, the GAITANA and JUAN TAMA, took his place at the vanguard of his people, in opposition to his enemies.

He fought against sharecropping, for the repossession of *resguardos*, for the *cabildos*, for the defense of our culture. When he came to the realization that nothing would come of petitions and legal briefs, he formed ARMED groups, that would force the respect of the exploiters and the bosses.

More than 100 times he was imprisoned by order of Cauca's landlords. When our enemies cornered him and prevented him from continuing his work in our department, he went to Tolima, where he continued his struggle in the service of the Indians.

We are proud to carry the name QUINTIN LAME and to follow the example that he left us. (Comando Quintín Lame 1986; emphasis in original)

The Quintín Lame Command has harnessed the memory of Juan Tama, who we shall see, is a culture hero in modern-day Tierradentro. Moreover, they have linked the memory of Lame to the image of the colonial *cacique*. It is too early to tell whether the Command will effectively revive its namesake's image among the Páez, whether the Polindara sharecropper will take his place next to Juan Tama in the oral tradition, but it is supposed that Lame's name comes up more frequently in Páez conversations nowadays. We will now turn to an examination of how Juan Tama has become so important in contemporary historical memory.

CONTEMPORARY ORAL HISTORY

Twentieth-century events have played an important role in the development of a contemporary historical consciousness among the Páez. Although modern indigenous historians employ images that are by now familiar to us, they are harnessed for the solution of the problems of a distinct historical juncture. Contemporary history attempts to link together the multiple collectivities that make up the Páez nation: a difficult task, given that unity has been fragmented, not only by the creation of smaller territorial units, but also by the shattering of political leadership after the fall of Quintín Lame and the ravages of the Violencia. In the nineteenth century the moral continuity posited by historical consciousness was replicated in the political and territorial unity forged by indigenous *caudillos*, a marriage of memory and political leadership that continued through the *Quintinada* and the Peasant Leagues. But since the 1940s, although moral continuity persists as a consistent theme in the oral tradition of the Páez, there are no pan-Páez leaders effectively implementing moral continuity in political practice. Instead, we see numerous political actors – leaders of rival wings of the Indian Movement, guerrilla organizations, local Liberal Party bosses, the Church – all competing for leadership without achieving the broad following of a Don Juan Tama, a Francisco Guainás or a Manuel Quintín Lame. Under such circumstances, historical consciousness becomes equally fragmented and, as we shall see, employs universal themes to bolster narrower local identities. Contemporary oral tradition serves as a source of inspiration and example for political leaders and their communities. Oral tradition and its translation into ritual are "rehearsals for revolution" (Nash 1979), frameworks for resistance for those who use and interpret them. Nevertheless, they are still but "rehearsals" among the Páez, and will not be fully operationalized until a more unified political structure develops in the region.

Images from the past

The images articulated by Páez storytellers are elaborations upon colonial documents, given life and breath by more recent experience. They are fragmentary stories, frequently accompanied by scant detail. Although they are told in discrete episodes that do not come together in a linear chronology, the images that guide them can be placed in temporal order, as we will do here. What follows are some of the key images of Páez political history as it is remembered by the people of Tierradentro.[6]

The birth of the *cacique*

All of Tierradentro's culture heroes, including Juan Tama of Vitoncó,[7] Angelina Guyumús of Togoima, Llíban and Juan Chiracol of Calderas, Tóens of Tóez and José Calambás of La Troja, were born in highland streams, the progeny of the stars. Juan Tama, for example, was born in the Stream of the Morning Star, to which he descended from the Heights of Tama, above the village of Cuartel. Fished out of the waters by shamans, he was entrusted to maiden nursemaids, whom he killed by sucking their blood. Some people trace their descent to these mythical ancestors: culture heroes occupy the fifth or ancestor level of their genealogies, just as did Juan Tama in Quintín Lame's family tree.

Caciques-turned-serpents

The young heroes must be baptized immediately, for if they are not, they are transformed into man-eating serpents. In the case of José Calambás, this is precisely what occurred. The cannibalistic activities of *caciques*-turned-serpents can only be halted through setting traps that cut snakes into pieces. Segments of vanquished serpents are hurled into waterways and tend to orient upstream, with their heads pointing toward the rivers' sources; their remains continue to exist in whirlpools. While some culture heroes are transformed into evil snakes, others are villains in human form. Such was the fate of Tóens, who was hated by his people for all the maidens he killed while he nursed. The *cacique* of Tóez died in the Páez River when the bridge he was crossing broke, and he drowned in the waters.

Caciques as saviors

The *caciques* saved the Páez from a host of indigenous and foreign enemies. Juan Tama is said to have banished the Guambiano to their modern territory in the west, because they sacrificed Páez children to San José Lake in return for gold. Llíban of Calderas liquidated Pijao invaders by killing all those within reach of his sling. The European invaders were kept at bay when the *caciques* climbed high mountains and traced the boundaries of their *resguardos*. Angelina Guyumús forged the *resguardo* of Togoima atop Chumbipe Mountain, to the south of Togoima; Juan Tama consolidated his possessions on the banks of Juan Tama Lake, in the *páramo* between Tierradentro and the western slopes of the cordillera. Culture heroes were empowered through their possession of land titles, which were born with them, serving as pillows as they floated downstream. The supernaturally-born titles constitute what the Páez call a "Greater Right" to their territories that they claim by virtue of being the first Americans.

Disappearance of the *cacique*

At the end of the *caciques'* lives, they disappeared into highland lakes, from whence they can be called should the need arise. Juan Tama lives till today in Juan Tama Lake. He has returned to aid his people, most recently after the Violencia, when he is said to have caused an explosion at the headquarters of the Third Brigade of the Colombian army in Cali in retaliation for the abuses committed by the military police. Tama disappeared a second time in the nineteenth century, when the Páez hid his title in Juan Tama Lake to protect it from civil war generals; the original title has never been retrieved from its watery grave.

Buried treasures

The Páez were once the holders of great riches, some of which were acquired when they decimated the colonial town of La Plata. When the Spaniards came, the Indians organized themselves in long chains and passed their gold from hand to hand, depositing it in Tumbichucue, where it is still hidden.

Historical referents in the *cacique* narratives

The general outline of the *cacique* stories is clearly based on eighteenth-century *resguardo* titles. Additional information, some historical, some contemporary and some quite ancient, fleshes out the skeletal outline provided by the documents. The thrust of the stories is also corroborated by other forms of evidence the Páez deem historical.

The bare bones of the story derive from Don Juan Tama's title to Vitoncó, where he calls himself the "son of the star of the Tama Stream." The elaboration contained in present-day stories reflects Andean notions of the *amaru*, the snake that travels downriver in a period of chaos to establish an era of equilibrium (Earls and Silverblatt 1978: 314), much as the *cacique* floated downstream in order to establish the *resguardo* system. Undoubtedly, biblical symbolism also informs the image. The Páez draw upon other evidence to establish the veracity of their account: every June, when

Plate 6 *Precolumbian snake motif.* This ceramic jar is a part of a collection owned by the Apostolic Prefecture of Tierradentro (Belalcázar, Cauca). It illustrates that the image of the snake in contemporary oral tradition has its roots in precolumbian cosmology.

the rivers flood, they hear little *caciques* cry as they are carried by the torrent.

The transformation of the *cacique* into a man-eating serpent is not directly stated in colonial land titles. Nevertheless, serpents were a central iconographic motif in the precolumbian period and in the regional cosmology in general (Plate 6). The serpent story as told by the Páez is an inversion of the myth of the primordial anaconda of the Northwest Amazon, who swam upstream, social units arising from the different parts of his body; social groups are ranked according to their proximity to the mouth of the river, groups with higher rank corresponding to the head of the primordial anaconda (Reichel-Dolmatoff 1971; Bidou 1972, 1977; Hugh-Jones 1978). The Páez snake's head, in contrast, is located upriver from its tail. But as in the Vaupés, it is located opposite the most important settlements: there are two such serpents in Tierradentro, their heads facing Vitoncó and Togoima, the two principal colonial *cacicazgos*. Thus, the snake myth articulates historical information regarding constellations of colonial power in Tierradentro. The historicity of the tale is demonstrated by the Páez through the presence of snake-heads in whirlpools.

The various narratives of confrontation between *caciques* and their enemies are also elaborations upon *resguardo* titles. The tale of Juan Tama's banishing the Guambiano from Tierradentro in retaliation for their sacrifice of Páez children, for example, is a case in point. Nevertheless, the story also articulates other historical information. The fact that the Guambiano occupied Tierradentro in the precolumbian period is substantiated in Aguado's chronicle. The Páez have their own evidence to confirm the account: they point to a number of ancient roads in the high mountains, that they say were built by the *Kalwash*, the ancestors of the Guambiano. The story also incorporates more recent history: in the late nineteenth and early twentieth centuries, gold prospectors flocked to the *páramo* to stake claims (ACC/P 1874; AFCN/C 1972a; Cuervo Márquez 1956), and so it is no accident that the tale focuses on the perils of extracting gold from a highland lake.

The second precolumbian enemy of the Páez were the Pijao, repelled by sling-hurling *caciques* who killed all the invaders living within reach of their arms. The historical presence of the Pijao is a living memory among the Páez and the non-Indians of Cauca, who frequently encounter precolumbian burial sites which they say belong to the Pijao. Respiratory difficulties and other infections are believed to be caused by the presence of Pijao bones under a house-site (Bernal 1954b; Nachtigall 1953).

The most lasting of the three invasions suffered by the Páez was the Spanish Conquest. Evidence for this event is more than available in the Indians' everyday lives. Likewise, evidence for Páez resistance is embodied in *resguardo* boundaries and in *cabildo* activities. Accounts of resistance to European rule do not parallel the contents of the titles, but recapitulate the act of the drawing up of these documents. Within the colonial titles there is an emphasis on walking boundaries and on sighting community borders; these activities continue to provide vehicles for territorial validation today (Rappaport 1985) and are also central components of the three myths of invasion outlined above. Each one describes movement through territory, whether walking into exile or the movement of a sling, or sighting boundaries from a high mountain, as means of territorial maintenance. It is not by chance that these key practices are central to the invasion stories.

Narratives of the disappearance of the great *caciques* and of nineteenth-century land titles into highland lakes embody deeper Andean themes. In essence, the power of the past was sent underground, much as Quechuas believe happened to the Inca king (*Inkarri*) after the Spanish Conquest (Ortíz Rescaniere 1973). What distinguishes Páez from Quechua accounts is their dating of the disappearance: while Inkarrí went underground at the time of the Spanish invasion, Juan Tama and his titles did so at Independence. The Páez adapt Andean themes and patterns to explain an historical fact: the Indians of Cauca lost most of their lands and a great deal of their political autonomy during the course of the nineteenth century, when semi-independent political units were discouraged in the interests of national consolidation.

The juxtaposition of information from colonial titles, experiences from nineteenth-century wars and the memories of twentieth-century life, grounded within the same mythic vehicles that we find in other parts of South America, does not result in an event history. In contrast, the oral narratives of Tierradentro create a feeling for the consequences of the past as they are lived today: the implications of the acquisition of power by the *caciques*, the realities of land-loss, the power of colonial titles. A number of groundrules direct the insertion of evidence into the skeleton of the *cacique* story:

1 The central figure of the narrative is always the *cacique*.
2 The *cacique*'s power is embodied in *resguardo* titles.
3 All enemies of the Páez are violent, and their resistance can only be quelled through the actions of the *caciques* or, in their absence, the titles.
4 Resistance frequently takes the form of territory-validating activities such as walking or moving through a territory, and sighting boundary-markers.

5 One enemy may be substituted for another, depending upon the location and needs of the narrator.

6 One *cacique* may also be substituted for another.

7 Large blocks of time may be condensed into a single time-frame, according to the needs and experience of the narrator.

8 Large expanses of past and future time may sometimes be organized according to a five-generational model, especially when history takes a non-narrative form.

History or myth: a question of style

The chiefly framework into which the Páez insert past experience provides a central image that organizes historical evidence for them. The framework has expanded over the centuries, the product of a layering of various models for historical interpretation. The juxtaposition of patterns permits narrators to give new twists to their accounts, to contrast events with other more well-known episodes, to evoke powerful images which are all the more potent in the absence of detailed accounts. The result is a familiar format containing new information, which can be expressed through a number of genres, some of which are more mythical in flavor, situating events in a kind of primordial era, while others are factual in character. A good example of this is the chain of stories related to culture heroes who meet their deaths in the Páez River.

Castillo y Orozco's eighteenth-century Páez–Spanish dictionary (1877: 53) tells of Guequiáu, who arrived among the Páez to teach them their law. As he was unduly harsh on his people, he was punished: as he was fording the Páez River, he drowned. A similar story was told of the nineteenth-century *caudillo*, Guainás, who fell into the Páez River near the town of Wila and drowned when the bridge he was crossing broke (Cross 1871; 36). A contemporary storyteller recounted to me the death of the *cacique* Tóens, who was punished in a similar fashion for having sucked the blood out of too many maidens.

These three figures, each one separated from his predecessor by at least a century, are strikingly similar. All three are central political figures of their times, powerful men who meet their deaths in the Páez River in the vicinity of the modern *resguardos* of Wila and Tóez. Guequiáu and Tóens are born of the supernatural; the Guainás family traced its descent to the already-mythical Calambás family. Guequiáu and Tóens are punished by higher supernatural authorities

– the Creator and the Christian God, respectively – for their transgressions, including cruel and unusual punishment and cannibalism; Guainás' death is not a punishment, but he is described as sympathetic to the Páez' greatest enemy, the whites.

The three narratives differ in the nature of their protagonists and in the pattern by which they conduct their lives. The colonial Guequiáu and the contemporary Tóens are mythical and universal characters,[8] while Guainás is an historical personality, documented in history books and in archival holdings. The 1755 Guequiáu story and the 1871 recounting of the death of Guainás conform to a single archetype of the death of a fallen savior. In contrast, Tóens' death is subordinated to a new pattern, the contemporary *cacique* tale.

Several implications for the study of Páez history emerge out of a comparison of these three episodes. We have before us two genres of historical discourse. Guequiáu and Tóens are described in a universal and "mythical" idiom, while Guainás' story is related in a more particularistic historical style. This does not mean that mythic discourse was never employed during the nineteenth century, nor that a more objective and event-oriented mode of narration is never used today. Instead, the two styles are interchangeable, depending upon the context of the narration: the identity of narrator and listener, the purpose of telling the story. Most frequently, the two genres are intermingled. Thus, the individualistic and historically particular tale of the death of Guainás, while recounted in more objective terms, still conforms to the basic archetype exhibited in the deaths of Guequiáu and Tóens. The mythic mode, which interprets process as opposed to event, frames even the most objective of tales. Hence, the two modes are not entirely interchangeable but instead, the mythic mode informs all accounts to some degree; in this way the particularities of past experience are contextualized through pattern, as opposed to chronology.

THE OPERATIONALIZATION OF HISTORICAL IMAGES

Sacred geography

Geography provides another means by which history is patterned and contextualized. The *cacique* tradition is an all-encompassing model for spatial organization in Tierradentro, linking individual small *resguardos* into a common, mythically-defined territory. Although the *cacique* tales do not generally take place at any specified

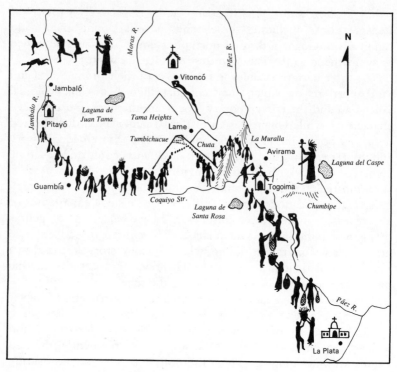

Map 7   Sacred geography of Tierradentro

time, they are linked to particular topographic sites that spatially
locate the places at which the culture heroes were born, lived and
fought major battles, created *resguardos* and finally disappeared from
human society (Map 7). Sacred geography is the medium in which
history is experienced in everyday life: as a fleeting image, a brief
mention, a vista, a resting-place, not a lengthy narrative. It fosters a
moral continuity with the past, more than a detailed knowledge of
it.

Considering that the oral tradition is an elaboration upon colonial
resguardo titles, it is appropriate that historically loaded sites are for
the most part located along community boundaries. They are
generally high mountains, perceived as ancestors by those who live
on their slopes and are guided by them. Some of these mountains are
of local significance, at once shared by two or three communities and
providing boundaries between them. Communities are thus united

on the sacred plane, while they remain divided in the political domain by allegiances to distinct *cabildos*. An example is Tek Kluus Tã' (Mountain of the Three Crosses) between San José and La Troja; it is the object of an annual pilgrimage each May. Other sites are of regional significance, uniting politically-divided *resguardos* through their common allegiance to these places. Some, like Juan Tama Lake, the final resting-place of the *cacique*, are located on the frontier of Páezdom, dividing Tierradentro from the Guambianos. Others, like Chumbipe, the heights from which Angelina Guyumús traced her *resguardo* boundaries, lie within Tierradentro, but along mythological frontiers: Chumbipe is located at the limits of Llíban's mythical Pijao-killing sling. The territorial unity created by regional sacred precincts conceptually recreates the great colonial *cacicazgos* of Togoima and Vitoncó.

But it is not enough to enumerate the sacred precincts that encode Tierradentro's history, nor to point out the moral continuity that they foster through the use of historical images. The grounding of Páez history in sacred space colors the modes by which knowledge of the past is experienced. Historical interpretation is intimately linked to space in a number of ways:

1   A non-linear notion of time emerges through references to sacred precincts, each of which encodes multiple historical referents as well as political boundary-markers, and each of which is related through narrative to neighboring sacred sites.
2   Tierradentro's sacred precincts are related to one another in calendrically significant ways, and a practice-based chronology emerges from the order in which they are experienced during the course of the year.
3   If the sacred geography of Tierradentro is approached from a regional perspective and the plot structure is superimposed upon the topography, spatial organization recapitulates the temporal relationships that link narrative episodes together.

Geography, history and chronology

Tierradentro is a mountainous region and many of the precincts sacred to the Páez are located atop mountain peaks. From one of these mountaintops, the observer can view many other mountains, some of which are also sacred. Villages or places of residence are also linked to sacred precincts in this manner. Because certain historically-

Plate 7   *Chumbipe.* This saddle-shaped mountain on the boundary of Togoima,
Cuetando and La Palma is a petrified Pijao chief, the peak from which Angelina
Guyumús viewed her dominions, and the object of modern pilgrimage to
appease a serpent that lives there.

significant mountains block the line of vision of a community,
forming its horizon and frequently the political limits of its domains,
many of these peaks are the focus of rituals that revalidate communal
identity. Even though the historical referents encoded in a series of
precincts and villages might not be connected by plot to the
narratives, visual or geographic relationships come to the fore when
these topographic features are visited, thus lending an immediacy to
non-narrative associations among them. Similarly, relationships are
forged among the multiple historical referents encoded in a single
sacred precinct, even though they may not appear together in a
narrated episode.

A good example of this breaking of an absolute narrative
chronology can be seen in Chumbipe Mountain, located along the
Páez River between La Palma and Cuetando (Plate 7). Chumbipe is
believed to be a petrified Pijao chief who was transformed into a
mountain after he was defeated by the Spanish invaders. St. Thomas,
precursor to the great *caciques*, hung his hammock on this peak. A
cannibalistic serpent lives at the summit. Here the *cacica* Angelina

Guyumús viewed her dominions and created the *resguardo* of Togoima; she also used to swim in a lake that is said to lie within the mountain. Given the close association between Doña Angelina and Chumbipe, it is not surprising that the gift she bestowed upon Simón Bolívar was a golden saddle: after all, Chumbipe has a distinctly saddle-like shape. The gift of the saddle symbolizes the *caciques'* relinquishing of their territorial autonomy to the new Colombian overlords. Thus, the mountain articulates a number of historical referents, including the primordial era of the Pijao and St. Thomas, the birth of *caciques* and their transformation into snakes, the years of glory, or "First Independence," when *caciques* ruled, *resguardos* were created, and lands were distributed and the post-Independence era, or "Second Conquest," when the *resguardo* system was threatened by the consolidation of the new Colombian nation.

Chumbipe is also related to neighboring sacred and historical precincts that can be viewed from its heights. It lies on the southern boundary of the *cacicazgo* of Togoima, the southernmost limit of the reach of Llíban's sling: beyond Chumbipe the Pijao were not killed and thus the mountain marks a frontier between the civilized Páez and the savage Pijao. The mountains of Calderas are visible from Chumbipe; similarly, Chumbipe is linked to Calderas because one of the community's *caciques* is said to have disappeared into a lake in La Palma, directly behind the mountain. Chumbipe is also a prime location for viewing Togoima, Angelina Guyumús' capital, founded at the *cacica's* visit to this historically significant peak. But Chumbipe encodes more than historical referents shrouded in mythic images; recent signposts can also be viewed from the mountain. Principal among these is Cuetando Bridge spanning the Páez River, which lies directly below the mountain: at this infamous site Páez Liberals were massacred during the Violencia. But even the bridge is of supernatural importance, since the tail of Togoima's supernatural serpent still lives nearby in a whirlpool.

And so the local residents, unversed in the sacred geography beyond their horizon, can "read" historical evidence atop Chumbipe. Their interpretation of these "documents" will be colored by their layout across the landscape they scan. The moral continuity affirmed by the oral tradition is acted upon in a special way through the sacred geography. It is not so much the temporal position of historical markers, as the practice of locating them in space, that binds the sacred geography into a common history and lends it significance.

Plate 8 *La Muralla*. La Muralla, the boundary between Calderas and Avirama, is believed to be a line of petrified human beings carrying the treasure of La Plata to its hiding place at Tumbichucue.

In her study of memory techniques in the western world, Yates (1966) describes how the classical Greeks utilized buildings as mnemonic devices, so that architectural features became repositories for facts which could be recalled in a fixed order corresponding to the order of the architectural features of the building. Harwood (1976) expands on Yates' example in her analysis of the arrangement of Trobriand mythic episodes within and across the sacred geography. She asserts that the temporal order of myth is recapitulated in geography: the chronology of myth is reflected in the order of episodes emerging from sites oriented in a single cardinal direction. The relationship between sacred place and mythic episode is not static; the myth is merely a reference to a whole series of further episodes which might be recalled, reformulated or recombined.

An interesting situation results when we apply Yates' and Harwood's ideas to Tierradentro's sacred geography and documentary history relating to Juan Tama (Map 7). The history of the northern Páez is one of migration up the cordillera and toward the northwest. Oral tradition and sacred space recapitulate this trajectory, lending it immediacy by framing it with mythic concepts. The riches of La Plata, destroyed by the colonial Páez, are said to have been transported in single file via a mountain called La Muralla to Tumbichucue, a clear northwesterly movement. The story is preserved in the rock formation, which is said to be a line of petrified Indians (Plate 8). Juan Tama, born in Cabuyo, also moved toward the northwest, battling the Guambiano in the Páramo de Moras and settling finally in the Juan Tama Lake. His unbaptized siblings were transformed into snakes whose fragments are also oriented upriver, toward the northwest.

The arrangement of Tierradentro's sacred geography recapitulates the historical migrations of the Páez nation. The individuals who walk from the market town of Belalcázar to Vitoncó via Avirama, Calderas, Tumbichucue and Lame, and continuing on via Mosoco to Pitayó, will pass numerous sites which encode Páez history. The order in which they pass them causes them to relive the historical migration of the Páez to the western slopes of the cordillera. Here again, through practice – this time, walking – temporal structure and history are experienced and enacted.

History and ritual practice

The historical significance of Tierradentro's sacred geography is experienced most actively through ritual. On the one hand, ritual links historical referents into new associations determined by position in the ceremonial calendar. On the other, ceremony invests historicity in sites that do not themselves embody events of the past. Ritual thus expands the range of space and time in the present, so that it can encompass the past.

The calendar and the oral tradition

As early as the eighteenth century, Father Castillo y Orozco (1877: 58–59) reported that the Páez of Tálaga revered two "seats of the sun," oracles of astronomical and historical significance. Contemporary Páez oral tradition, sacred geography and ritual are also closely linked to the calendar. Historical events and ritual activity consistently take place on calendrically significant dates, especially on the solstices. Numerous sacred precincts are markers for celestial and meteorological phenomena. Historical referents are best experienced through the calendar, their chronology modified by the timetable dictated by ritual practice and observation of the heavens.

Cultivation necessitates the elaboration of mechanisms for the development of an agricultural calendar through the temporal location of seasonal changes. This can be achieved in various ways. For example, the arrival of the rains clearly indicates the beginning of winter. The approach or the end of a planting season can also be fixed by the arrival of certain insects. The solstices are stronger indicators of seasonal change. Occurring in June and in December, they are marked by the arrival of the sun at its extreme northern and southern limits in the course of its travels across the sky; solstices can be located by reference to architectural features (Aveni 1981; Reichel-Dolmatoff 1975) or topographic sites.

Páez oral tradition is full of references to astronomical and calendrical phenomena, its culture heroes intimately related to the sun and the stars. Juan Tama's parents were the waters and the star. He is sometimes said to have been born on a day when Venus was very bright (Hernández de Alba 1963: 953). Tama was not the only *cacique* assoicated with astral bodies: various stars are said to have fallen into the water, especially at times when the river runs quickly – at the June solstice – and these stars are called *satjkwe*, or "little *caciques*."

Even as fragmentary texts, *cacique* stories structure time and aid in the formulation of a calendar. *Caciques* are born at the height of the June rainy season and the solstice. By this time, planting must have ended. After the solstice comes a long period of *hambruna*, or hunger, when there is no maize to eat. Chiefly birth thus divides the year into two seasons, winter and summer, and provides a very general temporal structure into which more specific markers might be incorporated.

Meteorological phenomena marking the change of the seasons are associated with historical sites and their ritual. One San Joseño remarked to me that when Juan Tama sang, the winter would come. For him, Juan Tama was the Thunder, coming from the north or from the south. To the southwest of San José lies the lake into which the *cacique* disappeared. To the north is the *páramo* and the spot at which he battled the Guambiano. Similarly, according to a resident of La Cruz de Vitoncó, located between Vitoncó and Taravira, the winter thunder comes from the mountain called Chuta. She is the "Mother of the Rains," since storms and clouds over her peaks foretell winter in La Cruz. Some sites are of astronomical importance: from Vitoncó, Juan Tama's capital, it is possible to observe the sunrise over his birthplace in Cuartel at the time of the

Plate 9   *Musicians from San José.* Musicians participate in many of the rituals and festivities associated with community boundaries, sacred sites and the Páez historical memory.

June solstice.[9] The close association between Tierradentro's sacred geography and the agricultural calendar is thus operationalized through the practice of looking, much as are the establishment of political and social boundaries and the expansion of social frontiers (Plate 9). Similarly, annual pilgrimages to Chumbipe to feed the serpent that lives there coincide with the June solstice; in this case, the relationship between space and time is operationalized through walking.

Ritual reenactments of history

The homes in which people live are frequently the most tangible repositories of historical information. The form in which a house is divided over the years among heirs, a process embodied in its ground-plan, is a living – and lived-in – piece of historical evidence (Behar 1986). The traditional Páez house embodies many of the elements which go into the formation of Tierradentro's sacred precincts. In fact, the house has always been a vehicle for remembering history, going back to pre-columbian times, when houses were abandoned at the birth or death of a resident (Rodríguez

Figure 3   Páez house

1684), and continuing to the present, when the presence of Pijao burials can harm a house's residents.

The traditional house is a wattle and daub structure with at least one, although sometimes several, rooms, roofed with straw thatch. Along the joints of the roof are a number of straw cushions into which small wooden crosses are fitted (Figure 3). The new house looks like a mountain, with its steep roof and its crosses: Tierradentro's slopes are similarly precipitous, and frequently have crosses planted at their summits to mark boundaries (Plate 10).

Historically-laden ritual associated with housebuilding endows houses with a practice-oriented kind of historicity. In La Ovejera, between Pitayó and Jambaló, ritual accompanies the completion of house construction (Diego Berrío, personal communication). When building activities are terminated, a straw opossum effigy is placed on the roof and a ceremonial battle takes place, dislodging and ceremonially killing the effigy. After the death of the opossum, bread-babies are taken out and are "baptized" by a man disguised as a Catholic priest. Once baptized, the bread-babies are broken in pieces, dipped in *chicha* (cane beer) and consumed by the participants.

Although ceremonial battles did take place in eighteenth-century Tierradentro (Castillo 1877: 64), there is no indication of any historical referents in the first portion of the ritual. But the baptism

Plate 10   *Crosses as boundary markers.* These crosses are located on a mountain between Togoima and Santa Rosa and are the object of pilgrimage in May. The image of the mountain is recapitulated in the Páez house, whose roof is steep and carries crosses at its apex.

of the bread-babies evokes a very clear historical image: the consumption of the bread-babies is interpreted by Páez participants as bringing to mind the time when Páez children were fed to a lake to free up the stores of gold which lay under its waters. This is a clear reference to the story of Juan Tama's triumph over the Guambiano, itself an elaboration upon Don Juan Tama's Vitoncó title. Through ritual and symbol, the story is recalled and reenacted: the bread-babies refer to the sacrificed Páez children and the yellow *chicha*, to the gold given in return for the infants. Furthermore, ritual practice links the village to historically-laden sites in much the same way as pilgrimage would.

Creating history

While offerings to the serpent of Chumbipe are a ritual insertion of a sacred site into the calendar-round, linking historical referents to practical agricultural time, the house-building ceremony evokes historical images at sites quite distant from those which mark these events. A third ritual, the refreshing of the *cabildo*'s staffs of office, lends historical significance to sacred precincts that were never the stage for events from the meaningful past.

Until the time of the Violencia, the *cabildo* climbed a sacred mountain each year to ritually refresh the staffs of office carried by its members. The ceremony ensured the well-being of the community and the integrity of its *cabildo*. The entire *cabildo*, accompanied by shamans, spent the night atop the mountain, burying their staffs of office there. Approximately a month later, or when the signs were right, the staffs were unearthed and taken home for use on political occasions.

Staff-refreshing ritually opened the political year of the *cabildo*. The ceremony, while linked to *cabildos*, was not necessarily conducted at a single site in each *resguardo*. For example, there are several staff-refreshing mountains in the *resguardo* of Vitoncó, each of which was used by the *cabildo* members that lived below its peaks. Not only were communities divided by this practice, but portions of *resguardos* were also united with neighboring political units that refreshed their staffs on the same mountains. Thus, the ceremony cut across political affiliations, fostering a broader political unity among Tierradentro's small *resguardos*.

In the more distant past, staff-refreshings were confined to two regional sites. The southern Páez travelled to Santa Rosa Lake and the northerners, to Juan Tama Lake. These earlier ritual foci grouped communities according to their colonial affiliations. More recent staff-refreshing centers, in contrast, created multiple foci that cut across colonial *cacicazgo* territories. Moreover, they are not necessarily historically-loaded sites, although they lie along political boundaries.

The staff-refreshing ceremony was not a mnemonic device for recalling an historical event. Nor was it a means of legitimizing the

Figure 4   Páez coat of arms

historicity of a place. It was, instead, a means of *extending* the scope of historical referents, investing local mountains with the history already retained by regional sacred precincts. It turned local boundaries into historically-significant markers, allowing the local community to share more completely in a regional history. Because historicity was not permanently invested in these mountains through documents or physical reminders, such as unique rock formations, it had to be periodically reasserted through ritual.

The staff-refreshing ceremony was revived in the 1980s by the Indian movement. CRIC sponsored pilgrimages to Juan Tama Lake, where some *cabildos* enacted the ritual collectively. The Movement of the Southwest reintroduced the ceremony through activities associated with political icons, such as a coat of arms (Fig. 4). The Páez logo depicts a hand holding a staff of office, superimposed over a circle containing a mountain-range. The circle is said to represent *resguardo* boundaries and the mountain range, the sacred peaks in which historical information is lodged. The hand holding the staff of office represents the *cabildo* united in struggle, like the fingers of a hand. The coat of arms is carried by Páez activists to political meetings and from community to community in marches and demonstrations.

The coat of arms can be understood as a regional extension of the traditional ritual of refreshing the *cabildo*'s staffs of office. Like the staff-refreshing ceremony which revalidated the historicity of sacred precincts, the logo also expands historically-loaded space by creating its own "movable sacred precinct." Movement through space with this innovative but traditional symbol lends a broader regional significance to localized sacred geographies which encode the history of individual *resguardos*. Beyond the strictly Páez sphere, the shield is used in demonstrations as distant as Cali, thereby creating Páez space far beyond the borders of Páezdom and underlining the greater right that the Páez claim by virtue of their status as the first Americans. A very simple innovation, the new symbol permits the continuation of a distant mode of interpreting the past within a new national context.

7

Julio Niquinás, a contemporary Páez historian

In 1971 and 1972, the Comité de Defensa del Indio conducted a series of Spanish-language interviews in the hamlet of El Cabuyo, *resguardo* of Vitoncó, with an aged activist, Julio Niquinás, who was well-known in the area as a good storyteller. Niquinás was an activist, conscious of the totality of the Páez world. He had been an associate of Quintín Lame as well as a close friend of José Gonzalo Sánchez, indigenous Communist Party organizer. He was believed to be a descendant of the culture hero Juan Tama. His narrations interweave historical information acquired through reading and discussion with non-Indians, with the traditional Páez patterns of historical understanding examined in the previous chapter, and clearly display his creativity and his agile interpretive abilities. Moreover, the stories demonstrate that Páez history is not a set of texts, but a constant movement between oral and written modes of expression, constantly altered by the knowledge and experience of the narrator and the context in which narration takes place.

Julio Niquinás' narrations are not simple repetitions of texts that he heard earlier. They are complex fabrics woven as the storyteller interacts with his listeners: they are negotiations with an audience (Blount 1975) that on the one hand, is cognizant of the broad configurations of the stories he recounts and of the images he paints and on the other, eagerly awaits the new descriptions and interpretations of this master storyteller. They accomplish in the narrative sphere what Niquinás' compatriots effect through ritual and icon.

In this chapter we will examine these samples of Páez historical thought in action. The conversations will be analyzed for the images they deftly interweave, the general contours in which historical thought emerges, the narrative patterns by which the histories are governed, their relationship to earlier histories, both written and oral, as well as the topography of the narrator's home.

THE HISTORIAN

Julio Niquinás, Cabuyeño and, according to some in Tierradentro, descendant of Juan Tama, was born in Tierradentro shortly before the War of the Thousand Days, in about 1893. He was a child at the turn of the century, observer and participant in the nineteenth century's last great civil war:

At that time I was like this little one, what else? I couldn't shoot because the guns were too heavy. But I sure did go everywhere with the soldiers. I was like a rabbit running. Yessir, I know war, I've been with soldiers. [Q: Were there many Indians?] Yessir, but little ones don't get hit by bullets; it's dangerous for the adults. [Rosalino] Yajimbo[1] had few soldiers and he was confronting thousands of government soldiers, yes. And we suffered a lot here during wartime. They destroyed all the houses, burned them, yes. But even that didn't stop them being Liberals.   (AFCN/C 1972a)

While Niquinás was too immature to serve as a soldier, his siblings were of fighting age: little Julio's brother fought in the war and went on to participate in the guerrilla forces that sprung up in post-war Tierradentro, while Julio himself was a guard for the irregular forces. His memories of the guerrilla war are vivid:

There were guerrillas here. Later there were only a few, just Víctor Mulcué one, Jacinto Mulcué two, Manuel Santos Hurtado three, Sergio Güeya four, Severo five. Who was the other one? Manuel from Honda's father. There were very few here. In San José one Isidro Muse, a Manuel Pacho, Francisco Pacho – there were about four from San José, very few. In La Troja, Manuel Cayoy, Jesús Ramos, Sebastián Ramos, José Yajimbo and Bernabé Calambás – he was the leader there. In Vitoncó, Carlos Gutiérrez, Venancio Fince, Manuel Fince, Joaquín Titicué, Juan Menza and Juan Yandy. There were very few, all told about forty soldiers. And they made horrible parades, the little pricks! That's all. [Q: In what year?] In 1901 and 1902. There was an attack. Yessir. I remember it so well. [Q: How were they armed?] With rifles. At one time they didn't have any rifles; the poor bastards defended themselves with sticks. So many good arms around and the poor guys fought with sticks. It was horrible. And even so, they marched and made a scandal and the people thought they were armed, but they weren't. Finally, when Juan Cloromiro Castillo came with the blacks he left them five rifles. With those five rifles, they made other rifles. Once, here in Cabuyo, Yajimbo caught 70 soldiers. With four soldiers and two behind, six, and the women and children making a scene: they thought there were a lot of Reds [Liberals], but they were ruined. But of the strongest ones, seven fell... Yajimbo was wounded and Juan Nepomuceno Saldarriaga from Medellín, he was black, he was a fierce one, he was short like you but damn it, he was a tough bastard! And when those Indians won they would make a dance, and I was a guard, watching for the enemy. They danced and I watched for the coming of the enemy. Yessir, there were a lot of bullets here! The damned skirmishes... right here on this slope, and they killed them; they even used rocks. Those Indians sure were strong! But who knows today with these youths, whether there are young people to take up arms if a war breaks out, yessir.   (ibid.)

Niquinás was an ardent Liberal at an early age, working for the party by the time he was 12; his political persuasion colors all his memories, including his feelings for Quintín Lame, who was a Conservative.

Niquinás did not have much of a childhood. Brought up in wartime Tierradentro, he did not play at soldiers: he was one. His mother died when he was a child, and like so many others, economic circumstance forced him to leave school before second grade, and to work for the family. Niquinás was thus a self-taught literate. He was fluent in Spanish at an early age and as an adolescent, served as an interpreter for white traders from Belalcázar and Silvia who passed through Tierradentro.

From the time of the civil wars through the *Quintinada*, Julio Niquinás, along with many of his compatriots, was a follower of the indigenous *caudillo* Rosalino Yajimbo. According to Niquinás, the Indians followed Yajimbo because he was a *caudillo*, and they continued to heed his command when he federated with the Lamista forces:

> [Q: Why did the people follow Yajimbo? Was he a *cacique* or something?] A colonel. [Q: A colonel in the army?] In the war. And since they'd already declared war, he started to lead us, believing that maybe this way Mr. Manuel Quintín Lame would become a Liberal, along with all the other Indians. That's it: he thought he would swell the ranks of Liberalism. [Q: So with the Indians, he wanted to take revenge for the Conservatives having won in the Thousand Days?] Yes, yes, yes, that's what happened. It's good to take hold of the story! That's it exactly! Yessir (AFCN/C 1971a)

Niquinás did not consider himself a follower of Lame, but of Yajimbo, and did not even know the sharecropper from Polindara until after Lame, Yajimbo and he were arrested in 1917 in the governmental backlash following the 1916 massacre in Inzá.

Quintín Lame remained imprisoned for three years after his 1917 arrest, accompanied by Niquinás, who became an interpreter for the Indians on trial, as well as Lame's secretary. Until then, Niquinás did not know Lame:

> I was not directly with [Lame], no? I was with Yajimbo... Since I could more or less write, keep accounts, all of that, they called me and they grabbed me in Popayán, because they needed me to work as a secretary. I said I didn't know how because I was still only a boy then. That's how life goes. That's how I met Mr. Quintín Lame. Then later I became his friend and we continued working. (ibid.)

As Lame's secretary, Niquinás learned to draw up legal documents, taking dictation from the *caudillo*.

During his prison years, Niquinás also grew to know José

Gonzalo Sánchez, who was at that time one of Lame's associates. Once the *Quintinada* was over, Sánchez travelled to the Soviet Union to study. Upon his return he began to organize Peasant Leagues among the Páez. Niquinás collaborated in the Communist organizing drive until generalized persecution decimated its ranks.

During the 1930s Niquinás also prospected for gold in the company of his German *compadre*, Eduardo Aloz. This association increased his awareness of international events; during the course of the interviews, he frequently mentions Hitler with regard to the dangers of war.

A Lamista and a Peasant League activist, Julio Niquinás was a target during the Violencia and was forced to leave Tierradentro, spending three years in the Cauca Valley.

Although Niquinás was never governor of his *resguardo* – because, he claims, he would have had to drink too much *chicha*, and alcohol was one of his weaknesses – he continued to participate in politics until his death in 1971, confronting the Monsignor of Tierradentro, Enrique Vallejo, and demanding that a school be built in Cabuyo, as well as supporting the nascent CRIC and fighting for Indian unity.

THE STORIES

Contours of the interviews

The Julio Niquinás interviews were conducted by Víctor Daniel Bonilla between July 1971 and August 1972, in Tierradentro. They were conversations as opposed to lengthy narrations, interviewer continually confronting narrator, forcing him to clarify points, raise up new memories, tell the complete story. Páez observers listened to these conversations, adding their own two cents: "He's telling the truth," "I know that story." In the earlier interviews, Niquinás claimed to know little of some stories. Later, as trust grew with his interviewers, he spoke openly and in more detail.

Unlike many of my own interlocutors, Julio Niquinás was a skilled historian. He did not repeat stories, he formed them. Throughout the transcripts he comments, "Yessir. I have lots of stories. Don't you see that we are forming stories?" (AFCN/C 1971a). Julio Niquinás' comments indicate that true history is a dialogue, an interpretation of the past within a particular social context, not a simple repetition of facts. This is especially clear in a series of stories he wove regarding the Spanish invasion.

The stories

Niquinás' knowledge of the mythical *caciques* came to the fore only after the interviewer asked him to share some of this wisdom. Sandwiched between accounts of the War of the Thousand Days and of the *Quintinada*, the stories contrasted with his personal reminiscences. Chock-full of details as are his own memories, his *cacique* tales are elegant, following one after another in a clear and symmetrical structure. While some will be new to the reader, containing only brief references to patterns we have already come to know, others present new twists on familiar models. Among these is Niquinás' rendition of the triumph of Juan Tama over Calambás:

[Q: The story of the *cacique* Fontana [Juan Tama] as told by Don Julio.] Who knows if the *caciques* or the Guambianos were sent before the *cacica* or the *cacique* realized it, because their last name was Calambás. So the Páez children were taken away, and the children were taken from their mothers. Then the Páez Indians became furious, and the *cacique* rose up against the *cacique* lords and there were wars. So as not to leave [Tierradentro], they made war. There were six years of war, did you know that? And they fought with slings. They collected stones from all over, stones from the river...and they killed each other. At the end of the six years, old Fontana won... The definitive battle took place in front of the village of Jambaló, where there is level ground, and that's where it ended. Yessir, that's the story... I've even seen old, old documents. [Q: Where did you see them?] Here in the village of Vitoncó the *caciques* themselves kept them, all rotting away. I used to say that if they'd saved them, they would've been very useful. [Q: Do any of these documents still exist?] Who knows? I haven't asked for them. Well, Fontana said, this is for only one woman and one man. The rest of the people, those who are not guilty because they were following orders, in that case they should stay right here. And for this reason he said: You don't have to leave for somewhere else. And he left a place on the other side [of the Cordillera], and this is why the Páez Indians don't marry the *Casucos* [Guambiano], and the *Casucos* don't permit marriage with Páez men or women, and it's respected nowadays, no? They respected each other. [Q: and now they marry?] Now they have to marry because civilization arrived and no more of that foolishness, right? They can marry. That's the story: six years of war. It's rough. (AFCN/C 1971b)

A year later, Don Julio made the weave of the tale more complex by including his own interpretation of the story of La Gaitana and of the Spanish conqueror Sebastián de Benalcázar's missions in Tierradentro. The story appeared in conjunction with his memories of the death of his brother following the War of the Thousand Days:

He was fighting General Uribe at Palonegro. After the Liberals were defeated, my brother came home and started another guerrilla group here and he finally died here at Segovia. [Q: The Páez have been great warriors. Before the Thousand Days, do you know any stories from the last century?] I don't know any, just stories of the *caciques* and things. Yes, we know that, about Juan Tama, with the *cacica* Calambás of the *Casucos*, those fighters: they're Peruvians. There was an invasion from Peru and old Juan Tama made war. There were six years of war. And after six years Juan Tama beat them and the rest died in the war. Its center was in Silvia. That's that. [Q: Was that before or after the Spanish arrival?] It was after the Spaniards.

(AFCN/C 1972a)

On the heels of his skeletal repetition of the battle of San José Lake, comes a new periodization of history, a temporal scheme at whose center lies the *cacica* Gaitana:

[Q: And what did the *cacica* do?] The *cacica* is an older story... Cayetana, when they made the First Independence. [Q: The First Independence, how's that?] That was because the old woman had a son, Prince Güiponga. That Güiponga was very rich. He was going to marry – he was very young – a very beautiful Indian woman. And all the Indians congregated in Avirama: that's where they were. Well, Pedro Ñasco was in the same village and he sent a commission to call the old lady and the prince to come to him. Prince Güiponga arrived there, and then: "Listen son, you have to tell me where you have your treasures. With that harvest, you'll save yourself." That's what Mr. Ñasco told him. So the Indian answered that he was poor: what did he have to pay with? what was he going to turn over? They got together a lot of wood, a burnt offering, damn it: they burned him alive. He was burning here [points to part of body]. "How do you feel, Indian?" "Just fine." What do you think? He's like a flower. And in the end he burned up. The old lady flew into a rage, damn it. She ran off. They were watching the young man burn, and they forgot about the old lady. She just bolted. That old lady walked for three days in Avirama! Well, Güiponga's bride died of sorrow and there was no wedding... Well, after Mr. Ñasco and his soldiers finished the party, there in Wila... Have you been to Wila? [Q: No, not yet.] In Wila there's a place called Caloto where the Spanish had their churches. What a pretty piece of ground! Well, the woman organized around Tacueyó and all those places where there were lots of Indians. There were 250,000 Indians. One day they got together and were preparing themselves. It was on a Sunday, not Saturday, because they were Adventists. When... [the Spaniards] were in church... [the Indians] fell on them. They killed the Spaniards. And they said not to kill Pedro Ñasco. They said they shouldn't hurt him. They caught him and gave him to the *cacica*. She had a gold tray and a stone awl. And she said: "Oh, here you are, Don Pedro! Tie him up well!" They tied him up and they held the golden tray and – tas! – they took out his eye and the other eye. And they gave him the gold tray and they said: "Is it tasty? How do you feel?" The poor man had no eyes. Then they tied him up and walked him all over, where all the Indians were. After two weeks of suffering, he died. The man died. Well, there were thousands of Indians who had to eat a little bit of meat. They skinned him but didn't throw away even a little piece of bone. They had to save them as relics. They saved all the bones. Then she said: "*Caciques*, chiefs, keep in mind that these are the greatest enemies of your race. You must roast these bones." They put some grease in a pot and roasted it all on the fire and ground it up, damn it! It turned into ashes. And then in front of all those people, she jumped into the Páez River and said: "Get out of here! Go to Spain! I don't want to see you! May the river take you and leave you in Spain!" That's what the old lady said. (ibid.)

From the story of La Gaitana, Niquinás shifts gears to recount the battle of the Páez and Sebastián de Belalcázar[2] at the Peñón de Tálaga, weaving the two tales into a single fabric:

[Q: What was the *cacica*'s full name?] Gaitana, no? That's all. That's the story. Do you remember that little story? [Q: Yes, but not in detail.] Well, Sebastián de Belalcázar was in Popayán. He came with 500 Spaniards to catch the old lady. He thought it was only the old lady, but there were thousands of Indians, just beyond [the town of] Belalcázar, where there's a little spring. There they [the Spaniards] camped for the night and the Indians planned to fall on them. That was in from Guadualta. And when he was surrounded he discovered, damn it, that he [Belalcázar] was surrounded by Indians. They [the Spaniards] shot some bullets. And the old lady thought: "That's it. Kill the Spaniards. They can kill all of us, but we'll finish them off. They'll finish us off or we'll finish them." And that woman flew into a rage. Belalcázar, damn it, Sebastián... And if he didn't work quickly, they [the Indians] would eat him [Belalcázar]. Because Belalcázar was angry, the name stuck [to the place]. But once it was called Pueblito ["Small Town"]. That's the story. And then a century and a half later, they [the Spaniards] returned from Spain and [the Indians] hid all the riches, the salt mines, the goldmines. The Indians ordered that the mines be covered up. Now we know what gold is worth, because when the Spanish came, damn it, the Indians sent them some gold. Instead of following the Indians, the Spaniards fought over the gold, ha, ha, ha, ha! In Honda, [the Spaniards] ordered [the Indians] to be killed, because gold's important and the Indians saw that it was worth something, because [the Spaniards] fought over it. So [the Indians] ordered it to be hidden. That's why here in Colombia, they hid the gold. There's a lot in Wila. Just in time. Who knows where they left it? There were 200,000 workers. Where did [the Indians] bury it? Where in the world did they cover it up? Who'll look for it now? They talk about the Treasure of Tumbichucue. It's there, but who knows where! I don't even know. That's why you have to look, but who knows where in those mountains! It's difficult...looking for it. And they've looked there. Look at Caca Negra[3]...looking for it. And he was with a German, spending money. It was my *compadre*, Eduardo Aloz. That's how I know... Yes, it's only a short story, but a good one.

Ending this lengthy narration is a brief rendition of the story of Juan Tama Lake:

[Q: And the one about... I've heard that there are some stories about a lake up there.] Ah, that's Juan Tama Lake. They say that Juan Tama bathed there and that he left offerings there, but who could ever look there! The lake is very big. They wanted to go search there but you can only search in summer because in the winter it's too cold – even here [in Cabuyo] it's cold. Yessir.   (ibid.)

Reading Niquinás' history

The series of stories recounted by Julio Niquinás parallels a number of historical accounts, which the narrator might have read at one time or heard recounted by another:

1 The Tama-Calambás battle: Niquinás rendition of the story of San José Lake closely parallels Don Juan Tama's own version in the title to Vitoncó (ACC/P 1883). Lacking in detail, the eighteenth-century *cacique* claimed to have battled an alien *cacique*, Calambás, who had attacked him, and to have won the war, thereby banishing Calambás' followers to the Piendamó River, now Guambía. Niquinás was well-versed in the colonial version of his tale, having read it as he perused ancient documents.

2 The Belalcázar missions: Sebastián de Benalcázar entered Tierradentro in 1537, supported by 200 Spanish soldiers. He was routed at the Peñón de Tálaga and 26 of his strongest combatants were killed by Páez warriors. He retreated to Popayán via the Páramo de Santo Domingo and the Palo River (Simón 1982: 233). A year later, the founder of Popayán accompanied Juan de Ampudia and Pedro de Añasco to the east to found the cities of Neiva and Timaná (ibid: 235).

3 La Gaitana: An elaborate mythology of Añasco's pacification of the Indians of Timaná began to develop in the early years of the colonial era. While contemporary documents give few details of Añasco's battles with the Indians (Friede 1953), a number of chronicles (Castellanos 1944; Simón 1982) weave a stirring tale of battle and intrigue, centering on La Gaitana, the Indian chieftainess who triumphed over Pedro de Añasco. The tale is well-known throughout southern Colombia, commemorated in a statue of the Gaitana in the city of Neiva. The story runs that the Gaitana was a great *cacica* with many followers. When Pedro de Añasco arrived in Timaná, he sent for her son, who he burned alive. In retaliation for the murder of her son, the Gaitana organized several thousand Indian warriors from the Páez, Pirama and Guanacas nations to do battle with Añasco, who was taken prisoner and turned over to the *cacica*. In the Spanish myth, an elaborate tale of the death of Añasco is spun: he is said to have been brutally tortured, his eyes removed and a rope strung under his tongue; he was led in this way from town to town, until he finally expired. But before attaining the peace of the grave, he was dismembered, limb by limb, by his Indian captors. Further battles with the indigenous forces followed the death of the brutal Spanish captain.

Full of Páez images and articulated into a unique sequence, the Niquinás tales transform these historical facts and myths, building upon the patterns that characterize the oral tradition and producing a novel and creative interpretation of the past.

Detail

Julio Niquinás' stories differ from their colonial forebears as well as from the traditions of other contemporary storytellers in the sheer wealth of detail they offer. The episodes are all grounded in specific topographic sites: Juan Tama's battle with Calambás takes place on a plain in front of Jambaló; the *cacica* met with her Indian forces in the village of Avirama, organized many thousand warriors in Tacueyó and fell upon Añasco at Caloto, Wila, throwing his ashes into the waters of the Páez River; Sebastián de Belalcázar did battle with the Gaitana at a stream behind the modern site of Belalcázar. Only the location of the treasure of Tumbichucue is not divulged: if Niquinás knew its whereabouts, he would certainly not reveal it to a tape recorder manned by non-Indians! A skilled storyteller, Niquinás paints a vivid picture of the geographic backdrop of historical events, evoking in knowledgeable listeners precise images grounded in the familiar topography of Tierradentro. Through this detail, he recreates the sacred geography from which his story can be read and expanded in the minds of his listeners.

Similarly, considerable detail is provided regarding the actions of the stories' heroes. We learn that Güiponga was wealthy and that a beautiful woman was promised him, that his mother was old; that Tama's war with Calambás lasted six years and was fought with slings; that the Gaitana organized 250,000 Indians to make war on Añasco and that Belalcázar had only 500 soldiers; that 200,000 Indians were needed to hide the Páez treasure from the Spaniards. This detail, some of which is reflected in other accounts and some of which is a product of Niquinás' fertile imagination, paints a reality, a tangible series of events to be imagined by his audience. Image is strengthened by the inclusion of dialogue, bringing Niquinás' heroes and villains to life. The dialogue is reminiscent of Lame's *Los pensamientos*, which also uses speech to drive a point home.

The bare skeletons of the narrations are indeed historical. They speak of relationships between Páez and Spaniard, between Guambiano and Páez. They reflect the military superiority of the Indians, the Europeans' lack of knowledge of aboriginal tactics, the

founding of Spanish settlements and their destruction by Indian
warriors, the existence of riches below the soil of Tierradentro and
the Indians' inability to exploit them autonomously. But the details
are fantastic, evoking images from other stories, bringing historical
facts to life through metaphor. All Páez oral tradition achieves this
goal, although the picture it paints is pale in comparison to
Niquinás' brilliant canvas.

Chronology

No numerical dates are employed in these stories, although the
duration of some events – three days, two weeks, six years, a century
and a half – is defined. Episodes relating the Gaitana's confrontations
with Añasco and with Belalcázar are sandwiched between accounts
of Juan Tama. The chronology of the narrative, specified at several
points in the course of the interview, does not correspond to the
order in which the episodes are recounted:

Order of episodes	*Chronology*
1 Juan Tama	1 Gaitana vs. Añasco
2 Gaitana vs. Añasco	2 Gaitana vs. Belalcázar
3 Gaitana vs. Belalcázar	3 Juan Tama
4 Juan Tama	

Lack of fit between the narrated order and the assumed chronology
was not determined by the interviewer's questions; Niquinás was
given ample leeway to spin his own tales. On the contrary, the
incongruence is intentional. The actions of La Gaitana, which do not
form a regular part of the oral tradition, are grounded in the more
accessible Juan Tama story, well-known to all Páez listeners. Two
episodes of Juan Tama's life are narrated: his battle with Calambás
and his travels to Juan Tama Lake. Although the two are distinct
episodes, they also reflect one another. In the first story, Tama
battles with the Guambiano, who kill Páez children in order to
extract offerings from the lake – this last bit of information would be
understood by the knowledgeable listener. In the second, the *cacique*
returns the offerings to the waters. The second episode is an
inversion of the first, effectively framing the Gaitana story against a
familiar backdrop.

There is yet another reason for the non-chronological nature of the narration, one which derives from the periodization employed by Niquinás. As Europeans, we have constructed our own periodization of Latin American history: the Conquest, the colonial era, Independence, the Republican period, the modern era. Julio Niquinás demonstrates that from the Indian perspective, this periodization is in error because it is European-focused. To call the Spanish invasion a conquest is to admit defeat. To label the creation of the Colombian nation a flowering of independence is to deny that indigenous autonomy was relinquished at this time. While colonial chroniclers decried the barbarities committed by the Páez against the Spaniards, the Indians themselves perceive them as celebrations of victory. The Gaitana's triumphs are a "First Independence" for Julio Niquinás because they are a first step towards regaining indigenous autonomy. How better could this pivotal step be framed than by the actions of Juan Tama, who drew a map of the road to future autonomy through the creation of the *resguardo*?

Images

The stories of Juan Tama and the Gaitana are remarkable for the diversity of images they contain, their references to other historical traditions, only tangentially related to the narrative. The density of Niquinás' imagery underlines the importance of cross-referencing in Páez historical thought. In his narratives this almost takes the form of the "formulaic utterances" known to Greek and Old English scholars:

Simple common sense tells us that an audience used to Homeric verse and listening to a performer composing or reciting the sixth book of the *Odyssey* would be affected, consciously or otherwise, by the formulaic epithet "white-armed," which serves here to describe King Alcinous' cute young daughter... but which we know from the *Iliad* to be associated with Queen Helen, whose regal beauty is such that she is easily mistaken for one of the immortal goddesses. (Renoir 1986: 104–105)

Páez cross-referencing, though, is equally practiced in the non-narrative sphere, particularly in the sacred geography, where the experience of a single sacred precinct will bring to mind a broad array of historical referents that are attached to the site or to neighboring ones linked by vision or ritual.

The Niquinás narratives incorporate a number of images linking the various episodes together, others bringing to mind associations with other stories and rituals, and yet others that draw up personal reminiscences of the past hundred years. Some of Don Julio's images succeed at several of these levels at once.

The Juan Tama–Gaitana–Belalcázar sequence reconstructs the ancient political unity of the Páez nation, much as does the ritual in which the *cabildo*'s staffs of office are refreshed. If we plot out the locations of the events recounted by Julio Niquinás, the territory encompassed in the narratives comprises the three great *cacicazgos* of the colonial era. To the northwest, Tacueyó and Jambaló are cited: in Tacueyó, Niquinás has the Gaitana organizing the Indians against Añasco; in Jambaló, Tama fights his battle with Calambás. To the north, Añasco is murdered in Wila in an episode that is more reminiscent of the Páez destruction of La Plata than of the Gaitana story of the colonial chronicles. Güiponga, Gaitana's son, is murdered in Avirama, to the south. Also in the southern sector, Sebastián de Belalcázar is defeated by Gaitana's hosts.

The individual episodes also evoke images of events. One of the unique details included in Niquinás' rendition of the Tama–Calambás battle is the use of slings and stones to vanquish the Guambiano forces. This brings to mind another battle, in which Llíban kills all the Pijao within reach of his sling. The Indians' burial of their riches at the second coming of Belalcázar conveys the image of capitulation to Spanish rule, along with an extended period of waiting before independence can once again be enjoyed. It is not difficult to imagine this episode and associate it with two other occasions on which the Indians buried something for safekeeping: the disappearance of the *caciques* into highland lakes at the close of the colonial period and the hiding of *resguardo* titles in these same bodies of water during the War of the Thousand Days. On a more factual level, the explanation provided by the narrator for the changing of Pueblito's name to Belalcázar is reminiscent of the not-so-distant past, when Republican legislation created *zonas de población* within Tierradentro's *resguardos*, as well as the establishment of the missionary bishopric at the turn of the century. Niquinás points to a transition in the nature of the town, much as the legislative measures effected wide-reaching changes in the nature of the municipal center, transformations lived by many of Niquinás' listeners.

The death of Pedro de Añasco, in particular, contains a number of signposts pointing to other Páez tales more central to the *cacique* tradition and to the personal experience of the audience. These "formulaic utterances" are, for the most part but not exclusively, included in his description of Añasco's death. Whereas colonial chroniclers do not elaborate on the Indians' treatment of the conqueror's remains, confining their attentions to the graphic description of the tortures he suffered before finally dying, Niquinás fashions an additional episode which treats this theme in considerable detail. His rewriting of the events that transpired after Añasco's death creates an opening for the incorporation of precisely those images that will elicit associations with other tales.

To recapitulate this portion of the story: Pedro de Añasco, having undergone two weeks of torture, including the extraction of his eyes and display of his bondage throughout the territory, finally expires. His flesh is cut into thousands of pieces which are consumed by the Indians. His bones are roasted and ground into ashes which are thrown into the Páez River and commanded to return to Spain.

The cutting to pieces of Añasco's corpse[4] is reminiscent of the death of the *cacique*-turned-serpent, the fragments of whose body, moreover, are thrown into the river, much like Añasco's bones. The removal of his bones from Tierradentro suggests the danger of other bones which lie buried in Páez territory: the bones of the ancient Pijao, that cause sickness among those who occupy homes built over these burials. Most striking is the Gaitana's act of hurling Añasco's bones into the Páez River, thus sending them off to Spain. This is reminiscent of another series of events that took place along the banks of the Páez, near Wila: the deaths of Guequiáu, Guainás and of Tóens, all of whom were carried away by this powerful river.

But other portions of Niquinás' recounting of the death of Añasco also incorporate images of oral traditions and personal experience. Colonial chroniclers highlight the extraction of the Spanish soldier's eyes, which is duly described by the Páez narrator. Despite its Spanish origins, this image takes on an added significance before a Páez audience. In some instances I have recorded, when an enemy is killed his eyes are removed from his corpse so that he cannot find his murderer and take revenge for his death. Thus, from a Páez perspective it is very fitting that Añasco be blinded. Other personal reminiscences are also stimulated by this episode. Primary among them is the memory of the War of the Thousand Days, where prisoners were hurled into the river by the Páez irregular forces led by Yajimbo, much as were Añasco's bones. The notion of the Gaitana war as a "First Independence" brings to mind the series of wars remembered as having followed the "Second Conquest," or the creation of the Colombian state. These wars would be remembered by Páez listeners as a single conflict, the War of the Thousand Days.

There are also crosscutting images in these episodes that refer the listener from one episode to another. In the first narrative, Tama defeats the Guambiano, who had transgressed by making offerings of Páez children. In the final episode, Tama himself makes offerings to Juan Tama Lake. Between these two Tama sequences, similar offerings are repeatedly referred to: Güiponga is asked to turn over his treasures to the Spanish conquerors and as he refuses, is burned alive; before Belalcázar's return to Tierradentro, 200,000 Indians bury these very treasures to hide them from the Europeans. Similarly, the killing of Páez children by the Guambiano is reminiscent of the cannibalism that disposes of Añasco's remains. Finally, when Añasco's body is cut into pieces, we think of the ceremony in which bread-babies are broken in pieces, dipped in *chicha* and eaten, a ritual which is itself reminiscent of the final battle of Calambás with the great chief Juan Tama. Before being eaten, these babies are "baptized" by Páez actors, evoking the memory of the transformation of unbaptized *caciques* into snakes.

Just as the sacred geography of Tierradentro evokes images of Páez history, Julio Niquinás' tales elicit memories of these same stories. Niquinás' creativity stems from his ability to interweave these familiar images with less well-known stories that are not a central part of the oral tradition. Ritual practice utilizes the relationship between geography and historical referents to create new sacred spaces that, through ceremony, embody the history of the Páez people, even if only for a short time. The mark of a great Páez historian is the achievement of a similar flexibility through the cross-referencing of images in narrative, permitting the incorporation of new tales and the interpretation of new events within a common framework. This is what Julio Niquinás achieves.

Pattern and interpretation

The cross-referencing of images so aptly executed by Julio Niquinás is structured by a coherent pattern, only partially apparent in the oral traditions of other storytellers. The central focus of his story, the death of Añasco, is reminiscent of the deaths of *caciques*-turned-serpents and of Tóens. Here, it is sandwiched between two *cacique* stories that frame the less familiar narrative, producing a ring sequence reminiscent of the form of Homeric, Old English and Yugoslav traditions (Lord 1986). If we list Don Julio's episodes, the sequence can be folded over itself, so that the episodes mirror each other as they advance toward and away from the central story:

Episode 1: Juan Tama fights and routs his Peruvian enemies
           (understood: they are stealing his gold)
Episode 2: Güiponga's marriage festivities are planned
Episode 3: Death of Güiponga at the hand of Añasco
+ Episode 4: Battle with Añasco (the First Independence)
Episode 5: Torture and death of Añasco at the hand of
           Gaitana
Episode 6: Festivities, ingestion of Añasco's remains
Episode 7: Gaitana fights and routs Spaniards, covering up
           Páez riches

The ring sequence is not accidental in Niquinás' account. Jorge
Mulcué Sandoval, another Páez historian and an associate of Don
Julio, tells his own story, strikingly similar in structure although
somewhat different in detail:

Well, I saw a little book about La Gaitana. Pedro Añasco was sent by the King of
Spain to attack the Pijaos who lived in Platavieja and in Pitalito. Well, he came with
30 soldiers from Bogotá to call on Gaitana and to tame her, like when you kill a
sheep. So he ordered that Gaitana be notified. She was at home. Gaitana flew into
a rage and said that she wasn't a white, that she was an Indian, she was from there,
and that she could order Añasco around: "He has to submit to me, because of who
I am. I don't [have to submit to him]." Then he ordered that her son Boiponga be
taken prisoner. Añasco caught Boiponga and hung him up and lit a fire under him.
Ah, the Gaitana became so angry that she made an agreement with all the *caciques*
and armed all those people. Then she said: "Go bring Pedro de Añasco. Bring him
here to me, but don't mistreat him. Just bring him to me." So the Indians caught
him and brought him to Gaitana. She put a chain here and she took out his eyes with
those painted rocks they'd tooled.

Well, the *Cacique* Tumbichucue was chief of Tumbichucue. I think that that treasure
from Platavieja was the treasure of Tumbichucue. It was in a cave they didn't build.
They say the cave was excavated by his Indians at Tumbichucue, for his cathedral.
So the *Cacique* Tumbichucue used the cathedral to live in. Boiponga was *Cacique*
Tumbichucue's son-in-law. In those days, they were going to make a banquet in
Tumbichucue. Chia, the wife, was in Tumbichucue, and she sent for her husband,
who was in Platavieja. The *Cacica* Gaitana was about to come to the Tumbichucue
banquet when they killed Boiponga and that *cacica* died of grief.

Yessir, since then it belongs to the Indians. Don't you see that not even the *Cacica*
Gaitana accepted the whites from Spain? If they'd let them, this place would be full
of Spaniards. Not even we Indians would be here. We would have become slaves,
because that's what the whites want.

I tell you: the *Cacica* Gaitana armed her Indians and all the caciques. She armed
them with stone lances. Here in Platavieja there was a big cathedral, the church.
Don't they say that if the Indians hadn't looted it, it would be the richest church
in Colombia? They came at 6 or 5.30 in the morning. They came in when the whites

were in mass. When all the patrons had come to mass, the cook who'd stayed at home cooking came out and saw that all around the town there were many Indians covered with branches: their faces covered, all around the town. They were half way through the mass when the Indians finished them off. The Indians came in and killed all the whites, except for the priest. They didn't kill him, but led him by a rope and said to all the Indians: "This white meat shouldn't be thrown out. It should be sliced up and dried to eat." And that's what they did. Don't they say that human meat tastes like pork? Well, they decapitated him and came back with the riches of the church of Tumbichucue. How many Indians there were, stretching from Platavieja to Tumbichucue! Passing the stolen gold from hand to hand from Platavieja to the cathedral of Tumbichucue. They passed it in their hands. And Pedro Añasco, with 30 soldiers sent by the King of Spain to tame the *Cacique* Tumbichucue... If they'd only let them be, they wouldn't have done wrong to the whites.

(AFCN/C 1972b)

Mulcué's account, which I will not analyze in any detail, is as symmetrical as is Niquinás', but its centerpiece is not the death of Añasco. Instead, it pivots around the construction of Tumbichucue. The structure of Mulcué's narration is as follows:

Episode 1: Añasco travels from Bogotá to Platavieja to tame the Indians
Episode 2: Añasco murders Boiponga
Episode 3: Gaitana organizes the Indians
Episode 4: Torture of Añasco
+ *Episode 5*: Excavation of Tumbichucue
Episode 6: Death of Boiponga
Episode 7: Gaitana organizes the Indians
Episode 8: Torture of priest at Platavieja
Episode 9: Transport of Platavieja treasure to Tumbichucue[5]

What is special about Mulcué's version of the Gaitana story is that it recapitulates the sacred geography of Tierradentro in its narrative order. The story begins to the north in Bogotá, moving south to Platavieja and ends by moving in the opposite direction, northward from Platavieja to Tumbichucue. At the sequential and geographic center lies Tumbichucue, the pivot of the other episodes. Mulcué's ring structure, therefore, is organized around the sacred geography, whose center is Tumbichucue, that encodes his episodes, much like the historical memory is structured by Tierradentro's broken topography.

The close relationship between the ring structure of Mulcué's narration and Tierradentro's geography, sheds light on aspects of Julio Niquinás' longer story, where the same identity between geography and narrative structure appears. Niquinás begins his story in the Páramo de Moras, where Juan Tama defeats the Guambiano. He then moves to the southeast, to Avirama, where Añasco confronts Gaitana and her son. The Spanish conqueror is tortured and killed in Wila. Niquinás then shifts to the environs of Avirama where, on the opposite bank of the Páez River, Gaitana battles Belalcázar. The final, brief story of Juan Tama Lake takes the listener back to the Páramo de Moras.

In this skeletal form, geography does not appear to recapitulate Niquinás' ring sequence. There seems to be a glaring error in the narrative structure: instead of moving neatly from northwest to southeast and back, the center of the narration takes place in Wila, to the north of Avirama and Belalcázar. Here, it is useful to return to the details of Niquinás' story, for his version of the death of Añasco more closely resembles chronicle descriptions of the Páez assault on La Plata, than the Spanish variant of the Gaitana tale. Read from this perspective, the central episode takes place in the far southeast, the narrative action moving toward the southeast and back. Thus, Niquinás recreates the mythical chain of human beings, carrying treasures to Tumbichucue from Pitayó in the northwest and La Plata in the southeast; he also retraces the axis of his people's historical migration. By restructuring his chronology, Don Julio posits an identity between geography and history, reproducing in narrative form the spatial referents that organize Páez historical consciousness.

Other narrators are not capable of producing the geographic structure inherent in the stories of Julio Niquinás and Jorge Mulcué. Their command of the sacred geography is more piecemeal and their knowledge of events outside of the oral tradition is more limited.

Why are Julio Niquinás and Jorge Mulcué so special? What facilitated the development of their interpretive skill? I would suggest that apart from Niquinás' obvious talent at narration and interpretation, his gift was nurtured by political experience in the civil wars, in the *Quintinada* and in the Peasant Leagues. Having lived through and helped to determine the course of these events, Don Julio gained a more global vision of the Páez geography, the Páez past and the Páez future. His overarching perspective aided him in analyzing discrete bits of information and fitting them into a more all-encompassing structure, highly suited to the political juncture and his audience. That is, Niquinás did not tell such good tales just by virtue of being a good storyteller: his tales are good because they were articulated with contemporary political concerns. Thus, to be a good Páez historian, one must have more than a grasp of the past: one must also be capable of articulating past and present in order to change the future. This is what made an historian out of Don Juan Tama and Manuel Quintín Lame, and what permitted this heritage to be carried on by Julio Niquinás.

8

Conclusion: narrative and image in a textual community

We have now come to the end of our anthropological excursion into the lives and thoughts of three men who, while products of their times, were instrumental in maintaining a moral continuity between past and present in an isolated corner of South America. Don Juan Tama, Manuel Quintín Lame and Julio Niquinás can clearly claim a place in the memory of the Páez, but how are their intellectual biographies significant for students of historical thought? The introduction to this book laid out some of the general concerns of historical anthropologists regarding the structure and nature of non-Western historical thought, as well as the various methodologies that can be employed to examine it. This constellation of ideas and theories has been applied to a concrete case in which works of the three indigenous intellectuals were examined in terms of their structure and their symbolic content, the relationship between the images they employ and the political activities through which images were filtered and finally, the nature and availability of channels for communicating these images across time and space. What is the relevance of the Páez case to the analysis of image, narrative and text, the study of literacy and the usefulness of distinguishing myth from history?

THE PAST IN THE PRESENT

The past is only useful insofar as it sheds meaning on the problems of the present. The Páez do not simply reflect on events of the past, they inquire into the relationship between past events and their manifestations in the present. The histories woven by Páez narrators contain time-worn images, but their contents are the product of new social situations and relationships, and the patterns that organize them are products of a gradual process of transformation over the centuries. The intellectuals who produced these histories built upon a range of documentary sources located at the interface of two cultural traditions. On the one hand, they based their interpretations upon legal documents and books written by members of the dominant society. On the other hand, they looked toward personal reminiscences and oral tradition, as well as the sacred geography within which history is cast in Tierradentro. The result was not so much an uncompromised reflection upon the past, as a vehicle for changing the course of history. The Páez are not interested in guarding pristine texts, but in incorporating the knowledge they acquire from the world around them into their reflections upon the events of former times, which in turn, are employed for transforming the present.

Interpretations of the past may be incorporated into a well-known narrative, or, in the hands of a skilled storyteller like Julio Niquinás, might take the form of the weaving of familiar images into a less familiar storyline. Historians like Manuel Quintín Lame disseminated their interpretations in book form, while Don Juan Tama and twentieth-century activists incorporated them into legal documents and judicial proceedings. Páez villagers, on the other hand, will interpret the past as they pass by those topographic sites in which historical referents are encoded.

Among all the varied genres of historical interpretation there are two elements in common: pattern and image. Whether an account be framed in fabulous imagery or cast in a more objective idiom, most Páez accounts refer, at least fleetingly, to images developed in more detail in more well-known stories, and most of these are related at least tangentially, to the *cacique* motif. Thus, for example, Don Juan Tama harked back to the chiefly history of the precolumbian period, summoning his people to draw relationships between the sixteenth-century *cacique* Calambás and their contemporary situation of domination. Quintín Lame drew upon the successes of Juan Tama to frame a more general Indian history in opposition to the history of and by non-Indians. Julio Niquinás produced a string of associations by including references to the Páez assault on La Plata, the deaths of Tóens and of Guainás, the heroic battle of Juan Tama against the Guambiano, all in an account of the death of Pedro de Añasco framed by the story of Juan Tama. These images, some new and some familiar, are contextualized through the use of well-known patterns relating to the life of the mythical *cacique*. Such images do not in themselves constitute full-blown histories; they are but brief references to the past, drawing their power from their articulation with the social and political contexts in which they are applied (Benjamin 1968).

The nature of the Páez' insertion into national structures colors the problems that these histories address, the mix of referents hailing from a range of time-periods, the medium in which the account is expressed. As the nature of the *resguardo* has been transformed, from a large and autonomous political unity to a small, isolated and powerless entity, historical interpretation has itself changed in order to incorporate the contemporary political entity, with an eye to constructing new forms of moral continuity with the past. Thus, we move from Don Juan Tama, who rebuilt the image of the warrior *cacique* into the character of a statesman ruling vast dominions in peacetime; to Manuel Quintín Lame, who reunited and extended Tama's domains by availing himself of presumed genealogical links to the *cacique*-turned-statesman, to be himself transformed into a *caudillo*-turned-*cacique*; and to Julio Niquinás, who by grounding the *cacique* tale in the regional geography, was able to conceptually recreate the conditions of Páez unity necessary for the forging of a pan-Indian organization with international connections. This involved the careful choice of political vehicles for the deployment of historical visions. Although each historian chose the *resguardo* as his starting-point, the nature of the institution was vastly different at each juncture, causing it to be employed distinctly in each period as a tool for achieving political unity: the *resguardo* as a vehicle for establishing territorial boundaries within an eighteenth-century expansionist ideology; *resguardos* as building-blocks for forging Republican military unity; small *resguardos* as components of a modern pan-Indian *cabildo*.

All of the historians we have met have been political activists of one sort or another, and this is not by chance. As a *cacique*, Don Juan Tama enjoyed the allegiance of a broad layer of the aboriginal population, while he also commanded the attentions of the Spanish administration. Of all the colonial *caciques*, he was most effective in interpreting history to contemporary ends, since he consolidated rule over a number of *resguardos*, each in different geographic, economic and political circumstances. Manuel Quintín Lame, by virtue of his civil war experience and his hispanicized upbringing, held a command of the Spanish language and of the history and institutions of the broader society. He understood how to gain

access to the means of communication of his epoch and accurately
appraised the implications of setting his interpretations in writing.
Moreover, like Don Juan Tama, he influenced a vast array of
communities, extending from his own Polindara, on the outskirts of
Popayán, to the more isolated Tierradentro, and finally to the
indigenous communities of the neighboring departments of Tolima
and Huila. Julio Niquinás acquired his command of national politics
and his global vision of the Páez people through his experiences with
Manuel Quintín Lame. Nevertheless, his personal history included
attempts at integration rejected by Lame, including participation in
the Communist Party, collaboration with foreigners in Tierradentro
and at the end of his life, the development of international contacts
and support for the growing Indian movement. Niquinás thus
acquired a more international vision within which he was able to
insert his knowledge of the past.

Amenable as contemporary oral tradition is to a minute analysis
of its structure and symbolism, it cannot be wholly understood
without a thorough grounding in the political conditions that
influenced its chain of transmission. Páez history is not a set of texts,
but an expression of goals informed by the Páez *habitus*. As outlined
by Pierre Bourdieu (1977), the *habitus* is a complex of calls to action
that orient members of a society toward particular practices as
opposed to others. These predilections arise out of experience and
are highly influenced by past events. A product of history, the *habitus*
is continually changing. The elements that make up the *habitus* arise
primarily from those considerations geared toward perpetuating or
reproducing the group and its members. Bourdieu thus encounters
the primary sources of the *habitus* in economic activity. In the Páez
case, where a conquered people is attempting to maintain autonomy
under colonial and neocolonial domination, we might look toward
the political sources of the *habitus*, which are expressed most
effectively in historical interpretation. The Páez *habitus* includes,
among other elements, the oral and written memory of the *caciques*,
the practiçal memory of forebears experienced through ceremony
and through geography, and the recollection of personal experiences
of resisting the State. Each Páez historian draws upon the *habitus*,
constructing interpretations geared to political action that reflect the
experience and knowledge of the storyteller and his audience. The
habitus of each historian is constrained by the political and social
constellation of the dominant society and of Páez society, which
limits the relevant past that can be drawn upon. Páez history is a

process of negotiation, not a fixed array of texts, and it must be studied in its historical, political and social specificity.

THE TEXTUAL COMMUNITY

At the beginning of this book, I explained some of the difficulties of diachronically defining the Páez as a social unit. Their territorial base has shifted in the course of the past 500 years. The nature of political units has been profoundly altered over the course of the centuries, and many of the political innovations embraced by the Páez are also shared by other indigenous communities. The population itself has grouped and regrouped, frequently with members of other ethnic units, whether they be Guambiano, Pijao or Guanacas. Many Páez no longer speak the aboriginal language, but continue to identify themselves with the ethnic group.

Thus, the historical continuity that defines the Páez as a distinct social and cultural unit is more moral than actual, drawing its nourishment from an active historical tradition. By studying the transformation of historical knowledge across the centuries, we can also facilitate the task of defining who the Páez are.

Recent investigations into the nature of literacy in Western society (Stock 1983; Ong 1986) provide us with angles for determining what binds the Páez together. Particularly useful is the notion of the textual community, comprised of a group of people whose activities revolve around the interpretation of key texts. The members of the textual community are not entirely literate; it is composed of both literate individuals and their listeners. The unit coalesces around those who interpret the texts that unify them. The interpretations generated by these communities are sometimes written, but frequently take on an oral form. The textual community *par excellence* is comprised of the followers of a world religion, united in the interpretation of sacred writings, such as the Christian gospels studied by Ong (1986). But the textual community could also take the form of a nation, whose means of social control are based on a series of interpretations of fundamental texts, such as a constitution.

The notion of the textual community is a useful point of departure for defining the Páez as an ethnic group in flux, for examining the interface between the oral and the literate worlds, and for getting to the root of the relationship between structure and event. The source of the moral continuity that the Páez have always drawn with their past is born of the interpretation of key texts, most important among them being the *resguardo* titles written with the collaboration of Don Juan Tama. The patterns of historical interpretation that have emerged over the centuries can be traced to these documents as they have been reinterpreted by various historical actors. But it is not only the texts themselves that define the textual community: of greater importance are the historians who interpret them, for the majority of Páez cannot read the original documents. These men, from their vantage point as observers of the global conditions of their people and as individuals conversant with history and law, and with the strengths and weaknesses of the dominant society, expand the documents in ways that make them more relevant to the problems at hand, the recent experiences of listeners and the geography within which they move in their daily and ritual lives. Textual communities revolving around such skilled individuals live in an everchanging world that they are able to understand and act upon, based on a continuity with the past that grows from a dynamic interpretation of it.

The texts written or dictated by Juan Tama, Quintín Lame and Julio Niquinás are by no means of the same order as the Christian gospels considered by Ong. Although the gospels were at one time created and interpreted in an oral medium and are still communicated to the faithful in spoken form, their broad diffusion across the globe was facilitated by their published nature and their association with political power and territorial expansion. Páez texts, in contrast, are essentially oral narratives put into writing and, like other oral texts, are more amenable to transformation and innovation than is a written source. In written form, they have only a limited diffusion, both due to the medium in which they are cast and the language in which they are written. The fact that they can only be made accessible to the majority through oral means demonstrates the lack of power of the Páez within Colombian society. Nevertheless, the use of texts reflects axes of power within Páez society itself. They are only effectively articulated by those who exert political control within Páez communities. They constitute a textual community based on many texts, as opposed to one authorative version, reflecting the diffuse nature of power in Tierradentro. Their contents are most frequently experienced through practical activity and through ritual, frequently tied to the legitimization of political power, and are not primarily communicated through narrative performance. Thus, they bind together a peculiarly Páez textual community, and not one in any European sense of the word.

Reference to the notion of the textual community leads to a consideration of the nature of literacy in societies such as the Páez. Given the process of continuous reinterpretation undergone by written texts in Tierradentro, can we still bestow fixity upon the written word? And in contrast, noting the perpetuation over time of key images and patterns in Páez oral tradition, can we maintain that oral communication is fluid, changing, and based entirely in the present? In Tierradentro, the written word opens a space in which creative impulses, both practical and narrative, can be realized. At the same time, it provides a constant foundation that is resighted generation after generation, forcing oral interpretation to assume patterns from the past. The creative space of the literate tradition is both a consequence of Colombian society's domination of the Páez, and a native vehicle for transcending this control. On the one hand, the subject matter of oral tradition is restricted by Indian legislation, which defines the means by which native communities can legitimize their identity. Hence, there is considerably more oral elaboration upon Don Juan Tama's titles, than on documentary evidence of messianic movements or narratives of such culture heroes as St. Thomas. But on the other hand, even given the limitations of Indian legislation, the oral transmission of the contents of eighteenth-century titles provides an opening for interpretations of the present, which would not be possible if the documents were maintained in purely written form. Oral elaborations upon written texts have the potential to create a distinct Páez collectivity, based not on the hierarchical power legislated by the dominant society, but on a native sense of political process marked by the decentralization of power. This is true, despite the fact that the very oral traditions have been used historically to bolster the aims of specific political actors. No political leader, including Don Juan Tama, has effectively used the *cacique* image to exert total political control over Tierradentro. Oral narrative thus presents a distinct advantage over the European-derived written form, because it limits quick and enveloping hierarchical control. But the power of certain oral narratives among the Páez is a function of their origins in written sources, and their efficacy derives from their location at the interface of the oral and written modes, as well as of two distinct cultural traditions.

Clearly, the sorts of generalizations that traditionally place the oral and written modes within sharply different domains, giving rise to distinct modes of thought, leave little room for the hazy middle ground in which Páez creativity occurs. The Páez exhibit what is undoubtedly a more general feature of the relationship between the oral and the written in colonial society. They live in a mix of the two modes of communication, one determining the nature of its counterpart as they are deployed across the political and social stage (Street 1984; Goody 1987). The Páez have been forced by colonialism to operate at the interface of the oral and the literate. On the one hand, they must survive within a society that fetishizes the written word and, consequently, bestows power upon those who manipulate it effectively. On the other hand, given that literacy is a necessary but inadequate tool for achieving power in Colombia, the Páez must also consolidate themselves as an ethnic group, working in the oral realm. This process is only partially fueled by narrative; the deployment in the landscape of historical referents constitutes a different type of written record, which can be read by everyone. The ways in which the Páez intermingle the oral and the written word are partially beyond their control, given their subordinate relationship to the dominant Colombian society (Rappaport 1987b). In other words, the nature of Páez orality and literacy is determined by social, political and linguistic factors, and not entirely by the medium itself. But the choices they must make in selecting from the oral and from the literate worlds are also fueled by a profound historical memory interacting with the exigencies of the present. The end result is a tradition that can neither be classified as oral nor literate, but as the interface of the two.

IMAGE AND TEXT ACROSS TIME

The historians we have been considering based their interpretations only in part upon written documents and books they might have read or oral histories handed down to them. Each of them fashioned his history around an image that was first articulated in non-narrative form; in façt, most of the central images we have been examining first emerged within the framework of political practice. Don Juan Tama's title to Vitoncó appeared only after he was successful in refashioning the prevailing image of a *cacique* to fit the juncture in which he lived; Quintín Lame traced his descent to Juan Tama, reinterpreting him as a nineteenth-century *caudillo* only after becoming a *caudillo* himself; Julio Niquinás employed the *cacique* archetype within a number of movements in his youth, sharing his observations as a venerated historian in his old age.

The treatment given in this book to Páez politicians has

emphasized their articulation of history *as it should have occurred*, and not the past as it happened. What colonial *caciques*, nineteenth-century *caudillos* and modern ethnic rights activists share is a propensity to reinvent tradition. Hobsbawm and Ranger (1983: 1) define invented tradition as

a set of practices, normally governed by overtly or tacitly accepted rules and of a ritual or symbolic nature, which seek to inculcate certain values and norms of behaviour by repetition, which automatically implies continuity with the past.

The Páez past is certainly symbolic and repetitive in its use of the *cacique* motif, fostering a moral continuity with the past through brief and stylized references, as opposed to detailed statements of historical process. Nevertheless, it is not Hobsbawm and Ranger's invented tradition, but a *reinvented* past. Unlike their examples, which focus on the creation of traditions by colonizers working in the service of domination, the Páez example illustrates the creation of a moral link to the past in order to defy the colonizing power. Moreover, the Páez past is not an invention originating in the present, but a selective process whereby the same images are consistently rearticulated, generation after generation: it is a continuous reinvention of the same tradition within everchanging circumstances.

While the chiefly motif is articulated in political action as a brief and stylized reference, what Tama, Lame and Niquinás recount appear to us as detailed statements of historical process. Despite their frequently mythic nature and their compression of linear time, they clearly explain the results of historical processes on Páez society through a deployment of historical referents. Moreover, we can trace many of their documentary and their experiential sources. In short, the narrative history that characterizes the Páez is not wholly invented and of the present, but is also a conscious interpretation of a vast array of historical evidence that is made sense of through recourse to images and patterns.

Páez historymaking is a two-phase process: a stage of image-making corresponding to what we might call the reinvention of tradition, in which historical symbols are given expression through political activity; and a subsequent phase of research and reflection that fills in the gaps left by the images, producing a more integrated text or set of episodes that no longer appear as purely invented. Neither of the two stages is unconscious. Both are grounded in historical reality, in the conscious choice made by an intellectual leadership. Their options are limited by the availability of source material, the social and political vehicles to which memory can be harnessed and above all, the ability to persuade the vast majority that innovation is indeed a return to the past. For this reason, I have concentrated on the work of individual intellectuals, as opposed to storymakers in general. Likewise, this contention has led me to juxtapose political action to text-making, instead of considering texts on their own: the latter would have supported the erroneous notion that Páez history is a continuous application of constant patterns arising from the collectivity, instead of a constant clash of innovation and tradition mediated by key individuals who reappropriate patterns they have acquired from written sources, in response to regional, national and even international, pressures.

RECONSIDERING THE MYTH–HISTORY DISTINCTION

This argument bears some implications for our choice of a classificatory approach for understanding the types of narratives that have been examined in this book. As timeless texts, divorced from the historical reality in which they were written, the sources at the disposal of their authors and the practical images upon which they are based, they are certainly amenable to an approach that might catalogue them as myth. They can legitimately be examined on the intellectual plane as solving conceptual problems that cannot be resolved on the ground, although I have not chosen to consider them in this light. But at the same time, if taken as part of a dialectical process of the creation, elaboration and re-elaboration of written and oral images within a power struggle, they do in fact solve precise practical problems. In this sense, Páez oral tradition is by no means myth produced by a "cold" society (Lévi-Strauss 1966), nor the constant reapplication of unconscious structures in novel circumstances (Zuidema 1982).

The Páez are not unique in their conscious reapplication of models from the past in the present. Although more research into the influence of legal documents on the construction of political strategy and history must yet be conducted in highland South America, trajectories similar to that of the Páez are now being analyzed in Bolivia. Here, early twentieth-century native resistance to anti-community Liberal legislation spurred a conscious revival of chiefly hierarchies, using information drawn from historical documents (Rivera 1986). Comparative research is needed to analyze the factors influencing the reinvention of history through oral elaborations upon written legal sources in Latin America; hopefully, this will provide us with a broader picture of what constitutes Andean society, taking into account not only continuing links with a pre-columbian past, but also the nature of the state under which communities have been forced to live since the sixteenth century.

If oral traditions are examined historically, Bloch's (1977) suggestion that we would do well to consider temporal reckoning in practical activity and not just in the ritual sphere, becomes a useful assertion. When linked to an ethnic strategy, these narratives take on a different light than they would if considered exclusively in the mythic or symbolic spheres. Moreover, their very contents are dictated by non-narrative political strategies and circumstances. But notwithstanding the centrality of the practical sphere in Páez historymaking, we cannot lose sight of the importance of ritual, symbol and pattern in insuring the efficacy of these narratives over space and time. While they are practical in that they derive from activities that solve problems on the ground, they accomplish this by articulating powerful symbols that move people to action by forging a moral link to a distant past. Their efficacy lies in their very merging of myth and history, and not in any separation of the two.

Glossary

baldío Tracts of land granted to homesteaders by the Colombian government during the nineteenth and twentieth centuries; also called public lands.

cabildo The elected council administering the *resguardo*.

cacica A female hereditary chief or culture heroine.

cacicazgo Hereditary chiefdom.

cacique A male hereditary chief or culture hero.

cascarillero Cinchona bark collector.

capitán Hereditary position on modern *resguardo* council, responsible for coordinating communal labor; the *capitán* is sometimes called *cacique*.

caudillo Nineteenth- and early twentieth-century politico-military leader.

Don, doña Colonial titles of nobility, commonly granted to aboriginal hereditary chiefs; modern term of respect.

encomendero Recipient of a colonial tribute grant awarded by the Crown to conquerors and administrators in recognition of services rendered.

indigenista A supporter of an Indian-oriented approach to indigenous rights, as opposed to a western-based ideology used to advance native claims.

new caciques Eighteenth-century chiefs who consolidated dominion over large expanses of territory, founding *resguardos*.

páramo Marshy plain at the top of the cordillera in the northern Andes.

principal Hereditary political leader under supreme *cacique*.

resguardo Indigenous territorial unit comprising communal and inalienable lands administered by elected councils and legitimized by colonial or nineteenth-century titles.

terrateniente Large landowner, frequently employing sharecroppers.

Notes

Note Unless otherwise indicated all translations are mine.

1 INTRODUCTION: INTERPRETING THE PAST

1 Indigenous organizations have been active in preparing treatises outlining their demands and their philosophies. Their writings frequently include statements of the importance of history in their projects. For some South American examples of indigenous statements regarding history, see Comité de Solidaridad con las Luchas Indígenas–Pasto 1982; Consejo Indio de Sud América 1982; Gobernadores Indígenas en Marcha 1981; Guambía 1980; Wankar 1981.

2 Ethnographers of the Páez include Bernal (1953, 1954a, 1954b, 1955, 1956), Hernández de Alba (1963), Nachtigall (1953, 1955), Ortíz (1973, 1979), Pittier de Fabrega (1907), Rappaport (1982, 1985), Findji and Rojas (1985) and Sevilla Casas (1976a, 1986). More exclusively historical treatments include Bonilla (1979), González (n.d.), Henman (1981) and Roldán (1974).

3 Historians of Africa have been active in retrieving historical information from oral tradition and have developed techniques for locating historical referents in even the most mythological of accounts, the creation stories (cf. Yoder 1980). Although history by the Páez contains clear historical referents and the relationship between history as *we* read it and as the *Páez* interpret it will be used in this analysis, it is not an end in itself, but a vehicle for understanding how the Páez construct their own historical vision.

4 One of the most intriguing examples of the use of historical information is documented by María Rostworowski (1977: 178–87), who describes a dispute over coca fields brought to a colonial Peruvian court, in which the disputants used evidence from *pre*-Incaic times that had been preserved in the oral memory.

5 In situations of domination, history and historical thinking have always been opposed to some other mode of talking about time. This is as true for our own society as it is for colonized ones, a fact recognized by Walter Benjamin who wrote that "history" was the domain of the ruling classes, while the downtrodden were relegated to the domain of "tradition" (Benjamin 1968; Eagleton 1985–86).

6 See also an earlier formulation of this argument in Goody and Watt (1963).

7 The importance of the past in the present and the past in the future is also an essential element of the Marxist theory of history (Marx and Engels 1964; Eagleton 1985–86), and it is thus no accident that many Third World novelists have embraced Marxism at some point in their careers.

191

8 The significance of the future for visions of the past was brought home to me in a discussion with Ron LaFrance of the Mohawk Nation. As he related his experiences in the Akwesasne Freedom School, an institution run by and for the community, he gave some advice for an indigenous community in Colombia which was embarking upon a similar enterprise. He spoke of the fact that it was necessary to think in units of seven generations back from the present and forward to the future, in order to set priorities for the school's curriculum. This type of all-encompassing vision can only be possible when history is understood as a tool for empowerment, and not an abstract object of reflection.

9 *Resguardo* titles include those of Pitayó (ACC/P [Archivo Central del Cauca, Popayán] 1881; NC/S [Notaría del Circuito, Santander de Quilichao] 1914) and Vitoncó (ACC/P 1883) of the *cacique* Don Juan Tama; Toribío and Tacueyó (Sendoya n.d.: 29–30), established by Don Manuel de Quilos y Sicos; and Togoima (AHT/B [Archivo Histórico de Tierradentro, Belalcázar] 1727), domain of the Gueyomuse family.

10 An English translation of Lame's work appears as an appendix to Castillo (1987) also the editor of the Spanish-language edition of the treatise and author of a biographical introduction to the book.

11 The Niquinás interviews, conducted by Víctor Daniel Bonilla, Trino Morales and other associates, form part of an extensive tape archive at the Archivo Fundación Colombia Nuestra (AFCN/C 1971a, 1971b, 1972a, n.d.b).

12 This does not really tell us anything about their levels of literacy, since scribes were routinely used for drawing up documents, as they knew the formulae to be used in legal writing.

2 THE RISE OF THE COLONIAL *CACIQUE*

1 Published documentary sources are listed according to the publication date of the edition consulted, followed at the first reference to the text by the date of the original publication or preparation in brackets. This procedure will also be used for archival sources which frequently contain copies of earlier documents.

2 Aguado's chronicle is organized in books and chapters, each with a regional focus. His description of the Páez is found in volume 2, book 16, and all citations are from there.

3 These alliances are documented extensively by chroniclers Andagoya (1892 [1544]), Aguado (1956), Castellanos (1944 [1589]), Ordóñez (1942 [1614]), Simón (1982 [1627]) and Piedrahita (1973 [1688]), and also appear in documents from the period (for example, FDNR 1559, 1576).

4 The Mesa de Páez, or Wila, is called *Kween Dyi'* (The Meeting of the Roads) in Páez. Suin is *Uswa'l* (Large Frijoles). Avirama is called *Pilamo* (*pil* = leg bone).

5 It is not the purpose of this book to define the nature of northern Andean society, although it is hoped that its characterization of the Páez will contribute to such a definition. The reader will note that comparisons are frequently made with Andean and Amazonian societies. Like other northern Andean peoples, the Páez absorbed a great deal of lowland influence, probably made possible by their considerable range of contacts with tropical forest peoples, but they have also shared in a common Andean ideology. Nevertheless, Páez society was more highly decentralized than those of the aboriginal population of Quito, the Pasto or the Chibcha, and may be more properly understood as a frontier community.

6 Within the province there also reigned Anabeima, supreme *cacique* of Guanacas (Aguado 1956). Anabeima was not Páez, but belonged to the Guambiano-Coconuco linguistic family whose main zone of settlement was located on the western slopes of the cordillera with its center in Popayán.

7 Pedro de Aguado's 1575 chronicle documented one of these wars in detail: the establishment and destruction of San Vicente de Páez at the Mesa de Páez. In the first volume of his history of the city of Caloto, Cauca, Mariano Sendoya (1975) traces the multiple foundations of this Spanish town, one of which was San Vicente de Páez. Most of these foundations were destroyed by Páez armies. Also of note was the 1577 destruction of the mining town of La Plata, in whose vicinity the precolumbian Páez had been settled.

8 It is quite possible that the Páez suffered even greater depopulation than that described by Sevilla. Working on the basis of chronicle sources, Earle (n.d.a: 3) calculates that there were 25,000 Páez in the 1540s.

9 Very illustrative of the loss of lands to the east was a series of disputes between the Páez of Togoima and a Spaniard, Don Diego González de la Sotta, over the lands of Itaibe, near La Plata (AHT/B 1729), which the Páez eventually lost. The Spaniards began to encroach on these lands in the early seventeenth century.

10 Páez settlements to the east in the Gobernación de Neiva were geared to gaining access to warm-country produce, including sugar cane, cotton and manioc (ANC/B 1739), as well as coca (ANC/B 1692). But many Páez also flocked to the Neiva area to pan gold for tribute payment (ANC/B 1752, 1784).

11 The same struggles for political hegemony were occurring beyond the borders of Tierradentro at the time that the Páez were forging their own political and territorial unity, for example, in Yumbo near Cali (AJC/Q 1646), in Pasto (AJC/Q 1739, 1751), among the Tama of Timaná (Friede 1953), in the Sibundoy Valley (Bonilla 1972) and in Popayán itself (AJC/Q 1679; Friede 1972).

12 A considerable number of Páez *resguardos* cropped up at this time in the Gobernación de Neiva, to the east of Tierradentro. These lands were settled by Páez migrants in the early seventeenth century (APFS/B [Archivo Provincia Franciscana de Santafé, Bogotá] 1657), who ostensibly won them from the Pijao (APFS/B 1701b). The population of such communities as Iquira, El Retiro and Nátaga equalled that of Tierradentro in the first half of the eighteenth century (ANC/B 1757).

13 Findji and Rojas also suggest that Tama was able to achieve broader legitimization because his lands were located along a frontier. This is not an adequate explanation of Don Juan Tama's success, given that Togoima and Tacueyó were also frontier *resguardos*. Tama's achievement of broader autonomy may have resulted from the relative lateness at which his *resguardos* were founded, and even more, might be attributed to his own very special political talents.

14 The Páez *caciques* of Neiva were by no means as effective as their Tierradentro compatriots in consolidating their rule. Eastern *resguardos* rarely encompassed more than a league of land (ANC/B 1692, 1739). Chiefly power more closely approximated that of precolumbian chiefs: the *caciques* of Neiva had trouble maintaining long-term control over their populations (ANC/B 1739), in part because of a high degree of intracommunity violence (APFS/B 1701a) and also

because *caciques* were implicated in the sale of subjects into slavery in the formerly Pijao communities to the north (ANC/B 1643, 1660). Perhaps the lack of chiefly authority was a major determinant in the disappearance of such ethnic communities in the Gobernación de Neiva: the heirs to the *resguardos* of Iquira, Nátaga, El Retiro and Los Organos no longer consider themselves to be Indians.

15 On this basis it can be suggested that many losses of territory originated in the new *caciques'* distinct worldview, which did not coincide with that of the Spaniards, and caused them to define their political and territorial autonomy in a manner that appeared contradictory to the Europeans.

16 It is indeed tempting on the basis of tribute lists which distinguish upper and lower portions of communities, to suggest that a moiety system existed among the Páez, as it did in Andean communities to the south. Nevertheless, Conquest-era documents make no reference at all to a moiety system and it is probable that these distinctions are the product of Spanish interpretation and not Páez reality.

17 For example, the *cacique* of Suin in 1733, Don Joseph Becuchi, was married to Doña Juana Pando, *cacica* of Tálaga (ACC/P 1733); while Suin was part of the *cacicazgo* of Vitoncó, Tálaga was not. Similarly, the same 1733 tribute list noted the marriage of Doña Josefa, another of Tálaga's *cacicas*, to Don Pedro Momosque, *cacique* of Avirama, located at quite a distance from Tálaga, and within the jurisdiction of the Gueyomuse of Togoima. Finally, the 1745 *cacica* of Guanacas, Doña Marta Cunchima, who was not Páez but a member of the Guambiano-Coconuco group, was married to Don Pedro Tonz, *cacique* of Paniquitá, located on the outskirts of Popayán, and part of Don Juan Tama's Pitayó dominions (ACC/P 1745).

3 THE BIRTH OF THE MYTH: DON JUAN TAMA Y CALAMBÁS

1 Indian-authored chronicles include Diego de Castro Titu Cusi Yupanqui (Titu Cusi Yupanqui 1973 [1570]), Joan de Santacruz Pachacuti Yamqui Salcamaygua (Pachacuti Yamqui 1967 [1613]), Felipe Guaman Poma de Ayala (Guaman Poma 1936 [1615]), Inca Garcilaso de la Vega (Garcilaso 1962 [1616]) and the late sixteenth-century Quechua manuscript of Huarochirí (Urioste 1983 [Anon.: n.d.]).

2 Colonial documents included only the Spanish transcript of legal proceedings, so it is unclear what terms the Páez witnesses actually used in their discussions with the colonial authorities. There was a word, *ongoi*, which meant "in ancient times" (Castillo 1877: 67), but we do not know if they used this term in pressing their claims. Furthermore, it is unclear whether *ongoi* referred to the recent or the very distant and mythical past.

3 References to precolumbian visits of Christian apostles are frequent in the colonial literature (cf. Pachacuti Yamqui 1967; Guaman Poma 1936).

4 THE CHIEFDOM TRANSFORMED: THE NINETEENTH-CENTURY PÁEZ

1 Within the first decade after Independence whites attempted to avoid prosecution for occupying Guambiano lands by claiming their right, as citizens, to a fair trial (ANC/B 1829).

2 The liquidation of communal properties through the creation of individual landholdings and the bestowal of citizenship rights upon the Indians to justify encroachment on their lands were the norm throughout nineteenth-century Spanish-speaking South America (see Smith [1983] for a description of nineteenth-century Indian policy in Peru and Platt [1982] on Republican Bolivia).

3 Nevertheless, many of the non-Páez *resguardos* surrounding Popayán, as well as communities in southern Cauca, were dissolved in the course of the nineteenth century (cf. Friede 1972).

4 The sheer volume of documentation relating to Indians available for the colonial period is unknown for Republican Colombia. Moreover, most nineteenth-century archives are uncatalogued and thus extremely cumbersome to work with, with the exception of expedients on public lands in the National Archive (ANC/B) and in the Archive of the Colombian Institute of Agrarian Reform (AINCORA/B). More readily available information can be found in the nineteenth-century periodical record, as well as in travel memoirs.

5 I am indebted to Findji for coining the term "*caciques* without *cacicazgos*". This is an especially useful concept from a methodological perspective, because it allows us to focus on *Páez* agency, instead of on non-Indian actions that impinged upon the Páez. Civil war also nurtured the rise of indigenous *caudillos* in other parts of the country, including the Cuna governor Victoriano Lorenzo, who operated in Panama during the War of the Thousand Days. (Jaramillo 1985).

6 Quoted from ANC/B, v. 42, f.177.

7 For a Spanish colonial treatise on the benefits, taxonomy and harvesting of cinchona bark, see Mutis (1983 [1809]).

8 Ironically, the time-consuming process of validating *baldío* grants doomed many of these would-be quinine entrepreneurs to failure. By the time they acquired title to the forests, the cinchona frontier had already moved to another location (ibid.).

9 For example, agents of the Arboleda family wrote up a contract regarding the lands of Asnenga, in dispute with Pitayó and Jambaló. A long chain of letters regarding quinine-barking in Asnenga appeared in *El Tiempo* (2 February, 20 April, 4 May, 11 May 1858; 14 September 1859).

10 On the Sant-Rose Compagnie, operating in neighboring Huila, a series of commentaries was published in *El Tiempo* (2 October, 27 November, 4 December, 11 December, 18 December, 25 December 1855; 1 January, 8 January, 15 April, 1856). The Compañía de Colombia was also engaged in quinine extraction in the eastern cordillera of Tolima (*La Reforma*, 6 September, 9 October, 30 October 1879). Whether or not Páez laborers participated in these enterprises is unclear.

11 This is not so unusual in many Páez areas, including the heartland of Tierradentro, where there are many monolingual Spanish-speakers in some of the southern *resguardos*.

12 Although the Lamistas never ran a presidential candidate, one of Lame's associates, Eutiquio Timoté of Coyaima, Tolima, was the 1934 candidate for President of Colombia on the Communist Party ticket (*El Espectador*, 8 January 1934). Lame broke with Timoté and José Gonzalo Sánchez over their

participation in the Communist Party, Lame preferring a more *indigenista* mode of organizing.

1 Lame's manuscript was edited by Gonzalo Castillo, who also wrote a biographical essay as an introduction to the treatise.

2 As is evident in the Republican notations on copies of colonial *resguardo* titles (see ACC/P 1883).

3 This passage comes from Book 1 of Lame's treatise and at the time he dictated it to Florentino Moreno he only expected the manuscript to contain six chapters. By the time he concluded his dictation, there were two books, containing a total of 20 chapters. At the end of this passage Lame makes reference to his years of activism in Tolima and to what was his most successful campaign: the reconstitution of the *cabildos* of Ortega and Chaparral in the late 1930s.

4 In contrast, the Colombian press and officialdom frequently did so, as did other Indians (ANC/B 1920: 534).

5 Nevertheless, official reports stated that Lame meant to establish a "Little Government" of his own in Tierradentro (Cauca, Gobernación 1916). It is unclear from these reports whether the officials believed that he planned to create an independent government, or a *cabildo*, a government within a government.

1 The captain of a *resguardo*, also occasionally called *cacique*, holds hereditary office, supervising communal work projects.

2 Guillermo León Valencia was a Popayán-born poet and politician, presidential candidate in 1914 and highly influential in regional and national circles. He was one of Lame's principal enemies.

3 Although I do not have population figures for the pre-Depression era, more recent statistics indicate the demographic shifts that began to be experienced in this period. By the mid-seventies, only 67 percent of Tierradentro was Páez, with most of the non-Indian population concentrated in the municipality of Inzá. By then, only 40 percent of Inzá was comprised of *resguardo* lands (Sevilla 1976a: 20).

4 The *cabildo* of San José was decimated by the military police. The only survivor was an adolescent who served as a messenger for the indigenous authorities. He was shot and left for dead in a river, but survived his wounds.

5 González (n.d.), who was a missionary in Tierradentro during the Violencia, includes his own personal reminiscences of the civil war in his book on the Páez. Testimonies by the survivors of the San José massacre are included in the Archivo Fundación Colombia Nuestra tape archive (AFCN/C 1971c, 1971d).

6 Páez oral narrative includes many themes other than those that will be described here. There are also numerous stories of very distant ancient times, of tricksters and of animals, of the introduction of fire and of the first earthquakes, of the Virgin Mary and of St. Thomas (Bernal 1953, 1956; Nachtigall 1955).

7 The Juan Tama of the documentary record will be distinguished from his counterpart in oral history by the use of the noble title *Don*, by which he was identified in the eighteenth century.

8 Don Ambrosio To was an eighteenth-century *cacique* in Tóez (Castillo 1877: 81), but there is no documentary evidence allowing us to surmise that To and Tóens are the same individual.

9 The significance of astronomical measurements was determined by inserting them in a chart prepared by Anthony Aveni (Aveni 1972) and revised to accommodate Tierradentro's precipitous geography by Professor Andrés Simar of the Universidad del Valle, Cali. After I had studied these measurements and noted the astronomical significance of Cuartel, the parish priest of Vitoncó, Father Jorge Escobar, showed me a photo of Cuartel that he had taken from Vitoncó at the June festival of San Juan, of the sun rising directly above the Heights of Tama.

7 JULIO NIQUINÁS, A CONTEMPORARY PÁEZ HISTORIAN

1 Rosalino Yajimbo was a Páez *caudillo* and Quintín Lame's foremost associate in Tierradentro. He is mentioned throughout the Niquinás interviews and the narrator looked up to him more than to Lame: it was only through Yajimbo that Lame was able to move the Indians of northern Tierradentro.

2 I have chosen to use the colonial spelling (Benalcázar) for reference to the historical figure and the contemporary spelling (Belalcázar) for the character in these narratives.

3 The Colombian officer who arrested Quintín Lame in 1916 at San Isidro (Popayán).

4 In the Spanish account, it takes place *before* his death and is a simple dismemberment, not the cutting into thousands of pieces.

5 The identity between episodes 1 and 9 stems from their cardinal orientations on the north–south axis.

References

UNPUBLISHED DOCUMENTARY SOURCES

Archivo Academia Colombiana de la Historia, Bogotá (AACH/B)
n.d. "La epopeya de los Mil Días."

Archivo Central del Cauca, Popayán (ACC/P)

Archivo Colonial
1583–89 "Providencias de alcaldes, regidores, procuradores y actos del Cabildo de Popayan, años de 1583–1589.
1684 "Autos sobre la declaracion y tasacion que se hizo de los tributos que deben pagar todos los indios de las Provincias de Paez." Signatura 1863.
1719a "Numeraciones de los indios encomendados a Don Cristobal Mosquera Figueroa de los pueblos de San Fernando de Vitonco..." Sig. 2899.
1719b "Numeracion de los indios de San Miguel de Abirama...por el juez Don Antonio Vallejo..." Sig. 2907.
1719c "Numeracion de los indios de San Pedro de Toboima, encomienda de Don Garcia Hurtado de Olarte y Ospina." Sig. 2908.
1721 "Comision de Vallejo para hacer el censo de San Pedro de Toboima." Sig. 2993.
1733 "Numeraciones y cartas cuentas hechas por Santiago Alvarez, corregidor de naturales." Sig. 3491.
1745 "Numeraciones completas de los pueblos de la Provincia de Paez, hechas por Pablo de Chaves Caizedo, comisario de la Junta de Real Hacienda 'en consorcio' del Maestro Eugenio del Castillo y otros curas." Sig. 4093.
1757 "Diligencias hechas por el cura de Talaga en virtud de un despacho de los Oficiales Reales de Popayan sobre tributos de los pueblos de Paez..." Sig. 4658.
1792 "Autos del remate de los tributos de los pueblos de Toboima...hecho por Don Juan Antonio de Ibarra." Sig. 6364.

Archivo de la Gobernación del Cauca ("Archivo Muerto")
1871 "Documentos relativos a la utilización de las quinas de Wila." Legajo 16, paquete 112.

Archivo Sergio Arboleda
1874 "Carta de Miguel A. Peñaranda a Sergio Arboleda (Vitoncó, octubre 13 de 1874)." Folder 5.

198

1888 "Carta de Ulpiano Obando a Sergio Arboleda (Toribío, marzo 28 de 1888)." Folder o.

Protocolos Notariales

1881 [1700] "Titulo de las parcialidades de Pitayo, Quichaya, Caldono, Pueblo Nuevo y Jambalo." Partida 843.

1883 [1708] "Titulo del resguardo de Vitonco." Partida 959.

1897 "Título de la parcialidad de indígenas de Yaquivá." Partida 757.

1898a "Diligencias relativas a unos terrenos pertenecientes a la parcialidad de indígenas del resguardo de Avirama." Partida 637.

1898b "Diligencias relativas a la propiedad que tienen los indígenas de Cohetando en unas tierras como pertenecientes a dicha parcialidad." Partida 505.

1898c "Título de la propiedad que tienen los indígenas de Tálaga en los terrenos de resguardos de esa parcialidad." Partida 709.

Archivo Fundación Colombia Nuestra, Cali (AFCN/C)

1971a "Entrevista con Julio Niquinás." Moras, 7/29/71. XII H 2, cas. 1, lado a, 8/71.

1971b "Entrevista con Julio Niquinás." Cabuyo, 7/30/71. XII H 2, cas. 2, lado a, 8/71.

1971c "Entrevistas varias." San José, 8/1/71, n.r.

1971d "Entrevistas varias." San José, 8/14/71, n.r.

1972a "Entrevista con Julio Niquinás." Mosoco, 8/13/72. XII H 2 (2), 8/72.

1972b "Entrevista con Jorge Mulcué Sandoval." N.p., 11/25/72. XII H 2, cas. 2, 11/72.

1973 "Entrevista con Pedro Pito." Bellavista, Pitayó, 3/2/73. XII F, 3/73.

n.d.a. "Entrevista con Paz Colmenares." N.p., n.d., n.r.

n.d.b "Entrevista con Julio Niquinás." San José, n.d. XII H 3.

Archivo General de Indias, Sevilla (AGI/S)

1558 "Tasacion hecha por el Licenciado Señor Tomas Lopez, oidor del Nuevo Reino y visitador de la Provincia de Popayan y los obispos de Pasto y Popayan, de la Gobernacion de Popayan." Audiencia de Quito, legajo 60.

1582 "Nicolas Hurtado de Medina, sobre los daños causados por paeces y pijaos." Audiencia de Quito, legajo 16.

1673 "Copia de una carta en que se refieren las violencias y vejaciones que los yndios paezes reciuen de sus encomenderos." Audiencia de Quito, legajo 210.

1717 "Confirmacion de las encomiendas de San Fernando de Vitonco y San Vicente de Paez en Cristobal Mosquera Figueroa." Audiencia de Quito, legajo 157.

Archivo Histórico de Tierradentro, Belalcázar, Cauca (AHT/B)

1729 "Tierras de los ocho pueblos…"

Archivo Instituto Colombiano de la Reforma Agraria, Bogotá (AINCORA/B)

1855a "Baldíos de Inzá." Vol. 9, ff. 197–211.

1855a "Título de tierras baldías de Inzá expedido a favor del Capitán Hipólito Maldonado." Vol. 1, f. 554.

1865 "Cuentas de las haciendas de La Bolsa, Quintero y Japio." Vol. 1, ff. 774–821.
1872 "Baldíos de Coconuco a nombre de Tomás Cipriano de Mosquera." Vol. 2, ff. 827–37.
1873 "Pleito sobre las quinas de San Agustín." Vol. 16, ff. 258–62.
1874 "Baldíos de Páez (Elías Reyes vs. *resguardo*.)" Vol. 16, ff. 606–10.
1875 "Baldíos del camino de Timaná-Coconuco (José Hilario López vs. Tomás Cipriano de Mosquera)." Vol. 16, ff. 404–19.

Archivo Jijón y Caamaño, Quito (AJC/Q)

1646 "Autos seguidos por Don Jacinto Mundo, indio, contra Don Sebastian Quindaquin sobre el cacicazgo del pueblo de Yumbo en la Provincia de Cali." Colección de Manuscritos, v. 18.
1679 "Autos seguidos por Don Luis Guaman y consortes pidiendo a nombre de Doña Beatris Calambas Timbio real provision sobre el cacicazgo de Timbio, pueblo de la jurisdiccion de Popayan." Colección de Manuscritos, v. 18.
1739 "Autos seguidos por Don Ventura Assa pidiendo se le posesione del cacicazgo de Guachocal en la Provincia de los Pastos." Colección de Manuscritos, v. 18.
1751 "Autos seguidos por Doña Estefania Pastas pretendiendo el cacicazgo del pueblo de Pastas en la Provincia de los Pastos para su hijo Don Gregorio Garcia Putag contra Don Tomas Sapuisaca." Colección de Manuscritos, v. 19.

Archivo Nacional de Colombia, Bogotá (ANC/B)

Archivo Colonial

1629 "Documentos judiciales referentes a la visita practicada por Diego de Ospina, alguacil mayor de la Real Audiencia, en Timana, Neiva y Saldaña." Visitas del Tolima, vol. 1, ff. 693–931.
1643 "Don Cristobal de Mosquera y Figueroa, vecino de Popayan, encomendero de los indios paeces, los cuales han dado en ausentarse e irse a reunir con los natagaimas, pide real provision para obligarles a que le paguen daños y perjuicios." Miscelánea de la Colonia, Encomiendas, t. 61, ff. 622r–v.
1660 "Sobre mision de paeces en Ataco de la Orden de Predicadores." Miscelánea de la Colonia, vol. 15, ff. 276r–278v.
1692 "Pleito seguido por los indios paeces del pueblo de San Francisco de Iquira contra el capitan Miguel Fernandez Tamayo, vecino de Neiva, sobre el sitio de Buenavista." Resguardos del Tolima, Cauca y Antioquia, vol. 1, ff. 95–223.
1699 "Mosquera y Figueroa, Cristobal, su titulo de encomendero de los indios de San Fernando de Vitonco y San Vicente de Paez." Encomiendas, vol. 29, ff. 856–70.
1739 "Pleito seguido por los indios del pueblo de San Juan del Hobo... contra Jose de Medina, por tierras de sus resguardos..." Resguardos del Tolima, Cauca y Antioquia, t. 1, ff. 54–194.
1751 "Informe del P. Eugenio del Castillo y Orozco al Señor Gobernador y Capitan General de la ciudad de Popayan y sus provincias." Cartas de Contrabando, vol. 14, ff. 228r–29v.
1752 "Traslado de los pobladores de Nataga al sitio de los Organos, Provincia de Neiva." Poblaciones Varias, vol. 10, ff. 706–11.
1757 "Hurtado y Ponton, Lorenzo Antonio, reclama la sucesion en la encomienda

de San Pedro de Toboima...de que fuera encomendero Garcia Hurtado de Olarte, su padre." Encomiendas, vol. 13, ff. 518-86.

1766 "Don Jose Victoria pide se les incorpore a los indios de Ambosta al pueblo mas cercano." Resguardos de Antioquia, Cauca y Tolima, one volume, ff. 772-804.

1768 "El ilustrisimo Obispo de Popayan da cuenta de la union de los tres pueblos de Jambalo, Pitayo y Quichaya en un solo curato..." Poblaciones del Cauca, vol. 2, ff. 81-109.

1784 "Indios del sitio de los Organoz, de la jurisdiccion de Neiva, informe de Fray Diego Garcia sobre el estado de miseria en que se encontraban y su absoluta ignorancia en cuestiones religiosas." Caciques e Indios, vol. 31, ff. 961-94.

1791 "Sobre el resguardo ce Santa Rosa de la Cañada y sus limites con Segovia." Tierras del Tolima, vol. 3, ff. 663-849.

Archivo Republicano

1825 "Al Secretario del Estado en el Interior, le comunica la Sala de Gobierno de Popayan sobre una solicitud del cacicazgo de Guambia." Indios, one volume.

1826 "Informe dirigido al señor Secretario en el despacho del Interior, sobre milicia de indígenas." Indios, one volume, f. 390.

1829 "Conocimientos que pide el gobierno sobre el expediente promovido por los indigenas de Guambia sobre la expulsion de las gentes de casta, avesindadas en aquella parroquia." Indios, one volume, f. 368-78, 407-35.

1881 "Estado Soberano del Tolima – informe sobre terrenos del Chaparral." Baldíos, vol. 3, ff. 183-88.

1915 "Carta de los cabildos de Tacueyoó y Toribío al Ministro de Gobierno (1 junio, 1915)." Ministerio de Gobierno, Sección 4, vol. 107.

1916 "Carta de Antonio Paredes al Presidente de la República (Popayán, 22 noviembre 1916)." Ministerio de Gobierno, Sección 4, vol. 108.

1917 "El Gobernador del Cauca al Ministerio de Agricultura y Comercio sobre los baldíos de Páez." Baldíos, vol. 41, f. 114.

1919a "Carta de Efraín de Navia, Secretario de Gobierno Encargado de los Asuntos Locales, al Ministro de Gobierno, Bogotá (Popayán, 8 noviembre, 1919)." Ministerio de Gobierno, Sección 4, vol. 131.

1919b "Carta del Secretario de Gobierno del Cauca, Encargado de los Asuntos Locales, al Secretario de Gobierno de la Presidencia de la República (Popayán, 18 noviembre, 1919)." Ministerio de Gobierno, Sección 4, vol. 129.

1920 "Memorial que los cabildos de indígenas de las Parcialidades de Colombia y demás miembros, dirigen al Excelentísimo Señor Presidente de la República, pidiendo un reconocimiento a favor de Lame y sus representantes legítimos (Calibío, 18 junio, 1920)." Ministerio de Gobierno, Sección 4, vol. 137.

1921 "Visita practicada por Julio R. Delgado, visitador fiscal en la Alcaldía municipal de Jambaló." Baldíos, vol. 48, ff. 499a-c.

1922a "El Alcalde de Silvia al Ministerio de Agricultura y Comercio." Baldíos, vol. 50, f. 122.

1922b "Memorial que yo José Gonzalo Sánchez elevo ante Su Señoría El Ministro de Agricultura y Comercio en defensa de los resguardos de las parcialidades de indigenas de 'La Laguna' y 'Topa' en el distrito de Inzá del Departamento del Cauca." Baldíos, vol. 57, ff. 445-53, 459-73.

Archivo Nacional de Historia, Quito (ANH/Q)

1663 "A esta Audiencia de las aiudas necesarias al Gouernador de Popayan para la convercion y poblacion de los yndios paeces y noanamaes." Cedularios, caja 4.

1699 "Don Cristobal Mosquera de Figueroa, sobre las encomiendas de Timbio, Paeces y Turibio." Fondo Popayán, caja 17.

1703 "Pleito seguido por Don Antonio del Campo Salazar con Don Juan de Miera sobre la encomienda de Guanacas." Fondo Popayán, caja 20.

Archivo Provincia Franciscana de Santafé, Bogotá (APFS/B)

1657 "El cabildo se de vacante: Lic. Cristobal de Villa Arevallano, presbitero de Unzueta, Lucas Fernandez de Piedrahita, canonigo provis. y vicario general, y maestro Juan Bernal de Salazar racionero, dicen que San Francisco de Iquira y Santiago de Nataga de indios paez infieles, estan poblados 'pero ningun clerigo ha querido ir'; acuden a la provincia franciscana para que los administre." Vol. 4, documento 5.

1701a "Fray Tomas de Almanza, a favor de los indios, contra los abusos de los blancos." Vol. 4.

1701b "Fray Tomas de Almanza OFM de las missiones de Paez escribe al provincial remitiendo varios informes acerca de dos traslaciones de pueblos." Vol. 5, document 4.

Archivo Provincial de los Padres Vicentinos de Colombia, Bogotá (APVC/B)

1905–06 "Cuaderno no. 1 de la historia de la fundación de Tierradentro. Diario de los misioneros." Tierradentro, document 2.

Biblioteca Luis Angel Arango, Bogotá (BLAA/B)

1863 "Relacion hecha en Agosto de 1.863 por don Ramon Guerra Azuala para uso del General Posada Gutierrez, de la campaña que termino en Segovia en Noviembre de 1.860." Colección de Manuscritos, ms. 98.

Notaría del Circuito, Santander de Quilichao, Cauca (NC/S)

1914 [1702] "Titulo de las tierras de Jambaló." Escritura no. 167.

Notaría de Silvia, Cauca (N/S)

1941 "Protocolización de unas diligencias relativas a las declaraciones hechas por miembros de los cabildos de las parcialidades de Mosoco, Vitoncó y Lame, municipio de Páez." Escritura no. 116.

NEWSPAPERS

El Bolchevique (Bogotá)
Boletín Militar (Pasto)
Boletín Militar del Cauca (Popayán)
Boletín Oficial (Bogotá)
El Colombiano (Bogotá)
El Comercio (Bogotá)

El Día (Bogotá)
Diario Oficial (Bogotá)
El Espectador (Bogotá)
Gaceta Oficial (Bogotá)
El Nuevo Tiempo (Bogotá)
La Opinión (Bogotá)
La Reforma (Bogotá)
Registro Oficial (Popayán)
El Tiempo (Bogotá)
El Trabajo (Popayán)

PUBLISHED PRIMARY SOURCES

Aguado, Fray Pedro de. 1956 [1575?]. *Recopilación historial.* 4 vols. Bogotá: Biblioteca de la Presidencia de Colombia.

Andagoya, Pascual de. 1892 [1544]. "Relación de los sucesos de Pedrarias Dávila en la Tierra Firme y de los descubrimientos en el Mar del Sur." In Antonio B. Cuervo (ed.) *Colección de documentos inéditos sobre la geografía y la historia de Colombia,* vol. 2, pp. 77–125. Bogotá: Casa Editorial de J. J. Pérez.

Anonymous. 1938 [n.d.]. "Varias noticias curiosas sobre la Provincia de Popayán." Appendix to J. Jijón y Caamaño, *Sebastián de Benalcázar,* vol. 2, pp. 177–82. Quito: Editorial Ecuatoriana.

Anuncíbay, Lic. Francisco de. 1963 [1592]. "Informe sobre la población indígena de la Gobernación de Popayán y sobre la necesidad de importar negros para la explotación de sus minas." *Anuario Colombiano de Historia Social y de la Cultura* 1 (1): 197–208. Bogotá.

Camacho Roldán, Salvador. 1983 [1878]. *Escritos varios,* vol. 1. Bogotá: Incunables.

Castellanos, Juan de. 1944 [1589]. *Elegías de varones ilustres de Indias.* Madrid: Biblioteca de Autores Españoles.

Castillo y Orozco, Fr. Eugenio del. 1877 [1755]. *Diccionario páez–castellano.* Paris: Collection Linguistique Américaine, no. 2.

Cauca, Gobernación. 1916. *Informe del Secretario de Gobierno del Cauca.* Popayán: Imprenta del Departamento.

Caycedo, General Domingo. 1943 [1819–20]. *Archivo epistolar del General Domingo Caycedo,* vol. 1 (ed. Guillermo Hernández de Alba *et al.*). Bogotá: Academia Colombiana de Historia, Biblioteca de Historia Nacional, vol. 67.

Colección de documentos inéditos relativos al Adelantado Capitán Don Sebastián de Benalcázar, 1535–1565 (CDSB) (ed. Jorge A. Garcés). Quito: Publicaciones del Archivo Municipal, vol. 10, 1936. [1544] "Dos cartas a Su Majestad, del Adelantado Benalcázar," (Cali, 20 December 1544). Appendix XVIII.

Colombia, República de. 1970. *Legislación nacional sobre indígenas.* Bogotá: Imprenta Nacional.

Comando Quintín Lame. 1986. "Por la defensa de los derechos indígenas." *Colombia Viva,* April 1986, p. 11.

Comisión Corográfica. 1959 [1859]. *Jeografía física y política de las provincias de la Nueva Granada.* Bogotá: Banco de la República.

Comité de Solidaridad con las Luchas Indígenas–Pasto. 1982. *Manifiesto autónomo cumbe.* Mimeo.

Consejo Indio de Sud América (CISA). 1982. "Primer seminario sobre: ideología, filosofía y política de la indianidad." *Pueblo Indio, suplemento ideo-político.* Lima.

Consejo Regional Indígena del Cauca (CRIC). 1973. *Nuestras luchas de ayer y de hoy.* Popayán: Cartilla del CRIC, no. 1.

Cross, Robert. 1866. "Collection of Seeds of Chinchona de Pitayo in South America." *Papers relating to the introduction of the chinchona plant into India,* in British Parliamentary Papers, Accounts and Papers, vol. 53, pp. 256–76.

1871. *Report on the Collecting of Seeds and Plants of the Chinchonas of Pitayo.* London: George E. Eyre and William Spottiswoode.

1879. *Report by Robert Cross of his Mission to South America in 1877–78.* London: George E. Eyre and William Spottiswoode.

Cuervo Márquez, Carlos. 1956 [1887]. *Estudios arqueológicos y etnográficos.* Bogotá: Biblioteca de la Presidencia de Colombia.

Douay, Leon. 1890. "Contribution a l'Américanisme du Cauca (Colombie)." *Congrès International des Américanistes, Compterendu de la Septième Session.* Berlin, 1888, pp. 753–86.

Escobar, Fr. Gerónimo de. 1938 [1582]. "Relación de Fray Gerónimo Descobar de la Orden de San Agustín sobrel carácter e costumbres de los yndios de la Provincia de Popayán." Appendix to J. Jijón y Caamaño, *Sebastián de Benalcázar,* vol. 2, pp. 147–76. Quito: Editorial Ecuatoriana.

Fuentes documentales para la historia del Nuevo Reino de Granada (FDNR) (ed. Juan Friede). Bogotá: Banco Popular, 1975–76 [1559]. "Extensa carta del licenciado Tomás López informando sobre la tasación de los indios de la Provincia de Popayán..." t. 3, doc. 507, pp. 381–90 [AGI/S, Quito 188].

[1564]. "Relación anónima con descripción de la gobernación de Popayán." t. 5, doc. 718, pp. 107–11 [Colección Muñóz, Madrid, t. 89. Sin fecha].

[1576]. "Acta hecha en Popayán ante el gobernador Bartolomé de Mazmela, en presencia del obispo fray Agustín de Coruña y otros, en la que se toman medidas contra los indios pijaos." t. 7, doc. 1059, pp. 96–98 [AGI/S, Patronato 233, ramo 1].

Garcilaso de la Vega, El Inca. 1962 [1616]. *Historia general del Perú.* 4 vols. Lima: Universidad Nacional Mayor de San Marcos.

Gobernadores Indígenas en Marcha. 1981. *Cómo recuperamos nuestro camino de lucha.* Publicación no. 2. Mimeo.

González, Fr. David. n.d. *Los paeces o genocidio y luchas indígenas en Colombia.* n.p.: La Rueda Suelta.

Guaman Poma de Ayala, Felipe. 1936 [1615]. *Nueva corónica y buen gobierno.* [Facsimile version]. Paris: Institut d'Ethnologie.

Guambía, Cabildo de la Parcialidad de. 1980. *Manifiesto guambiano: ibe namuiguen y ñimmereay guchá.* Mimeo.

Hazañero, Fr. Sebastián. 1645. *Letras anvas de la Compañia de Iesus en la Provincia del Nvevo Reyno de Granada desde el año de mil y seyscientos y treinta y ocho, hasta el año de mil y seyscientos y quarenta y tres.* Zaragoza.

Helguera, J. Leon. 1983 [1835]. "Los resguardos indígenas en el sur: un aporte documental del año de 1834." *Anuario Colombiano de Historia Social y de la Cultura* 11: 342–49. Bogotá.

Henao, Jesús María and Gerardo Arrubla. 1938 [1910]. *History of Colombia.* (Trans. J. Fred Rippy). Port Washington, NY: Kennikat Press.

Lame, Manuel Quintín. 1971 [1939]. *En defensa de mi raza.* (ed. and with an introduction by Gonzalo Castillo) Bogotá: Comité de Defensa del Indio. (English translation in Castillo 1987).

Lugari, Mariano. 1936. "Informe agrícola de Tierradentro." *El Agricultor Caucano* 3 (27–28): 685–711. Popayán.

Magnin, Fr. Jean, S. J. 1964 [1725]. "Le première traversée de la Colombie par un missionnaire suisse (1725), le père Jean Magnin, S. J." *Annales Fribourgeoises* 46: 1–65. Fribourg.

Markham, Clements R. 1867. *The Chinchona Species of New Granada...* London: George E. Eyre and William Spottiswoode.

Molina, Cristóbal de (El Cuzqueño). 1959 [1573]. *Ritos y fábulas de los Incas.* Buenos Aires: Editorial Futuro.

Mollien, Gaspar. 1944 [1823]. *Viaje por la República de Colombia en 1823.* Bogotá: Biblioteca Popular de Cultura Colombiana.

Mosquera, Tomás Cipriano de. 1866. *Compendio de geografía general, política, física y especial de los Estados Unidos de Colombia.* London: Imprenta Inglesa y Extrangera de H. C. Panzer.

Mutis, José Celestino. 1983 [1809]. *Mutis y la Expedición Botánica: documentos.* Bogotá: El Ancora.

Navia, Estanislao. 1908. *La Rebelión.* Popayán: Imprenta de "La Tarde."

Ordóñez de Ceballos, Pedro. 1942 [1614]. *Viaje del mundo.* Bogotá: Biblioteca Popular de Cultura Colombiana, vol. 8.

Osorio, Nicolás. 1880. *Estudio sobre el cultivo de las quinas.* Bogotá: Imprenta de Medardo Rivas.

Pachacuti Yamqui Salcamaygua, Joan de Santacruz. 1967 [1613]. "Relación de antigüedades deste Reyno del Pirú." In *Crónicas peruanas de interés indígena.* Madrid: Biblioteca de Autores Españoles, vol. 209, pp. 281–319.

Piedrahita, Lucas Fernández de. 1973 [1688]. *Noticia historial de las conquistas del Nuevo Reino de Granada.* 2 vols. Bogotá: Editorial Kelly.

Polo de Ondegardo, Juan. 1917 [1567]. "Traslado de un cartapacio a manera de borrador que quedó en los papeles de lic. do. Polo de Ondegardo cerca del linage de los Incas y como conquistaron." [Attributed to Luis López]. *Colección de libros y documentos referentes a la historia del Perú,* vol. 4, pp. 95–138. Lima.

Rodríguez, Fr. Manuel. 1984. *El Marañón y Amazonas...* Madrid: Imprenta de Antonio Gonçález de Reyes.

Saffray, Charles. 1984 [1869]. *Viaje a Nueva Granada.* Bogotá: Incunables.

Simón, Fr. Pedro de. 1982 [1627]. *Noticias historiales de las conquistas de Tierra Firme en las Indias Occidentales.* 8 vols. Bogotá: Banco Popular.

Titu Cusi Yupanqui, Diego de Castro. 1973 [1570]. *Relación de la conquista del Perú.* Lima: Ediciones de la Biblioteca Universitaria.

Uribe Uribe, Rafael. 1907. *Reducción de salvajes.* Bogotá: El Trabajo.

Urioste, George L. 1983 [Anon: n.d.]. *Hijos de Pariya Qaqa: la tradición oral de Waru Chiri (mitología, ritual y costumbres).* 2 vols. Syracuse: Foreign and Comparative Studies Program, Latin American Series, no. 6.

Velasco, Juan de. 1977–79 [1789]. *Historia del Reino de Quito en la América Meridional.* 3 vols. Quito: Editorial Casa de la Cultura Ecuatoriana.

Wankar (Ramiro Reynaga). 1981. *Tawantinsuyu: cinco siglos de guerra Qheswaymara contra España.* Mexico: Nueva Imágen.

SECONDARY SOURCES

Adorno, Rollena (ed.). 1982. *From Oral to Written Expression: Native Andean Chronicles of the Early Colonial Period.* Syracuse: Foreign and Comparative Studies, Latin American Series, no. 4.

1986. *Guaman Poma: Writing and Resistance in Colonial Peru.* Austin: University of Texas Press.

Allen, Catherine J. 1984. "Patterned Time: The Mythic History of a Peruvian Community." *Journal of Latin American Lore* 10 (2): 151–73.

Americas Watch Committee. 1986. *The Central-Americanization of Colombia? Human Rights and the Peace Process.* New York: Americas Watch.

Arcila Robledo, Fr. Gregorio, OFM. 1951. *Las misiones franciscanas en Colombia: estudio documental.* Bogotá: Imprenta Nacional.

1954. *Apuntes históricos de la Provincia Franciscana de Colombia.* Bogotá: Imprenta Nacional.

Arvelo Jiménez, Nelly. 1973. *The Dynamics of the Ye'cuana ("Maquiritare") Political System: Stability and Crisis.* Copenhagen: IWGIA document, no. 12.

Aveni, Anthony F. 1972. "Astronomical Tables Intended for Use in Astro-Archaeological Studies." *American Antiquity* 37 (4): 531–40.

1981. "Tropical Archaeoastronomy." *Science* 213 (4504): 161–71.

Barre, Marie-Chantal. 1983. *Ideologías indigenistas y movimientos indios.* Mexico: Siglo XXI.

Behar, Ruth. 1986. *Santa María del Monte: The Presence of the Past in a Spanish Village.* Princeton University Press.

Benjamin, Walter. 1968. *Illuminations* (ed. Hannah Arendt). New York: Schocken.

Bergquist, Charles W. 1968. *Coffee and Conflict in Colombia, 1886–1910.* Durham, NC: Duke University Press.

Bernal Villa, Segundo E. 1953. "Aspectos de la cultura páez: mitología y cuentos de la parcialidad de Calderas, Tierradentro." *Revista Colombiana de Antropología* 1 (1): 279–309. Bogotá.

1954a. "Economía de los páez." *Revista Colombiana de Antropología* 3: 291–309. Bogotá.

1954b. "Medicina y magia entre los paeces." *Revista Colombiana de Antropología* 2 (2): 219–64. Bogotá.

1955. "Bases para el estudio de la organización social de los páez." *Revista Colombiana de Antropología* 4: 165–88. Bogotá.

1956. "Religious Life of the Páez Indians of Colombia." MA thesis. Columbia University, New York.

Bidou, Patrice. 1972. "Représentations de l'espace dans la mythologie tatuyo (Indiens Tucano)." *Journal de la Société des Américanistes* 61: 45–105. Paris.

1977. "Naître et être tatuyo." *Actes du XLII Congrès International des Américanistes,* vol. 11: 105–20. Paris: Fondation Singer-Polignac.

Bloch, Maurice. 1977. "The Past and the Present in the Present." *Man* (n.s.) 12: 278–92.

Blount, Ben G. 1975. "Agreeing to Agree on Genealogy: A Luo Sociology of Knowledge." In Mary Sanches and Ben G. Blount (eds.), *Sociocultural Dimensions of Language Use,* pp. 117–35. New York: Academic Press.

Bonilla, Victor Daniel. 1972. *Servants of God or Masters of Men?* Harmondsworth: Penguin.

1979. "¿Qué política buscan los indígenas?" In Guillermo Bonfíl Batalla (ed.), *Indianidad y descolonización en América Latina: documentos de la Segunda Reunión de Barbados*, pp. 325–56. Mexico: Nueva Imagen.

1982. "Algunas experiencias del proyecto 'Mapas Parlantes.'" In Juan Eduardo García Huidobro (ed.), *Alfabetización y educación de adultos en la región andina.* Pátzcuaro, Mexico: UNESCO.

Borofsky, Robert. 1987. *Making History: Pukapukan and Anthropological Constructions of Knowledge.* Cambridge University Press.

Botero Páez, Sofía. 1982. "Tras el pensamiento y pasos de los taitas guambianos: intentos de aproximación a su historia, siglos XVI–XVII–XVIII." BA thesis in Anthropology. Universidad Nacional de Colombia, Bogotá.

Bourdieu, Pierre. 1977. *Outline of a Theory of Practice.* Cambridge University Press.

Bovenschen, Silvia. 1978. "The Contemporary Witch, the Historical Witch and the Witch Myth: The Witch, Subject of the Appropriation of Nature and Object of the Domination of Nature." *New German Critique* 15: 83–119.

Bricker, Victoria R. 1981. *The Indian Christ, the Indian King: The Historical Substrate of Maya Myth and Ritual.* Austin: University of Texas Press.

Brockway, Lucile H. 1979. *Science and Colonial Expansion: The Role of the British Royal Botanic Gardens.* New York: Academic.

Bunker, Stephen G. 1985. *Underdeveloping the Amazon: Extraction, Unequal Exchange, and the Failure of the Modern State.* Urbana; University of Illinois Press.

Burns, E. Bradford. 1980. *The Poverty of Progress: Latin America in the Nineteenth Century.* Berkeley: University of California Press.

Bushnell, David. 1954. *The Santander Regime in Gran Colombia.* Westport, Ct: Greenwood Press.

Castillo Cárdenas, Gonzalo. 1971. "Manuel Quintín Lame: luchador e intelectual indígena del siglo XX." In Manuel Quintín Lame, *En defensa de mi raza*, pp. xi–xlv. Bogotá: Comité de Defensa del Indio.

1987. *Liberation Theology from Below: The Life and Thought of Manuel Quintín Lame.* Maryknoll, NY: Orbis.

Castrillón Arboleda, Diego. 1973. *El indio Quintín Lame.* Bogotá: Tercer Mundo.

Chaves, Alvaro and Mauricio Puerta. 1976. *Tierradentro.* Bogotá: Ediciones Zazacuabí.

1980. *Entierros primarios de Tierradentro.* Bogotá: Fundación de Investigaciones Arqueológicas Nacionales.

Clanchy, M. T. 1979. *From Memory to Written Record: England, 1066–1307.* Cambridge, MA: Harvard University Press.

Clastres, Pierre. 1977. *Society Against the State.* New York: Urizen.

Cohen, David William. 1989. "The Undefining of Oral Tradition." *Ethnohistory* 36 (1): 9–18.

Cohn, Bernard S. 1981. "Anthropology and History in the 1980s: Toward a Rapprochement." *Journal of Interdisciplinary History* 12 (2): 227–52.

Collingwood, R. G. 1946. *The Idea of History.* London: Oxford University Press.

Colmenares, Germán. 1970. *La Provincia de Tunja en el Nuevo Reino de Granada – ensayo de historia social – (1539–1800).* Bogotá: Universidad de los Andes.

1975. *Historia económica y social de Colombia, 1.537–1.719.* Bogotá: La Carreta.

1979 *Historia económica y social de Colombia, t. 2: Popayán, una sociedad esclavista, 1680–1800.* Bogotá: La Carreta.

Dasenbrock, Reed Way. 1985–86. "Creating a Past: Achebe, Naipaul, Soyinka, Farah." *Salmagundi* 68–69: 312–32.

Eagleton, Terry. 1978. *Criticism and Ideology*. London: Verso.

1985–86. "Marxism and the Past." *Salmagundi* 68–69: 217–90.

Earle, David D. 1985. "Producción agropecuaria y organización del trabajo en el Cauca central, 1925–1950." Paper presented at the 45th Congreso Internacional de Americanistas, Bogotá, Colombia.

n.d.a. "The Dynamics of Confrontation and Accommodation on a Cultural Frontier: Guambía and Tierradentro (Colombia) 1550–1700." Manuscript.

n.d.b. "Political Organization of Indian Groups in the Popayán Area at the Time of the Spanish Conquest." Manuscript.

Earls, John and Irene Silverblatt. 1978. "La realidad física y social en la cosmología andina." *Actes du XLII Congrès International des Américanistes* IV, pp. 299–326. Paris: Fondation Singer-Polignac.

Eder, Phanor James. 1959. *El fundador Santiago M. Eder (recuerdos de su vida y acotaciones para la historia económica del Valle del Cauca)*. Bogotá: Antares.

Errington, Shelly. 1979. "Some Comments on Style in the Meanings of the Past." *Journal of Asian Studies* 38 (2): 231–44.

Findji, María Teresa and José María Rojas. 1985. *Territorio, economía y sociedad páez*. Cali: Universidad del Valle.

Finley, M. I. 1965. "Myth, Memory, and History." *History and Theory* 4 (3): 281–302.

Fowler, Loretta. 1987. *Shared Symbols, Contested Meanings: Gros Ventre Culture and History, 1778–1984*. Ithaca: Cornell University Press.

Friede, Juan 1953. *Los Andakí, 1538–1947: historia de la aculturación de una tribu selvática*. Mexico: Fondo de Cultura Económica.

1972. *El indio en lucha por la tierra*. Bogotá: La Chispa.

Fuentes, Carlos. 1985–86. "Remember the Future." *Salmagundi* 68–69: 333–52.

Gilhodès, Pierre. 1970. "Agrarian Struggles in Colombia." In Rodolfo Stavenhagen (ed.), *Agarian Problems and Peasant Movements in Latin America*, pp. 407–51. Garden City, New York: Anchor.

González, Margarita. 1979. *El resguardo en el Nuevo Reino de Granada*. Bogotá: La Carreta.

Goody, Jack. 1977. *The Domestication of the Savage Mind*. Cambridge University Press.

1987. *The Interface between the Oral and the Written*. Cambridge University Press.

Goody, Jack and Ian Watt. 1963. "The Consequences of Literacy." *Comparative Studies in Society and History* 5: 304–45.

Harwood, Frances. 1976. "Myth, Memory, and the Oral Tradition: Cicero in the Trobriands." *American Anthropologist* 78 (4): 783–96.

Henige, David P. 1974. *The Chronology of Oral Tradition: Quest for a Chimera*. Oxford: Clarendon Press.

Henman, Anthony. 1981. *Mama Coca*. Bogotá: El Ancora.

Hernández de Alba, Gregorio. 1963. "The Highland Tribes of Southern Colombia." In Julian Steward (ed.), *Handbook of South American Indians*, vol. 2, pp. 915–60. New York: Cooper Square.

Hobsbawm, Eric and Terence Ranger (eds.) 1983. *The Invention of Tradition*. Cambridge University Press.

Hugh-Jones, Christine. 1978. *By the Milk River*. Cambridge University Press.

Janes, Regina. 1985–86. "Past Possession in Latin America." *Salmagundi* 68–69: 219–311.

Jaramillo, Carlos Eduardo. 1985. "Victoriano Lorenzo: el guerrillero invencible de Panamá." *Tolima, Revista de la Contraloría General del Tolima* 2 (1): 32–69. Ibagué.

Kaplan, Joanne. 1981. "Amazonian Anthropology." *Journal of Latin American Studies* 13 (1): 151–64.

Lederman, Rena. 1985. "Changing Times in Mendi: Notes Toward Writing Highland New Guinea History." *Ethnohistory* 33 (1): 1–30.

LeGrand, Catherine Carlisle. 1980. "From Public Lands into Private Properties: Landholding and Rural Conflict in Colombia, 1870–1936." Ph.D. dissertation, Stanford University.

1986. *Frontier Expansion and Peasant Protest in Colombia, 1850–1936*. Albuquerque: University of New Mexico Press.

Lehmann, Henri. 1963. "The Moguex-Coconuco." In Julian Steward (ed.), *Handbook of South American Indians*, vol. 2, pp. 969–74. New York: Cooper Square.

Lévi-Strauss, Claude. 1966. *The Savage Mind*. University of Chicago Press.

Llanos Vargas, Héctor. 1981. *Los cacicazgos de Popayán a la llegada de los conquistadores*. Bogotá: Fundación de Investigaciones Arqueológicas Nacionales.

Lockhart, James. 1968. *Spanish Peru, 1532–1560: A Colonial Society*. Madison: University of Wisconsin Press.

Long, Stanley and Juan Yánguez. 1970–71. "Excavaciones en Tierradentro." *Revista Colombiana de Antropología* 15: 11–127. Bogotá.

López Baralt, Mercedes. 1979. "Guamán Poma de Ayala y el arte de la memoria en una crónica ilustrada del siglo XVII." *Cuadernos Americanos* 224: 119–51.

Lord, Albert B. 1986. "The Merging of Two Worlds: Oral and Written Poetry as Carriers of Ancient Values." In John Miles Foley (ed.), *Oral Tradition in Literature: Interpretation in Context*, pp. 19–64. Columbia: University of Missouri Press.

Löwy, Michael. 1985. "Revolution Against 'Progress': Walter Benjamin's Romantic Anarchism." *New Left Review* 152: 42–59.

Lucena Salmoral, Manuel. 1962. "Mitos, usos y costumbres de los indios pixaos." *Revista Colombiana de Antropología* 11: 143–52. Bogotá.

Mantilla Ruiz, Luis Carlos, OFM. 1980. *Actividad misionera de los Franciscanos en Colombia durante los siglos y XVIII: fuentes documentales*. Bogotá: Editorial Kelly.

Marx, Karl and Frederick Engels. 1964. *The German Ideology*. Moscow: Progress Publishers.

Miller, Joseph (ed.) 1980. *The African Past Speaks*. Hamden, CT: Archon.

Moreno Yánez, Segundo. 1978. "Los 'caciques mayores': renacimiento de su concepto en Quito a finles de la Colonia.' *Antropología Ecuatoriana* 1: 31–39. Quito.

Morphy, Howard and Frances Morphy. 1985. "The 'Myths' of Ngalakan History: Ideology and Images of the Past in Northern Australia." *Man* (n.s.) 19: 459–78.

Nachtigall, Horst. 1953. "Shamanismo entre los indios paeces." *Revista Colombiana del Folclor*, 2 época, 2: 223–41. Bogotá.

210 *References*

1955. *Tierradentro: Archaologie und Ethnographie einer Kolumbianischen Landschaft.* Zurich: Origo Verlag.

Nash, June. 1979. *We Eat the Mines and the Mines Eat Us.* New York: Columbia University Press.

Ocampo, José Antonio. 1980–81. "La quina en la historia de Colombia." *Revista de Extensión Cultural (Universidad Nacional de Colombia, Seccional de Medellín)* 9–10: 27–46. Medellín.

Ong, Walter J., S. J. 1982. *Orality and Literacy: The Technologizing of the Word.* London and New York: Methuen.

1986. "Text as Interpretation: Mark and After." In John Miles Foley (ed.), *Oral Tradition in Literature: Interpretation in Context*, pp. 147–69. Columbia: University of Missouri Press.

Ortíz, Sutti R. 1973. *Uncertainties in Peasant Farming: A Colombian Case.* London School of Economics, Monographs on Social Anthropology, vol. 19. London: The Athlone Press.

1979. "The Estimation of Work, Labour and Value among Páez Farmers." In Sandra Wallman (ed.), *Social Anthropology of Work* (ASA, vol. 19), pp. 207–28. London: Academic Press.

Ortíz Rescaniere, Alejandro. 1973. *De Adaneva a Inkarrí: una visión indígena del Perú.* Lima: Retablo de Papel.

Ossio, Juan M. 1970. "The Idea of History in Felipe Guaman Poma de Ayala." B. Litt. thesis, Oxford University.

1973. *Ideología mesiánica del mundo andino.* Lima: Ignacio Prado Pastor.

1977. "Myth and History: The Seventeenth-Century Chronicle of Guaman Poma de Ayala." In R. K. Jain (ed.), *Text and Context: The Social Anthropology of Tradition*, pp. 51–93. Philadelphia: ISHI.

Otero, Jesús M. 1968. *Monografía histórica de Silvia.* Popayán: Imprenta Departamental.

Pacheco, Juan Manuel, S. J. n.d. *Los Jesuitas en Colombia*, vol. 1 (1567–1654). Bogotá: Editorial "San Juan Endes."

Padilla, Silvia, M. L. López Arellano and Adolfo González. 1977. *La encomienda en Popayán: tres estudios.* Sevilla: Escuela de Estudios Hispano-Americanos, Consejo Superior de Investigaciones Científicas.

Parmentier, Richard J. 1987. *The Sacred Remains: Myth, History, and Polity in Belau.* University of Chicago Press.

Pécault, Daniel. 1987. *Orden y violencia: Colombia 1930–1954.* Mexico: Siglo xxi.

Pérez de Barradas, José. 1943. *Colombia de norte a sur.* Madrid: Ministerio de Asuntos Exteriores.

Phelan, John Leddy. 1967. *The Kingdom of Quito in the Seventeenth Century.* Madison: University of Wisconsin Press.

Pineda Camacho, Roberto. 1980–81. "El rescate de los tamas: análisis de un caso de desamparo en el siglo XVII." *Revista Colombiana de Antropología* 23: 327–63. Bogotá.

Pittier de Fabrega, H. 1907. "Ethnographic and Linguistic Notes on the Páez Indians of Tierradentro, Cauca, Colombia." *Memoirs of the American Anthropological Association* 1: 301–56.

Platt, Tristan. 1982. *Estado boliviano y ayllu andino: tierra y tributo en el Norte de Potosí.* Lima: Instituto de Estudios Peruanos.

Poole, Deborah A. n.d. "From Pilgrimage to Myth: Miracles, Memory and Time in an Andean Pilgrimage Story." Manuscript.

Popular Memory Group. 1982. "Popular Memory: Theory, Politics, Method." In Richard Johnson *et al.* (eds.), *Making Histories: Studies in History-Writing and Politics*, pp. 205–52. Minneapolis: University of Minnesota Press.

Price, Richard. 1983. *First-Time: The Historical Vision of an Afro-American People.* Baltimore: Johns Hopkins University Press.

Rappaport, Joanne. 1980–81. "El mesianismo y las transformaciones de símbolos mesiánicos en Tierradentro." *Revista Colombiana de Antropología* 23: 365–413. Bogotá.

1982. "Territory and Tradition: The Ethnohistory of the Páez of Tierradentro, Colombia." PhD dissertation, University of Illinois at Urbana.

1984. "Las misiones protestantes y la resistencia indígena en el sur de Colombia." *América Indígena* 44 (1): 111–26. Mexico City.

1985. "History, Myth and the Dynamics of Territorial Maintenance in Tierradentro, Colombia." *American Ethnologist* 12 (1): 27–45.

1987a. "Los cacicazgos en America: el caso páez." In Robert Drennan and Carlos A. Uribe (eds.), *Chiefdoms in the Americas*, pp. 271–88. Lanham, MD: University Press of America.

1987b. "Mythic Images, Historical Thought, and Printed Texts: The Páez and the Written Word." *Journal of Anthropological Research* 43 (1): 43–61.

Reichel-Dolmatoff, Gerardo. 1971. *Amazonian Cosmos: The Sexual and Religious Symbolism of the Tukano Indians.* University of Chicago Press.

1975. "Templos kogi: introducción al simbolismo y a la astronomía del espacio sagrado." *Revista Colombiana de Antropología* 19: 199–245. Bogotá.

1978 "Colombia indígena: período prehispánico." In J. C. Cobo and S. Mutis (eds.), *Manual de Historia de Colombia*, vol. 1, pp. 31–114. Bogotá: Instituto Colombiano de Cultura.

Renoir, Alain. 1986. "Oral-Formulaic Rhetoric and the Interpretation of Written Texts." In John Miles Foley (ed.), *Oral Tradition in Literature: Interpretation in Context*, pp. 103–35. Columbia: University of Missouri Press.

Rivera Cusicanqui, Silvia. 1986. *"Oprimidos pero no vencidos": luchas del campesinado aymara y qhechwa, 1900–1980.* La Paz: HISBOL.

Roldán Ortega, Roque. 1974. *Antecedentes históricos del Resguardo de Jambaló.* Mimeo.

Rosaldo, Renato. 1980. *Ilongot Headhunting: 1883–1974. A Study in Society and History.* Stanford University Press.

Rostworowski de Diez Canseco, María. 1977. *Etnia y sociedad: costa peruana prehispánica.* Lima: Instituto de Estudios Peruanos.

Sahlins, Marshall. 1981. *Historical Metaphors and Mythical Realities: Structure in the Early History of the Sandwich Islands Kingdom.* Ann Arbor: University of Michigan Press.

Salomon, Frank L. 1982. "Chronicles of the Impossible: Notes on Three Peruvian Indigenous Historians." In Rollena Adorno (ed.), *From Oral to Written Expression*, pp. 9–40. Syracuse: Foreign and Comparative Studies, Latin American Series, no. 4.

1986. *Native Lords of Quito in the Age of the Incas: The Political Economy of North Andean Chiefdoms.* Cambridge University Press.

Sánchez, Gonzalo *et al.* 1988. *Colombia: violencia y democracia (informe presentado al Ministerio de Gobierno)*. Bogotá: Universidad Nacional de Colombia/ Colciencias.

Sanjinés, Jorge and Grupo Ukamau. 1979. *Teoría y práctica de un cine junto al pueblo.* Mexico: Siglo xxi.

Sendoya M., Mariano. 1975. *Caloto ante la historia.* 2 vols. Cali: Imprenta Departamental.

n.d. *Toribío, Puerto Tejada.* Popayán: Talleres Editoriales del Departamento.

Sevilla-Casas, Elías. 1976a. *Anthropological Studies of Tierradentro.* Cali: Fundación para la Educación Superior.

1976b. "Lame y el Cauca indígena." In Nina S. de Friedemann (ed.), *Tierra, tradición y poder en Colombia: enfoques antropológicos*, pp. 85–105. Bogotá: Instituto Colombiano de Cultura.

1986. *La pobreza de los excluidos: economía y sobrevivencia en un resguardo indígena del Cauca – Colombia.* Quito: Abya-Yala.

Smith, Richard. 1983. "La ideología liberal y las comunidades indígenas en el Perú republicano." *América Indígena* 43 (3): 585–600. Mexico.

Sperber, Dan. 1975. *Rethinking Symbolism.* Cambridge University Press.

Stock, Brian. 1983. *The Implications of Literacy: Written Language and Models of Interpretation in the Eleventh and Twelfth Centuries.* Princeton University Press.

Street, Brian. 1984. *Literacy in Theory and Practice.* Cambridge University Press.

Taussig, Michael. 1984. "History as Sorcery." *Representations* 7: 87–109.

Tello Lozano, Piedad Lucía. 1982. "Vida y lucha de Manuel Quintín Lame." BA thesis in Anthropology, Universidad de los Andes, Bogotá.

Tirado Mejía, Alvaro. 1976. *Aspectos sociales de las guerras civiles en Colombia.* Bogotá: Instituto Colombiano de Cultura.

1982. "El Estado y la política en el siglo xix." In J. C. Cobo and S. Mutis (eds.), *Manual de Historia de Colombia*, v. 2, pp. 325–84. Bogotá: Instituto Colombiano de Cultura.

Tovar Zambrano, Bernardo. 1984. *La colonia en la historiografía colombiana.* Bogotá: La Carreta.

Trimborn, Hermann. 1949. *Señorío y barbarie en el Valle del Cauca.* Madrid: Consejo Superior de Investigaciones Científicas, Instituto Gonzalo Fernández de Oviedo.

Uribe, Carlos Alberto. 1988. "Nuestra cultura de la muerte." *Texto y Contexto* 13: 53–67. Bogotá

Vansina, Jan. 1973. *Oral Tradition.* Harmandsworth: Penguin.

Vidal, Hernán. 1985. *Socio-historia de la literatura colonial hispano-americana: tres lecturas orgánicas.* Minneapolis: Institute for the Study of Ideologies and Literatures.

Villamarín, Juan and Judith. 1979. "Chibcha Settlement under Spanish Rule: 1537–1810." In David J. Robinson (ed.), *Social Fabric and Spatial Structure in Colonial Latin America*, pp. 25–84. Department of Geography, Syracuse University.

Wachtel, Nathan. 1973. "Rebeliones y milenarismo." In Juan Ossio (ed.), *Ideología mesiánica del mundo andino*, pp. 103–42. Lima: Ignacio Prado Pastor.

White, Hayden. 1973. *Metahistory: The Historical Imagination in Nineteenth-Century Europe.* Baltimore: Johns Hopkins University Press.

1978. *Tropics of Discourse: Essays in Cultural Criticism.* Baltimore: Johns Hopkins University Press.

Yoder, John C. 1980. "The Historical Study of a Kanyok Genesis Myth: The Tale of Citend A Mfumu." In Joseph Miller (ed.), *The African Past Speaks*, pp. 82–102. Hamden, CT: Archon.

Yates, Frances. 1966. *The Art of Memory*. University of Chicago Press.

Zuidema, R. Tom. 1964. *The Ceque System of Cuzco*. Leiden: E. J. Brill.

1977. "The Inca Kinship System: A New Theoretical View." In R. Bolton and E. Mayer (eds.), *Andean Kinship and Marriage*, pp. 240–81. Washington, DC: Special Publication of the American Anthropological Association, no. 7.

1982. "Myth and History in Ancient Peru." In Ino Rossi *et al.* (eds.), *The Logic of Culture*. New York: J. F. Bergin.

Index

Abirama (Conquest-era *cacique*), 30, 31
Aguado, Fr. Pedro de, 30–34, 38, 67, 144, 192n
Amazonia, 74–75, 143–44
Ambostá, San Antonio de (today Belalcázar), 75
Añasco, Pedro de: historical figure, 38, 83; in oral tradition, 166, 168–70, 172–77.
Andakí (ethnic group), 34, 74–75
Arboleda, Julio, 85, 95, 101
Asnenga, 101–2
astronomical symbolism, 153–55, 196
Avirama (community), 31, 47, 51, 153, 169, 172, 177

baldíos (public lands): of Asnenga, 101–2; in Colombia, 94–95; and great estates, 94; legislation, 94; and quinine extraction, 100–2; and *resguardos*, 95; in Tierradentro, 103
Belalcázar (municipal center), 102–3, 136, 153, 169, 177
Belalcázar, Sebastián, *see* Benalcázar, Sebastián de
Benalcázar, Sebastián de: historical figure, 38, 165, 168; in oral tradition, 167, 169–70, 172, 174, 177
Benjamin, Walter, 14, 190n
bilateral descent: among Inca, 68–69; among Páez, 53, 69
bilingualism, 23, 57, 71, 75, 82, 135, 163
Bloch, Maurice, 14, 189
Bogotá, 175–176; *see also* Chibcha

Bolívar, Simón, 151
Bonilla, Víctor Daniel, 164
Bourdieu, Pierre, 182

cabildo (reservation council: colonial, 45; contemporary, 134–35, 137, 144–45; as labor contractor, 103–4; nineteenth-century, 7, 87, 89–90; and privatization of lands, 131; and quinine extraction, 99–100, 102; reconstitution of, 110–11, 135; *see also* staffs of office
Cabuyo, El, 153, 161
cacicazgos (chiefdoms): among Andakí, 34–35; in Cauca Valley, 35; among Chibcha, 32, 34–35; colonial survival of, 48; evolution of, 35; among Guambiano, 35–37; in pre-Incaic Quito, 32–35; among Pijao, 34–36; among Pubenense, 32, 34, 36–37; succession, 42, 52–53; territories of, 30–31; *see also caciques*; *parcialidad*
caciques/cacicas (precolumbian hereditary chiefs), 32; economic power of, 35–36, 38; generational relationships among, 32–33; memory of, 9, 87–90; migration of sons, 33, 42; as military leaders, 34, 36, 51; political power of, 34–36; relationship to followers, 32, 35–36; relationship to *principales*, 31–34, 51; sibling relationships among, 31–33; supernatural power of, 36; use of chiefly titles, 63, 68–69; *see also cacicazgos*

215

Mulcué, Jorge, 175–77
Muñoz, Ignacio, 103–4
Muscay, Jacinto, 47, 65, 71–72, 75
myth: and fiction, 16; and history,
    10–14, 146–47, 188–89, 190n; and
    structure, 13; *see also* history

Ñasco, Pedro *see* Añasco, Pedro de
Nátaga, 52, 103
national symbols, 159–60
Neiva, 168
Neiva, Gobernación de, 74, 192n–93n;
    see also Huila; Tolima
new *caciques*: and *cabildo*, 45; chiefly
    hierarchy, 51–52; degrees of
    ethnic autonomy, 48; as leader of
    confederation, 51–52;
    legitimization for Spaniards, 48;
    legitimization for followers, 49,
    70–76; marriages, 193n; memory
    of precolumbian *cacicazgo*, 44,
    50–51, 70–73, 185; as outsiders,
    70, 72–75; as permanent
    authorities, 47, 70; privileges,
    45–46; relation to *principales*,
    51–52; as representatives of
    community, 51, 60; subordination
    to state, 61; succession, 52–53,
    65, 71–72, 75; and Tama slaves,
    74; territorial expansion, 44,
    50–52, 70; use of chiefly titles,
    51, 61–63, 65–70, 75; *see also*
    Gueyomuse; Quilo y Sicos;
    resguardo; Tama, Don Juan
Niquinás Julio, 19: cross-referencing
    in stories, 171–74, 180;
    descendant of Juan Tama, 21,
    161–62; as exile, 164; and
    geography, 176–77, 181;
    historical detail in stories,
    169–170; literacy, 20; as political
    activist, 20, 163–64, 181–182,
    186; ring structure, 174–77;
    story of La Gaitana, 165–67;
    story of Juan Tama, 165, 167;
    temporal framework, 166,
    170–71, 173; use of evidence,
    168; use of images, 171–74; war
    memories, 162

northern Andes, 191n
novels, *see* fiction
Nuesga, 32, 63
Nuevo Reino de Granada, 45

oral tradition: groundrules, 145–46;
    historical referents in, 142–45;
    and literacy, 161; and practice,
    145–46; use of images, 141–42;
    see also culture heroes; evidence;
    resguardo titles
Ortega, 105, 108, 110–11

Páez (Conquest-era *cacique*), 30–32
Páez (ethnic group): contemporary
    lack of unity, 140; dispersed
    settlement, 30; ethnographies,
    190n; as "First Americans",
    46–47, 49, 70; geographic
    localization, 2–5; of La Plata,
    29; military tactics, 30;
    population, 5, 40, 195n; relations
    with Guambiano, 36–38;
    relations with Pijao, 38;
    subsistence base, 8, 30; as
    warriors, 8, 82–83; on western
    slopes of cordillera, 33, 37; *see
    also* Tierradentro
Páez (municipality), *see* Belalcázar
Páez River, 30, 32, 146, 166, 169, 173,
    177
Paniquitá, 41–42
Páramo de Moras, 153, 177
parcialidad: localization of in
    Tierradentro, 30–31; *see also*
    cacicazgos
Peasant Leagues, *see* Communist Party
personal contribution, *see* tribute
Pijao, 30; alliance with Páez, 38–39;
    cacicazgos, 34–36; mythical beings,
    141, 144, 149–51, 172–73
Pisimbalá, San Andrés de, 47, 134
Pitalito, 175
Pitayó (*cacicazgo* and colonial *resguardo*),
    47, 65–67, 70–73, 75–76
Pitayó (community), 42, 47, 85, 87–89,
    92, 95–97, 100–2, 105, 153, 177
Platavieja, 175–76
Polindara, 104

CAMBRIDGE LATIN AMERICAN STUDIES